Drawn by George Varian

FROM THE
COLLECTION OF
ROBERT B. THOMSON
1912-1983

THE RAYMOND H. FOGLER LIBRARY

Foot Ball played at Market Place Barnet

Guide To Football Literature

Edited by

Anton Grobani

With Introductions by
Dick Gallagher, Director,
Pro Football Hall of Fame,
and
David Nelson, Athletic Director,
University of Delaware

Gale Research Company
Book Tower • Detroit, Michigan 48226

Copyright © 1975 by Gale Research Company

**Library of Congress
Cataloging in Publication Data**

Grobani, Anton.
   Guide to football literature.

     Includes index.
     1. Football–Bibliography. I. Title
Z7514.F7G76   016.79633'2'0973   75-1478
ISBN 0-8103-0964-5

Contents

INTRODUCTION BY DICK GALLAGHER, DIRECTOR,
PRO FOOTBALL HALL OF FAME..................... vii

INTRODUCTION BY DAVID NELSON, ATHLETIC DIRECTOR,
UNIVERSITY OF DELAWARE ix

ACKNOWLEDGMENTS xi

EXPLANATORY NOTES xiii

REFERENCE SOURCES xv

  1. GENERAL WORKS 1

  2. GUIDES 7

  3. EARLY BRITISH WORKS 15

  4. RECORD BOOKS 17

  5. ANNUALS 25

  6. GENERAL HISTORIES 35

  7. TEAM HISTORIES 41

  8. BIOGRAPHIES 59

  9. INSTRUCTIONALS 83

10. ANTHOLOGIES 113

11. PERIODICALS 115

12. FICTION 121

13. HUMOR 161

Contents

14.	DRAMA, VERSE, BALLADS	163
15.	PICTORIALS	167
16.	SCHEDULE AND RECORD BOOKLETS	169
17.	RATING SYSTEMS	177
18.	ECONOMIC MATTERS	179
19.	YEARBOOKS	183
20.	BOYS AND HIGH SCHOOL	195
21.	SIX-MAN AND TOUCH	209
22.	RULE BOOKS	213
23.	OFFICIATING	217
24.	POST-SEASON GAMES	221
25.	CONFERENCE AND SECTIONAL	227
26.	DICTIONARIES AND SPECTATORS' GUIDES	237
27.	ANECDOTES AND RECOLLECTIONS	245
28.	CONDITIONING AND INJURIES	247
29.	CONTROVERSIES	251
30.	ADMINISTRATIVE WORKS	255
31.	ALL-TIME AND ALL-AMERICAN	257
32.	SCOUTING	259
33.	MISCELLANEOUS	261
	GENERAL INDEX	263
	PROFESSIONAL INDEX	303

Introduction

by Dick Gallagher, Director, Pro Football Hall of Fame

Guide to Football Literature should be welcomed with great enthusiasm by just about anybody who is even remotely interested in delving into the history of this unique and exciting sport. Whether a person's primary interest centers around amateur, high school, college, or professional football, this guide will be an absolutely priceless aid in helping him to learn more about his favorite team.

History -- and specifically pro football history -- is the business of the Pro Football Hall of Fame. This is reflected in just about every corner of this pro football showplace. In each of three colorful and entertaining exhibition areas, in the action movie theater, and in the research library, history is the name of the game.

This is particularly true in the research library which, as the name implies, has been established for the use of football researchers from everywhere. Accredited professional writers and researchers and dedicated amateurs all find a treasure house of football publications in this large part of the Pro Football Hall of Fame.

We are proud -- justifiably proud, we hope -- of this facility which already contains thousands of publications -- general histories, books on coaching techniques, team histories, biographies and autobiographies of the game's great stars, photographic histories, yearbooks, game programs, press guides -- you name it, and if it is on the subject of professional football, chances are good that we have it.

One missing, and most-needed, link, however, has been a truly complete bibliography covering not only the material that may be on hand at the Pro Football Hall of Fame but also that material which is available but not yet added to our collection. Guide to Football Literature will be extremely valuable to the Hall in many ways, not the least of which will be in its quest for new items. Literally hundreds of new publications are being added to our research library every year.

Introduction

We can readily appreciate the many long and tiring hours Dr. Grobani must have spent in preparing this rare research aid.

We congratulate him on a production that fills a most prominent void in the football research field. Guide to Football Literature is something that will not only be appreciated but, even more importantly, it is needed and it will be used.

Introduction

by David Nelson, Athletic Director, University of Delaware

It is a wise individual who uses a guide for hunting, fishing, sightseeing and the search for anything that is difficult to discover. Football literature is a far cry from being a close relative to hunting, fishing, or sightseeing but it is a blood relative of anything that is difficult to discover. Football writings are scattered near and far and run a pattern that ranges from the fictional to the technical. Gridiron publications run the reader to daylight through writings programmed for boys, high school, college, and professional levels of competition.

Football is woven so tightly and widely into the American culture that the "good word" about football is published by everybody from breakfast food manufacturers to the country's most prestigious publishing houses. Football carries a "prestige by association" tag and because the game carries an aura of charisma, it has brought forth a variety of authors and publishers that is unique.

Searching and finding all that has been published about football requires guides of the stature of Kit Carson or Davy Crockett. Guide to Football Literature has accomplished this feat in the mold of the greatest guides by corralling most of the data about the writings associated with American football.

This work, together with the articles and films about football, will provide the researcher, the coach, the athletic administrator, or just plain devotees of the game (football nuts) with all the information available about "The Game."

Acknowledgments

A.P. DeWeese, The New York Public Library.

Dick Gallagher, Pro Football Hall of Fame.

Goodwin Goldfaden, Adco Sports Book Exchange.

Jack Horrigan, The American Football League.

Jim Kensil, The National Football League.

R.M. Lamb, The Football Information Bureau.

James Lucas, Pro Football Hall of Fame.

Ron Menchine, Washington, D.C.

David Nelson, University of Delaware.

Roy Nelson, All-American Sports Books.

W.R. Schroeder, Helms Athletic Foundation.

James Tobin, The New York Public Library.

Al Ward, The American Football League.

The sports information directors and librarians of numerous colleges, the publicity directors of the various professional teams, and various sportswriters throughout the country.

Explanatory Notes

In cases where a publication bears different title page and cover titles, the one by which the work is best known is given in the heading. The variant title is listed in the descriptive paragraph, and both are included in the index.

Works listing A.G. Spalding & Brothers as publisher include those published by the American Sports Publishing Co.

Works listing The Sporting News as publisher include those published by Charles C. Spink & Son.

Unless otherwise stated, the first entries appearing in a chapter are collegiate titles, followed by professional titles.

In the bibliographic references, "to date" means through 1972.

Reference Sources

Allegheny College Library

Cleveland Public Library

Detroit Public Library

Harvard College Library

Library of Congress

National Union Catalogue

New York Public Library

Ohio State University Library

Pro Football Hall of Fame Library

Material gathered from the Editor's private collection.

1. General Works

1-1 Beadle's Dime Book of Cricket and Football. Henry Chadwick. Beadle & Co. 1866. Booklet.

    First American publication on football. Laws, technical terms, rules of the Rugby and Eton games.

1-2 Wehman's Book on Football. Henry J. Wehman. 1880. Title page: Football, Rules of the Game. Paperbound.

    Duties of each player, descriptions of the Rugby and Association games, advice to officials.

1-3 Poe's Football. Street & Smith. 1891. Paperbound.

    Football at Princeton, American Intercollegiate Association rules. The play of each position, the referee, rugby rules.

1-4 American Football. Walter Camp. Harper & Brothers. 1891-96. Clothbound.

    The 1895 edition bears an 1896 printing date, but an 1895 copyright date. The 1891 edition was the first clothbound book on American football. The play of each position, signals, training, spectating. Historical background, interference, and wedge plays, team play.

1-5 University Football. James R. Church, ed. Charles Scribner's Sons. 1893. Clothbound.

    The play of each position, described by star players. Training, the referee, and umpire, American Intercollegiate Association rules and constitution.

1-6 A Scientific and Practical Treatise on American Football for Schools and Colleges. Amos Alonzo Stagg and Henry Williams. Case, Lockwood & Brainard Co. 1893. Clothbound. D. Appleton & Co. 1894. Clothbound. Finch Press. 1972, reissue. Clothbound.

    General discussion of the game, the play of each po-

General Works

sition. Plays, tactics, signals, axioms, rules.

1-7   Football. Walter Camp and Lorin F. Deland. Houghton Mifflin Co. 1896. Clothbound.

History, explanation of the game, fine points. Spectating, the effects of the game on the players, technical terms. The player's daily routine, organizing a team, training, the play of each position. Blocking, rushing, kicking, team play. Plays, coaching, tactics, game preparations. Signals, officiating, rules.

1-8   The Book of Football. Walter Camp. Century Co. 1910. Cover title: Walter Camp's Book of Football. Clothbound.

History, personality in football, general strategy, training, the play of each position, kicking, catching, passing. The captain and coach, All-America teams.

1-9   Official Football and Soccer Rules. Frank Haggerty. Stall & Dean. 1926-31. Title pages: Official Intercollegiate Football Schedules and Rules. 1926-28. Official Football Rules and Guide. 1929. Official Intercollegiate Football Rules. 1930, 1931. Paperbound.

Scores, schedules, playing instructions, rules.

1-10   Football, Today and Tomorrow. William Roper. J.W. Duffield & Co. 1927, 1928, reissue, 1929, reissue. Clothbound.

General discussion, training, quarterbacking, plays. Between the halves, psychology, requisites, the value of football. The modern game, criticism of pro football.

1-11   Small College Preview. Robert Adlam and Robert Lassanske. Football News Service. 1941. Paperbound.

Rosters, critiques, schedules, potential stars.

1-12   Football Cartoons and Features. Spencer Co. 1942, 1949, 1956-58. Booklet.

A catalogue issued by the printer of the official football programs. Articles on a variety of football topics. Signals, explanation of penalties, other data.

1-13   A Handy Illustrated Guide to Football. Samuel Nisenson. Permabooks. 1948, 1949, reissue. Paperbound.

History, instructions, plays, and strategy. Officials' signals, rules, terms. Pictures of famous players, digest of outstanding feats.

1-14   A Handy Football Library. Louis Oshins. Blue Ribbon Books.

General Works

	1949. Clothbound.
	Boxed set of four volumes.
1-14A	Offensive Football.
1-14B	Defensive Football.
1-14C	Football Rules and How They Are Applied.
1-14D	Famous Names in Football.
1-15	Football Facts and Fun. Hugh L. Ray. Borden Publishing Co. 1949. Booklet.
	History, fundamentals, techniques, formations, rules. Humorous illustrations.
1-16	The 1959 Football Story. Zander Hollander. Phillies Cigars. 1959. Booklet.
	Previews, reviews, schedules, terms, other data.
1-17	Football from the Ground Up. Station KMPC. Golden West Broadcasters. 1958, 1959. Booklet.
	History, glossary, photos.
1-18	Saturday's America. Dan Jenkins. Little, Brown & Co. 1970. Clothbound.
	A description of the atmosphere surrounding college football and the life styles of its fans.

Professional Titles

1P-1	Inside Pro Football. Joe King. Prentice Hall. 1958. Clothbound.
	Growth and development. General discussion covering coaching, scouting, kicking, finances, other aspects. What to look for on television, with tips by Lujack, Harmon, Grange.
1P-2	The NFL and You. The National Football League. 1960-65. Bert Rose, Jr. 1960. Jim Kensil. 1961-65. Cover titles: The National Football League/The NFL and You. 1960, 1961. The NFL and You. 1962-64. The Ball Is Snapped. 1965. Magazine.
	Designed for recruiting collegiate draft choices. Illustrated story of the game, player sketches, history of each team, all-time records. Accounts of players' successful business careers.

General Works

1P-3   The American Football League. The American Football League.
       1962-64. Al Ward. 1962. Jack Horrigan. 1963, 1964. Cover titles: American Football League. 1962, 1963. This Is the American Football League. 1964. Magazine.

   Designed for recruiting collegiate draft choices. League and team histories, features, photos.

1P-3A Your Future - The AFL. Al Ward and Jack Horrigan. The American Football League. 1965. Magazine.

   Continuation of 1P-3.

1P-4   The Pros. Robert Riger and Tex Maule. Simon & Schuster. 1960. Clothbound.

   A pictorial documentary of the game. Key plays, techniques, important games, outstanding players.

1P-5   Pro Football Scouting Reports. Sports Illustrated. Travelers Insurance Co. 1962. Booklet.

   Team previews reprinted from the 1962 Sports Illustrated pro football issue.

1P-6   Best Plays of the Year. Robert Riger. Prentice-Hall. 1962. Clothbound. 1963. Paperbound.

   National Football League action photos and game reports. Inside information from players and coaches.

1P-7   NFL Appointment Book. Tom Gorman. 1962-64. Clothbound.

   Accommodations in National Football League cities. Records, facts, other data.

1P-7A Pro Football Desk Diary. Tom Gorman. 1965, 1966. Clothbound.

   Continuation of 1P-6.

1P-8   Pro Football Hall of Fame Appointment Calendar. National Football League Properties. 1971. Paperbound.

   Player sketches, photos, calendar.

1P-9   The Blue Book of Professional Football. McNitt's, Inc. 1964. Paperbound.

   Directory and rosters of major, minor, and Canadian league teams.

1P-10 NFL 1964. David Boss. National Football League Properties. 1964. Paperbound.

   National Football League team histories, chronology, records, photos. Sketches of all-stars.

General Works

1P-11 The Gridiron Baedeker. M. Gold. Whisenant-Glenn. 1964. Paperbound.

    A guide to the cities with pro football teams. Accommodations, points of interest, etc. Playing records, statistics, schedules.

1P-11A Gridiron Guidebook. Peter Glenn. 1965-to date. Paperbound.

    Continuation of 1P-11.

1P-12 Nelson's Encyclopedia of Pro Football. Bill Wallace. Thomas Nelson & Sons. 1964. Clothbound.

    Informal history of the National Football League. Life among the pros, the championship game, the business of pro football. National and American Football League all-time records and rosters.

1P-13 The Pro Quarterback. Murray Olderman. Prentice-Hall. 1966. Clothbound.

    Evolution, training, general discussion of quarterbacking. Sketches and records of twenty-one past and present stars. Appendix, index, photos.

1P-14 The Players. Tex Maule. New American Library. 1967. Clothbound.

    A discussion of great players and the prerequisites for outstanding play at each position. Photos.

1P-15 Playing Pro Football to Win. John Unitas and Harold Rosenthal. Doubleday & Co. 1968. Clothbound. Signet. 1971, reissue. Paperbound.

    Insight into the game by an all-time great quarterback. Accounts of great games of the past and present, autobiographical notes.

1P-16 This Is NFL Football. National Football League Properties. 1967, 1968. Booklet.

    An advertising supplement containing articles and photos.

1P-16A The National Football League. National Football League Properties. 1969. Booklet.

    Continuation of 1P-16.

1P-17 Pro Football Forecast. John J. Plunkett. Macfadden - Bartell. 1970-to date. Paperbound.

    Team previews, rosters.

General Works

1P-18 The Vince Lombardi Pro Football Guide. Vince Lombardi and Ray Siegener. Aurora Publishers. 1970. Paperbound.

      Team previews, schedules, scores, explanations of the game, play diagrams.

1P-19 A Thinking Man's Guide to Pro Football. Paul Zimmerman. E.P. Dutton & Co. 1970, 1971. Clothbound. Paperback Library. 1972, reissue. Paperbound.

      An analysis of the game and its players. Anecdotes.

1P-20 Home Stadium Program - Record Book. Michaelson Press. 1971. Magazine.

      Rosters, records, data.

1P-21 Pro: The Official National Football League Television Magazine. National Football League Properties. November 14, 1971; January 16, 1972. Booklet.

      An advertising supplement containing rosters and articles.

1P-22 Pro Football Strategy '71. Pro Football Weekly. 1971. Paperbound.

      Discussions of game plans and strategy involved in games played during the 1970 season.

1P-23 Pro Quarterback Handbook. Pro Football Weekly. 1972. Paperbound.

      Quarterback sketches, ratings, statistics.

1P-24 Locker Room Talk. National Football League Properties. 1972. Magazine.

      Articles, interviews.

1P-25 Pro Football: The World of the NFL. Mike Rathet, ed. Henry Regnery Co. 1972. Clothbound.

      Articles on a variety of topics. 1971 statistics, photos.

1P-26 Inside Pro Football. Don Smith. Stadia Sports Publishing, Inc. 1972. Paperbound.

      Articles on a variety of topics.

2. Guides

2-1   American Inter-Collegiate Association Rule Book. American Intercollegiate Association. 1876-82. Booklet.

2-1A   Rugby Football Rules. 1876-81.

2-1B   The American Intercollegiate Football Rules. William F. Morgan. 1882.

    First official rule book and forerunner of the official guide.

2-2   Wright & Ditson Football Guide. Wright & Ditson. 1883-90.

2-2A   Football Rules, American Intercollegiate Association. Walter Camp. 1883. Booklet.

    Successor to 2-1 as the official rule book. Rules divided into three sections.

2-2B   Football Rules and Referee's Book. Walter Camp. 1884-89. Booklet.

    Official rule book. Rules, referee's duties, rule interpretations. The 1888 and 1889 editions contained the constitution of the American Intercollegiate Football Association.

2-2C   Wright & Ditson's Rugby and Association Football Guide. 1890. Paperbound.

    Rules and constitutions of the American Intercollegiate Association, Eastern Intercollegiate Football Association and the Interscholastic Football Association Football. Reprint of How to Coach A Football Team by Camp. Schedules of leading teams.

2-3   Spalding Football Guide. A.G. Spalding & Brothers. 1885-1940.

2-3A   Football Rules and Referee's Book. Walter Camp. 1885, 1886, 1888-90. Cover title: Spalding's Inter-Collegiate Association Football Rules. 1885, 1886. Booklet.

Guides

The Spalding editions for 1885, 1886, 1888 and 1889 were identical to the Wright & Ditson Guides for these years, a situation which has produced much bibliographical confusion. The Library of Congress lists the Wright & Ditson editions under the heading "Spalding's Official Football Guide," but this is incorrect. The 1888 Spalding edition bears the title page imprint "Entered according to Act of Congress 1888 by the American Intercollegiate Football Association and published for them by Wright & Ditson, Boston, Mass." The 1889 Spalding edition bears the imprint "Copyright in the year 1889 by Wright & Ditson, Boston, Mass." These editions contained a diagram of the playing field and the rules of the game. The editions from 1888-90 also contained the constitution of the American Intercollegiate Association. Beginning in 1890, the Spalding Guide became the official publication of the Association.

2-3B   The Game of Football. Henry Chadwick. 1887. Paperbound.

Revised rules of the American and English games. Technical terms, definitions. Since the format of this edition differed from that of the first two, which were simply copies of the Wright & Ditson Guide, the preface stated that "We present to the Football players of the United States and Canada the first work of the kind yet published on this continent." Because the 1885 and 1886 Spalding editions are extremely rare, it was in later years erroneously assumed from this statement that the 1887 edition was the first Spalding Guide.

2-3C   Spalding's Official Football Guide. 1891-1940. Walter Camp. 1891-1924. E.K. Hall. 1925-32. Walter R. Okeson. 1933-40. Cover titles vary. Title pages: Football Rules and Referee's Book. 1891-95. Football Rules as Recommended to the University Athletic Club by the Rules Committee. 1896-99. Football Rules as Recommended by the Rules Committee. 1900-92. Spalding's Official Football Guide. 1903-40. Paperbound.

The 1891 edition contained rules and the constitution. The 1892 edition included an introductory chapter for beginners, with playing instructions. The 1893 edition was the first to include scores, and was therefore the first true Spalding "Guide." Subsequent editions were enlarged to include national and sectional reviews and previews, statistics, All-American selections, all-time records, photos, etc. Sectional Editions: Eastern. 1906-32. Western. 1906-32. Midwestern. 1910. Mideastern. 1910. Pacific Coast. 1910, 1923, 1924, 1930-32. From 1906-26 the sectional editions con-

Guides

2-4 Official National Collegiate Athletic Association Football Guide. A.S. Barnes & Co. 1941-49. National Collegiate Athletic Association. 1950-to date. Walter R. Okeson. 1941-43. W.J. Bingham. 1944-47. Earl C. Krieger. 1948. A.R. Hutchens. 1949. Cover titles vary. Paperbound.

tained different minor college coverage. From 1927-32 the editions differed only in the team photos.

Sectional reviews and previews, bowl game summaries, All-American selections, team and player records and statistics, rules.

2-5 Official Collegiate Football Record Book. National Collegiate Athletic Association. 1951-to date. Paperbound.

Contains all material found in 2-4 except the rules.

2-6 Intercollegiate Football Review. S.M. Meyer and R.W. Baremore. 1904. Paperbound.

Reviews, previews, and rosters of eastern college and prep teams. Scores, All-American teams, photos.

2-7 Wilson's Football Guide and Annual Review. Harry W. Wilson. Werner Co. 1907. Paperbound.

Scores, schedules, accounts of major 1906 games. Team reviews, rules, photos.

2-8 Rawlings Official Football Guide. Rawlings Manufacturing Co. 1921. Paperbound.

All-America teams, rules, data.

2-9 Football Record and Rule Book. The Sporting News. 1945. Paperbound.

College and professional coverage. Scores, records, All-America selections, chronology.

2-10 Intercollegiate and Professional Football. J.J. Banta, ed. Dell Publishing Co. 1948-50. Paperbound.

Records, statistics, schedules. Team reviews, top plays, photos, questions and answers, glossary.

2-11 Conley's Football Guide. Roy Nelson. Conley Sports Publications. 1967. Paperbound.

Scores, schedules, rosters. Team and player statistics, post-season game summaries.

2-12 Hughes' Collegiate Football Guide. Palmer W. Hughes, ed. Hughes Sports Publications. 1971-to date. Paperbound.

Guides

Rosters, schedules, scores for all major schools.

Professional Titles

2P-1 Official Guide of the National Football League. A.G. Spalding & Brothers. 1935-40. Joe F. Carr. 1935-38. Carl Storck. 1939-40. Cover titles: The National Football League Professional Football Rules. 1935, 1936. Official Guide, National Football League. 1937-40. Paperbound.

Team reviews, statistics, records, schedules. Post-season game summaries, rules, photos.

2P-2 National Football League Manual. The National Football League. 1941-71. Paperbound. Signet. 1972. George Strickler. 1941-46. Joseph Labrum. 1947-61. Jim Kensil. 1962-65. Don Weiss. 1966-68. Jim Heffernan. 1969. Don Weiss, Seymour Siwoff, Jim Heffernan, and Harold Rosenthal. 1970, 1971. Weiss, Siwoff, Heffernan, Rosenthal, and Joe Browne. 1972. Cover titles: Official National Football League Roster and Record Manual. 1941, 1943. Official National Football League Record and Roster Manual. 1942. Official National Football League Record and Rules Manual. 1944. National Football League Record and Rules Manual. 1945-61. National Football League Record Manual. 1962-to date. Title pages: Roster and Record Manual. 1941. Record and Roster Manual. 1942, 1943. Record and Rules Manual. 1944. National Football League Record and Rules Manual. 1945-61. National Football League Record Manual. 1962-to date. Paperbound.

Statistics, rosters, all-time player, and team records. Post-season game summaries and records, all-time scores, other data.

2P-3 Official National Football League Pro Record and Rule Book. The Sporting News. 1947-50. Paperbound.

Records, statistics, rosters, rules. The life of Glenn (Pop) Warner was featured in the 1947 edition, Frank Leahy in 1948, Sammy Baugh in 1949, Earle Neale in 1950.

2P-4 Press and Radio Information Book. All-American Football Conference. 1946. Paperbound.

First AAFC publication. Conference officers, officials, schedules. Team rosters, chronology, scores of exhibition games.

2P-5 All-America Football Conference Record Manual. Joseph Petritz. All-America Football Conference. 1947-49, 1949 supplement. Paperbound.

10

Guides

Scores, rosters, rules. Team and individual records and statistics.

2P-6   Pro Football Handbook. Pocket Books. 1959-62. Paperbound. Thomas Nelson. 1961, reissue. Clothbound. J. Lowell Pratt. 1963-64. Paperbound. Don Schiffer. 1959-62. Dave Anderson. 1963-64.

        Team analyses, player sketches, rules interpretations. Rosters, records, statistics.

2P-7   Pro Football. Pocket Books. 1963-to date. Don Schiffer. 1963, 1964. Jack Zanger. 1965-70. Brenda Zanger and Dick Kaplan. 1971. Brenda Zanger. 1972. Paperbound.

        Team analyses, rosters, sketches of rookies. Team reviews, previews, statistics, records.

2P-8   American Football League Press, Radio, TV Guide. American Football League. 1960. Booklet.

        First AFL publication. History, directory, schedules, rosters.

2P-9   American Football League Record and Press Manual. Al Ward. American Football League. 1961. Paperbound.

        Directory, draft lists, league history. Records, scores, statistics, rosters.

2P-10   American Football League Official Guide. The Sporting News. 1962-69. Al Ward. 1962. Al Ward and Jack Horrigan. 1963. Jack Horrigan. 1964-66. Mike Rathet. 1967-68. Harold Rosenthal. 1969. Cover title: Official American Football League Guide. Paperbound.

        Rosters, scores, statistics, all-time player and team records. Historical background, post-season games, other data.

2P-10A   American Football League Official History. Harold Rosenthal, ed. The Sporting News. 1970. Paperbound.

        Continuation of 2P-10.

2P-11   Official Pro Football Almanac. Bill Wise. Fawcett Publishing Co. 1963-65. Paperbound.

        Rosters, records, statistics, player sketches, reviews.

2P-12   NBC Sports Pro Football. William Mehlman. National Broadcasting Co. Grosset & Dunlap. 1966. Paperbound.

        Playing instructions, spectating, team reviews, and previews. Rosters, statistics.

Guides

2P-13   Frank Gifford's NFL CBS Football Guide. Frank Gifford. Signet. 1967. Title page: NFL CBS Football Guide. Paperbound.

National Football League rosters, statistics, team reviews, play analyses. Spectators' guide.

2P-13A   Frank Gifford's NFL-AFL Football Guide. Frank Gifford. Signet. 1968-69. Paperbound.

Continuation of 2P-13.

2P-13B   Frank Gifford's Pro Football Guide. Frank Gifford. Signet. 1970- to date. Paperbound.

Continuation of 2P-13A.

2P-14   First Official Illustrated Digest. Ed Croke. Poretz-Ross. 1967. Paperbound.

National Football League team rosters, records, statistics, player sketches. Feature articles, photos.

2P-14A   Official Illustrated Digest. Don Smith and Ed Croke. Poretz-Ross. 1968. Paperbound.

Continuation of 2P-14.

2P-14B   First NFL-AFL Illustrated Digest. Don Smith, Ed Croke, and Art Poretz. Poretz-Ross. 1969. Paperbound.

Continuation of 2P-14A.

2P-14C   Illustrated Digest of Pro Football. Ed Croke and Art Poretz. Poretz-Ross. 1970. Stadia Sports Publishing. 1971-to date. Paperbound.

Continuation of 2P-14B.

2P-15   Conley's Pro Football Guide. Roy Nelson. Conley Sports Publications. 1967, 1972. Paperbound.

Rosters, scores, schedules. Team and player statistics.

2P-16   The Sporting News National Football Guide. The Sporting News. 1970-to date. Joe Marcin. 1970, 1971. Marcin and Larry Wigge. 1972. Paperbound.

Statistics, records, rosters, scores.

2P-17   Official National Football League Record Book. National Football League. Fawcett World Library. 1970, 1971. Paperbound. Signet. 1972. Paperbound.

Statistics, rosters, all-time player and team records. Post-season game summaries and records, all-time scores, other data.

Guides

2P-18　　Official National Football League Guide. National Football League Properties. Signet. 1972. Paperbound.

　　　　　Player statistics, records, previews, rosters, photos.

2P-19　　The Complete Handbook of Pro Football. John Devaney. Lancer Books. 1972. Paperbound.

　　　　　Player sketches, team previews, schedules, rosters, statistics.

3. Early British Works

3-1 Football, a Popular Handbook of the Game. G.A. Hutchison, ed. Religious Tract Society. 1877. Paperbound.

    Chapters by W.N. Irvine, C.W. Alcock, and others. Football songs.

3-2 The Laws of Football. Heckmondwike. 1886. Paperbound.

    Revised and corrected, with all recent alterations by the Football Association and Rugby Football Union.

3-3 Athletics and Football. Montague Shearman. Badminton Library. 1888. Clothbound.

    History, school games, the Rugby Union and Association games. Football as a sport.

3-4 Rugby Football. Harry Vassil. George Bell & Sons. 1890. Title page: Football, the Rugby Game. Clothbound.

    Background, the play of each position, referee's duties. Rules and regulations, discussion of professionalism.

3-5 Football, the Rugby Union Game. Francis Marshall. Cassell & Co., Ltd. 1892, 1895. Clothbound.

    History, playing instructions.

3-6 Baseball and Football. John Ward and Ralph D. Paine. Macmillan Co. 1905. Paperbound.

    General explanations of the games.

3-7 History of Football from the Beginnings to 1871. Francis P. Magoun, Jr. Bochum-Langendreer. 1938. Paperbound. Johnson Reprint Co. 1966, reissue. Paperbound.

    From earliest times to the nineteenth century. Football at the universities, the Football Association, the Rugby Football Union. Football in Scotland.

4. Record Books

4-1 Football Records of American Teams. Walter Camp. Wright & Ditson. 1883. Booklet.

Rosters and scores of Columbia, Harvard, Princeton, Yale, Stevens, Penn, Wesleyan, Michigan, Lafayette, City College of New York, Rutgers, Williams, and Hopkins from 1876-83. Referees, addresses of teams.

4-2 Gulf Football Manual. Parke Davis, ed. Gulf Oil Co. 1933. Booklet.

Historical background, series summaries, All-America teams, photos.

4-3 Intercollegiate Football. Christy Walsh. Doubleday, Doran & Co. 1934. Clothbound.

Major and small-college all-time scores and lettermen. All-America teams, chronology, all-time records, other facts.

4-4 Supplement to Intercollegiate Football. Glenn Whittle. Intercollegiate Football Association. 1935, 1936. Clothbound and Paperbound.

Designed to provide supplementary information to 4-3. Articles, scores, schedules, conference reviews, and previews. Longest plays, All-Americans. Contents of the 1935 edition are identical to the 1935 edition of 5-3.

4-4A Intercollegiate Football Annual. Glenn Whittle. 1937. Clothbound and Paperbound.

Continuation of 4-4.

4-5 College Football. Christy Walsh. Murray & Gee. 1949. Clothbound. House-Warven. 1951, reissue. Clothbound.

All-time scores and rosters for all major and many small colleges. Bowl results, All-America teams.

Record Books

4-6   <u>All American Football Dope Book.</u> Don Neth. All American Football Book Co. 1936. Paperbound.

         Scores, schedules, prospects, ratings, All-Americans. Pro coverage.

4-7   <u>American Football Statistical Bureau.</u> 1938-42. Paperbound.

4-7A   <u>Summary of Nation-Wide 1937 Football Statistics.</u> American Football Statistical Bureau. 1938.

4-7B   <u>Intercollegiate Football Summary.</u> American Football Statistical Bureau. 1939.

4-7C   <u>Official Intercollegiate Football Statistical Summary.</u> American Football Statistical Bureau. 1940-42.

         Extensive individual and team statistical records and performance rankings. Divided into geographical sections.

4-8   <u>What's What in Football Supplement.</u> H.A. Marple. What's What Publishing Co. 1938, 1939. Paperbound.

         Summaries covering previous season. See 11-2.

4-8A   <u>What's What in Football Yearbook.</u> H.A. Marple. What's What Publishing Co. 1940, 1941. Paperbound.

         Continuation of 4-8.

4-9   <u>Football Review Scrapbook.</u> Richard Poling. 1938-to date. Paperbound.

         Cumulative and season scores, ratings, statistics, facts.

4-9A   <u>Football Review Scrapbook Supplement.</u> Richard Poling. 1938-to date. Paperbound.

         Supplements to 4-9.

4-10   <u>Norman Sper's Football Almanac.</u> Norman Sper. Greenberg. 1942. Three editions: Eastern, South-Southwestern, Midwestern. Paperbound.

         Records, statistics, team analyses, predictions.

4-11   <u>The Football Review.</u> Byron Boyd, ed. Football News. 1942-45. Magazine.

         Cover titles vary. Articles, ratings, All-America selections, statistics, scores.

4-11A   <u>Football Scorebook.</u> Football News. 1946, 1953-60. Magazine.

         Cover title varies. Continuation of 4-11.

Record Books

4-12   Football: Facts and Figures. Dr. L.H. Baker. Farrar and Rinehart. 1945. Clothbound.

> Historical background, famous players, all-time player and team records. Coaches, lettermen, dual series standings and scores for all major colleges. Chronology of rule changes, bowl games, other data. History and records of pro football.

4-12A   Football: Facts and Figures Supplement. Dr. L.H. Baker. Rinehart & Co. 1948. Paperbound.

> Supplement to 4-12. Records, rosters and scores brought up to 1948.

4-13   Football Thesaurus. Deke Houlgate. Nash-U-Nal Publishing Co. 1946. Clothbound. Houlgate House. 1954. Clothbound. Yearly supplemental inserts, 1947-53.

> Yearly scores of all major and many small colleges. Coaches, famous plays, All-America players, other data. 1954 edition contains yearly history of football from 1869-1953, yearly highlights of each college, and photos.

4-14   Atlas Football Handbook. American Football Coaches Association. Wells Publishing Co. 1947. Booklet.

> Schedules, scores, plays, All-American players, leading teams, bowl games.

4-15   Football Data for Associated Sportcasters and Commentators. Tidewater Associated Oil Co. 1948. Paperbound.

> Scores, schedules, data, sketches of coaches for all major colleges.

4-16   Ronald Encyclopedia of Football. Harold Claassen and Steve Boda, Jr. Ronald Press. 1960, 1961, 1963. Clothbound.

> College: history, records, conference standings, bowl games, rankings. All-America teams, players in the Hall of Fame. Scores, individual records, coaches' records. Pro: history, records, standings. All-Star and Pro Bowl game results, all-league teams. High school: history, All-America players.

4-17   Collegiate Football Summary. A.B.A. Enterprises. 1962-65. Paperbound.

> Team analyses for coming season based on scores against each opponent for previous five seasons.

4-18   Tom Harmon's Book of Sports Information and Football Almanac. Tom Harmon and Jim Benagh. J. Lowell Pratt. 1965. Cloth-

Record Books

	bound. 1966. Paperbound.
	College and pro coverage. Reviews, previews, records, schedules.
4-19	College and Pro Football Guide. Jack Clary. Snibbe Sports Publications. 1967-to date. Booklet.
	Reviews, previews, schedules, rosters, records.
4-20	College Football All-Time Record Book. Steve Boda, Jr., ed. National Collegiate Athletic Association. 1969-to date. Paperbound.
	All-time team and player records.
4-21	College Football All-Time Galaxy. National Collegiate Sports Services. National Collegiate Athletic Association. 1970. Paperbound.
	Yearly statistics covering the college careers of all-time great players and coaches.

Professional Titles

4P-1	A Survey of Eleven 1939 National Football League Games. Hugh L. Ray. National Football League. 1940. Paperbound.
	A comprehensive survey of game statistics, records, and penalties.
4P-1A	A Survey of the 1940 National Football League Season. Hugh L. Ray. National Football League. 1941. Paperbound.
	Continuation of 4P-1.
4P-1B	National Football League Football Up to Date. Hugh L. Ray. National Football League. 1946-52. Paperbound.
	Continuation of 4P-1.
4P-2	National Football League Roster Manual. National Football League. 1942-47. Paperbound.
	Editions of 1942-45 contained team rosters. Editions of 1946 and 1947 were collections of team press guides.
4P-3	The Official National Football League Football Encyclopedia. Roger Treat. A.S. Barnes & Co. 1952. Clothbound.
	Historical background, coaches, rosters, sketches of star players. All-time roster, player and team records. All-time scores, summaries of post-season games, other

Record Books

data. Coverage of the All-American Football Conference.

4P-3A   The Encyclopedia of Football. Roger Treat. A.S. Barnes & Co. 1959, 1961. Clothbound.

    Continuation of 4P-3.

4P-3B   The Official Encyclopedia of Football. Roger Treat. A.S. Barnes & Co. 1964, 1965, 1967, 1968, 1969. Clothbound and Paperbound. Suzanne Treat. A.S. Barnes. 1972. Clothbound.

    Continuation of 4P-3.

4P-4   Pro Football Factbook. Pat Livingston. 1960, 1963. Paperbound.

    Yearly records and statistics of NFL players. The 1960 edition was included in the 1960 Pittsburgh Steeler Press Guide.

4P-5   National Football League Individual Statistics. National Football League. 1960. Paperbound.

    Yearly individual and team statistics since 1950.

4P-6   Pro Football Encyclopedia. B.R. Ampolsk. Reese Publishing Co. 1964. Paperbound.

    Team reviews, rosters, statistics, all-time records.

4P-7   Pro Football Record Book. Complete Sports. 1964. Paperbound.

    Yearly player records and statistics.

4P-7A   NFL and AFL Pro Football Record Book. Complete Sports. 1965-66. Paperbound.

    Continuation of 4P-7.

4P-7B   Official Pro Football Record Book. Complete Sports. 1967, 1968. Paperbound.

    Continuation of 4P-7A.

4P-8   Pro Football Guide. Snibbe Sports Publications. 1965-to date. Norman Miller. 1965. Jack Clary. 1966-to date. Booklet.

    Reviews, previews, schedules, rosters, records.

4P-9   Football Register. The Sporting News. 1966-to date. Joel Bussert, John Duxbury and Clifford Kachline. 1966. Bussert and Duxbury. 1967. Duxbury and Larry Shainman. 1968, 1969. Joe Marcin and Gary Shreve. 1970. Joe Marcin. 1971. Marcin and Donald J. Smith. 1972. Paperbound.

    Yearly statistics for each active pro player, as well as for many former stars. Team rosters.

Record Books

4P-10	NFL Appointment Calendar. Bob Oates. National Football League Properties. 1967. Magazine.
	Team reviews and previews, schedules, records, photos.
4P-10A	NFL Appointment Yearbook. Bob Oates. National Football League Properties. 1968-to date. Magazine.
	Continuation of 4P-10.
4P-11	Profile of a Season. Dave Gardner. Kimberly-Clark. National Football League Properties. 1968. Magazine.
	A pictorial weekly review of the 1967 NFL season. Game resumes and statistics.
4P-12	Pro Football Forecast for 1969. Berry Stainback. Grosset & Dunlap. 1969. Paperbound.
	An analysis of each team. 1968 statistics.
4P-13	Miller Falls Pro Football Fact Book. The Benjamin Co., Inc. Rutledge Books, Inc. 1969. Booklet.
	All-time records.
4P-14	National Football Conference Media Information Book. National Football League. 1970-to date. Don Weiss. 1970, 1971. Weiss, Joe Browne and Harold Rosenthal. 1972. Paperbound.
	Rosters, records, schedules of teams in the National Conference of the NFL.
4P-15	American Football Conference Media Information Book. National Football League. 1970-to date. Don Weiss, 1970, 1971. Weiss, Joe Browne and Harold Rosenthal. 1972. Paperbound.
	Rosters, records, schedules of teams in the American Conference of the NFL.
4P-16	Prolog: The National Football League Annual. Bob Oates, Jr., ed. National Football League Properties. Follett Publishing Co. 1971-to date. Clothbound and Paperbound.
	A review of the season. Team analyses, rosters, statistics.
4P-17	Pro Quarterback Annual. SCH Publications. 1971-to date. Paperbound.
	Reviews, previews, statistics, records.
4P-18	Gridiron Pro Yearbook. Champion Sports Publishing Co. 1972. Paperbound.
	Articles, statistics, photos.

Record Books

4P-19   Pro Football Review. Sports Illustrated. Pro Football Weekly. 1972. Paperbound.

      A review of the 1971 season. Game charts, rosters, team and player statistics, previews. Coverage of Canadian and Atlantic Coast Leagues.

5. Annuals

5-1 Illustrated Football Annual. Fiction House, Inc. 1930-53. Jack Byrne. 1930-35. Malcolm Reiss. 1936-37. Eddie Dooley. 1938-42. Jack Byrne and Malcolm Reiss. 1943-53. Magazine.

    Schedules, photos, articles, team reviews, and previews. Team scores carried from 1938 on.

5-2 Football Review. Writers' Digest Publishing Co. 1931. Magazine.

    Articles, schedules, photos. First coverage of pro football in an annual.

5-2A Football Digest. Writers' Digest Publishing Co. 1932, 1933. Magazine.

    Continuation of 5-2.

5-3 The Intercollegiate Football Pictorial. Glenn Whittle. Intercollegiate Football Association. 1935, 1936. Magazine.

    Contents of the 1935 edition are identical to the 1935 edition of 4-4. Articles, schedules, scores, records, photos.

5-4 Football Forecast. Eric B. Roberts, ed. Ric Roberts Publishing Co. 1939. Magazine.

    Team previews, sectional roundups, feature articles on Negro college football.

5-5 Street and Smith Football Yearbook. 1940-to date. Street and Smith. 1940-61. Conde Nast. 1962-to date. Magazine.

5-5A Street and Smith's Football Pictorial Yearbook. 1940-46, 1951-58.

5-5B Pic Quarterly Football Pictorial. 1947-49.

5-5C All-Star Sports Football. 1950.

5-5D Street and Smith's Football Yearbook. 1959-to date.

Annuals

Reviews, team analyses, schedules, scores, forecasts, photos. Pro coverage since 1947. Two regional editions published, 1963.

5-6   Football Prevues. Gorham Press and Athletic Publications. 1944-48. Magazine.

Reviews, previews, records, schedules.

5-7   College Football Illustrated. Elbak Publishing Co. 1946-49. Magazine.

Reviews, scores, schedules, photos.

5-7A   Sports Review College Football. Elbak Publishing Co. 1950. Magazine.

Continuation of 5-7.

5-8   Sports Review Football. Elbak Publishing Co. 1951-62. Magazine.

College and pro coverage. Reviews, previews, statistics, photos.

5-9   Complete Football. Ray Robinson, ed. Interstate Publishing Corp. 1949, 1950. Magazine.

Reviews, schedules, photos.

5-10   Stanley Woodward's Football. Dell Publishing Co. 1949-57. Magazine.

Scouting reports, forecasts, team ratings, All-America selections, photos.

5-10A   Dell Sports: Stanley Woodward's Football. Dell Publishing Co. 1958, 1959. Magazine.

Continuation of 5-10.

5-10B   Dell Sports Magazine: Stanley Woodward's Football. Dell Publishing Co. 1960-62. Magazine.

Continuation of 5-10A. Pro coverage included.

5-10C   Dell Sports. Dell Publishing Co. 1963-68. Magazine.

Continuation of 5-10B.

5-11   Football Stars. Dell Publishing Co. 1952, 1953. Magazine.

The ten best at each position. College and pro coverage.

5-12   True Football Yearbook. Fawcett Publishing Co. 1950-53, 1956- to date. Magazine.

Annuals

5-12A Football Yearbook. 1950-53. 1956-61.

5-12B True's Football Yearbook. 1962-to date.
Forecasts, sectional reviews, schedules, photos. Pro coverage.

5-13 Football Forecast. Fawcett Publishing Co. 1962, 1963. Magazine.
Articles, team reviews, statistics. College and pro coverage.

5-14 Real Magazine's Football Yearbook Kickoff. Popular Library, Inc. Literary Enterprises, Inc. 1956, 1957. Magazine.
Reviews, schedules, outstanding players.

5-14A Football Yearbook Kickoff. Popular Library, Inc. 1958-71. Magazine.
Continuation of 5-14.

5-14B Popular Sports Kickoff. Popular Library, Inc. 1972. Magazine.
Continuation of 5-14A.

5-15 Sports Forecast Football. O'Malley Publishing Co. 1958, 1959. Magazine.
College and pro coverage, 1958. Separate college and pro issues, 1959. Articles, scores, reviews, previews, photos.

5-16 Football Roundup. Counterpoint Publishing Co. 1960-64. Magazine.
Sectional reviews, schedules. College and pro coverage. Pro statistics.

5-16A Sports Quarterly Presents Football Roundup. Counterpoint Publishing Co. 1965-to date. Magazine.
Continuation of 5-16.

5-17 Inside Football. Sport Magazine. MacFadden-Bartell. 1961-70. Magazine.
Articles, photos, reviews, previews. College and pro coverage.

5-18 Complete Sports College Football. Natlus, Inc. 1961. Magazine.
Reviews, previews, articles, photos.

5-18A College Football. Complete Sports Publications. 1962-67. Mag-

27

Annuals

5-18B   azine. Continuation of 5-18.

         Complete Sports. Complete Sports Publications. 1968-to date. Magazine.

         Continuation of 5-18A. Material appeared in fall issue.

5-19   Who's Who in Football. Topical Magazines, Inc. 1964. Magazine.

         College, pro, and high school coverage. Player sketches, articles, statistics, photos.

5-20   Pro and College Football. Whitestone Publishing Co. 1965-67. Magazine.

         Previews, schedules.

5-21   College and Pro Football. Hewfred Publishing Co. 1968-to date. Magazine.

         Team previews, schedules.

5-22   Game Plan College Football. Game Plan Magazines. 1970-to date. Magazine.

         Team previews, rosters, statistics, records.

5-23   Ben Strong Football. Stanley Weston. 1972. Magazine.

         Articles on a variety of topics. Photos.

5-24   All-Star Sports Special. Reese Publishing Co. 1972. Magazine.

         Collegiate football preview issue. Articles, photos.

Professional Titles

5P-1   Who's Who in Major League Football. B.E. Callahan. 1935, 1936. Harold (Speed) Johnson and Wilfred Smith. 1935. Johnson. 1936. Paperbound.

         Team previews, player sketches, articles. Sketches of officials, terms, statistics, schedules, photos.

5P-1A   Who's Who in the Major Leagues Football. Harold (Howard) Roberts. B.E. Callahan. 1939, 1940. Booklet.

         Continuation of 5P-1.

5P-2   Pro Football Illustrated. Elbak Publishing Co. 1941-48. Magazine.

Annuals

	Official National Football League publication, 1941, 1942. Articles, rosters, records, statistics, photos.
5P-2A	Sports Review Pro Football. Elbak Publishing Co. 1949-50. Magazine.

Continuation of 5P-2. Coverage continued in 5-8 after 1950.

5P-3   Professional Football Yearbook of the National Football League. National Football League. Don Spencer Co. 1953. Stadium Publishing Co. 1955. Magazine.

Official National Football League Yearbook. Records, statistics, reviews.

5P-4   Pro Football Yearbook. Herb Elk and George Girsch, eds. Jay Publishing Co. 1954. Magazine.

Official National Football League yearbook. Rosters, statistics, team analyses, photos.

5P-4A   N.F.L. Pro Football Yearbook. Herb Elk and George Girsch, eds. Jay Publishing Co. 1959. Magazine.

Continuation of 5P-4, but not designated as the official yearbook.

5P-4B   National Football League Yearbook. Herb Elk and George Girsch, eds. Jay Publishing Co. 1960, 1961. Magazine.

Continuation of 5P-4A.

5P-5   American Football League Yearbook. Herb Elk and George Girsch, eds. Jay Publishing Co. 1960. Magazine.

First AFL publication available to the general public. Rosters, player sketches, photos.

5P-6   Pro Football. Petersen Publishing Co. 1956-64, 1970-to date. Magazine.

Articles, team analyses, rosters, statistics, records, scores, photos.

5P-7   Pro Football Yearbook. Rensart Publishing Co. 1957. Magazine.

Team analyses, records, player sketches, photos.

5P-8   Pro Football Stars. Whitestone Publishing Co. 1957, 1960-68. Magazine.

Articles, sketches, team reviews, photos.

5P-9   Pro Football All-Stars. Maco Magazine Corp. 1957. Magazine.

Statistics, rosters, reviews, previews, photos.

Annuals

5P-9A	**Sports All-Stars Football.** Maco Magazine Corp. 1958. Magazine.	

        Continuation of 5P-9.

5P-9B   <u>Sports All-Stars Pro Football.</u> Maco Magazine Corp. 1958-to date. Magazine.

        Continuation of 5P-9A.

5P-10   <u>All Pro Football.</u> Maco Magazine Corp. 1961-to date. Magazine.

        Team analyses and statistics. Photos.

5P-11   <u>Dell Pro Football Annual.</u> Dell Publishing Co. 1958. Magazine.

        Records, rosters, reviews, previews, photos.

5P-11A   <u>Dell Sports Magazine Pro Football.</u> Dell Publishing Co. 1959, 1960. Magazine.

        Continuation of 5P-11.

5P-11B   <u>Dell Sports Pro Football.</u> Dell Publishing Co. 1961. Magazine.

        Continuation of 5P-11A.

5P-11C   <u>Dell Sports Pro Football Preview.</u> Dell Publishing Co. 1962. Magazine.

        Continuation of 5P-11B.

5P-11D   <u>Dell Pro Football.</u> Dell Publishing Co. 1963-69. Magazine.

        Continuation of 5P-11C.

5P-12   <u>Dell Sports.</u> Dell Publishing Co. 1963-68. Magazine.

        Pro football issue.

5P-13   <u>Professional Football Annual.</u> Don Schiffer. Grosset & Dunlap. 1959. Magazine.

        Rosters, records, schedules, previews. Player sketches, chronology, photos.

5P-13A   <u>A Complete Guide to Pro Football.</u> Don Schiffer. Grosset & Dunlap. 1960. Magazine.

        Continuation of 5P-13. Reviews, previews, records, rosters, photos.

5P-14   <u>Sports Forecast Football.</u> O'Malley Publishing Co. 1959. Magazine.

        See 5-15.

Annuals

5P-15   Great Moments in Sports. Four Star Management Corp. 1960, 1961. Magazine.
Pro football issues. Outstanding games and plays.

5P-16   Who's Who in Pro Football. Agard Publishing Co. 1961. Magazine.
National Football League player sketches and photos.

5P-17   Sports Action Magazine Pro Football Thrills. Cape Magazine Corp. 1961. Magazine.
Articles, photos.

5P-18   Pro Football. Fawcett Publishing Co. 1961, 1963. Magazine.
Articles, photos.

5P-19   Frank Gifford's All-Pro Football. Popular Library. 1961. Magazine.
Team previews, statistics, photos.

5P-19A   Charley Conerly's All-Pro Football. Popular Library. 1962. Magazine.
Continuation of 5P-19. Articles, player sketches, statistics, quarterback ratings, photos.

5P-19B   All-Pro Football. Popular Library. 1963. Magazine.
Continuation of 5P-19A. Reviews, previews, photos.

5P-19C   Touchdown. Popular Library. 1964. Magazine.
Continuation of 5P-19B. Articles, player sketches, statistics, team analyses.

5P-19D   All-Pro Football Annual, Touchdown. Popular Library. 1965-71. Magazine.
Continuation of 5P-19C. Articles, player sketches, statistics, team analyses.

5P-19E   Popular Sports Touchdown, All-Pro Football. Popular Library. 1972. Magazine.
Continuation of 5P-19D.

5P-20   Pro Football Illustrated. Complete Sports Publications. 1961-to date. Magazine.
Ten sectional editions. 1963. Three sectional editions, plus one on the 30 top pro quarterbacks. 1964. Reviews, previews, articles, color photos.

Annuals

5P-21　Sport Heroes. Complete Sports Publications. 1964-to date. Magazine.

Pro football issue. Two 1965 editions. Sketches, photos, statistics.

5P-22　Pro Football. Complete Sports Publications. 1967. Magazine.

Articles, color photos.

5P-23　Paul Hornung's Football Magazine. Inside Sports. H.S. Publications. 1962. Magazine.

Two editions. Articles, photos.

5P-24　Sports Quarterly Presents Pros Football. Counterpoint Publishing Co. 1962-66. Magazine.

Team analyses, statistics, rosters, photos.

5P-24A　Sports Quarterly Presents Pro Football. Counterpoint Publishing Co. 1967-to date. Magazine.

Continuation of 5P-24.

5P-25　Sports Reviews Pro Football. M.F. Enterprises, Inc. 1963. Magazine.

Previews, sketches, statistics.

5P-26　Street and Smith's Pro Football Yearbook. Conde Nast Publications. 1963-to date. Magazine.

Team analyses, statistics, rosters.

5P-27　Sports Special: Pro Football. Tempest Publishing Co. 1963-to date. Magazine.

Articles, reviews, previews, ratings, statistics, photos.

5P-28　Sports Extra: Pro Football. Tempest Publishing Co. 1968-to date. Magazine.

5P-29　Official Pro Football. Official Sports. 1964. Magazine.

Team analyses.

5P-30　Pro Football Almanac. Sport Magazine. MacFadden-Bartell Corp. 1964-to date. Magazine.

Articles, reviews, photos.

5P-31　Sports Review's Pro Football. Splendid Publications. 1965-to date. Magazine.

Articles, photos.

Annuals

5P-32 Official AFL Autograph Yearbook. Coy Williams. NFL Properties: Sports Underwriters, Inc. 1968, 1969. Magazine.

    Team reviews, records, statistics, autographed player photos.

5P-33 Official NFL Autograph Yearbook. Coy Williams. NFL Properties: Sports Underwriters, Inc. 1968, 1969. Magazine.

    Team reviews, records, statistics, autographed player photos.

5P-34 Pro Football Sports Stars. Hewfred Publishing Co. 1968-to date. Magazine.

    Player sketches, team previews.

5P-35 Pro Football. Editors of Sports Today. Hewfrew Publishing Co. 1971. Magazine.

    Team previews.

5P-36 Pro Football Stars Photostamp Album. Glendale Publishing. 1969, 1970. Magazine.

    Player sketches and color stamps. Records, articles.

5P-37 Pro Football Report. Cord Communications. 1969-to date. Magazine.

    Articles, player sketches, team previews, photos.

5P-38 Pro Football Guide. Cord Communications. 1969-to date. Magazine.

    Team previews, rosters, statistics, photos.

5P-39 The Complete Televiewer's Guide to Pro Football. John Devaney. Magnum-Royal Publications. 1970. Magazine.

    Rosters, records, player sketches, statistics, schedules.

5P-40 Mainliner: Pro Football Issue. United Air Lines. August 1971. Magazine.

    Interviews with players and Commissioner Rozelle. Articles on rookies and the fans.

5P-41 Action Sports Pro Football. Rostam Publishing Co. 1971-to date. Magazine.

    Player sketches, team previews.

5P-42 Game Plan Pro Football. Game Plan Magazines. 1971-to date. Magazine.

    Team previews, rosters, statistics, records.

Annuals

5P-43   <u>Pro Football Guide.</u> Goldwin Publications. Sports Collectors, Inc. 1971. Magazine.

               Schedules, rosters, statistics, feature articles, color stamps of players.

5P-44   <u>All-Star Sports Special.</u> Reese Publishing Co. 1972. Magazine.

               Pro football preview issue. Articles, photos.

6. General Histories

6-1   Football, the American Intercollegiate Game. Parke Davis. Charles Scribner's Sons. 1911, 1912, reissue, 1917, reissue. Clothbound.

      The history of each era to 1910. Accounts of great games, proceedings of intercollegiate conventions and conferences. A series of individual treatises extracted from the book were published in 1911.

6-1A   Football from 1800-1868. Booklet.

6-1B   Traditional Rules from 1868-1870. Booklet.

6-1C   First Common Set of Rules from 1873-1874. Booklet.

6-1D   Concessionary Rules from 1873-1874. Booklet.

6-1E   Football Rules from 1876-1878. Booklet.

6-1F   Football Rules from 1880. Booklet.

6-1G   Evolution of Formations from 1880-1910. Booklet.

6-2   Development of Intercollegiate Football. Frank Haggerty. Stall & Dean. 1924. Booklet. George G. Renneker Co. 1936. Paperbound.

      Historical sketch, all-time teams. The 1936 edition included pro coverage.

6-3   American Football, Its History and Development. Alexander M. Weyand. D. Appleton & Co. 1926. Clothbound.

      Divided into sections, each covering an era: The old association, beginning of modern football, expansion, etc. All-time records and teams, photos.

6-3A   Supplement to "American Football." Alexander Weyand. 1929. Booklet.

      Errata, 1926-28 season reviews, 1925-28 All-America teams.

General Histories

6-4 The Saga of American Football. Alexander M. Weyand. Macmillan Co. 1955. Clothbound.

  Narrative history divided into eras. All-America players, yearly scoring leaders. Diagrams, photos.

6-5 Football through the Years. Dean Hill. Gridiron Publishing Co. 1940. Clothbound.

  A pictorial history by a former member of the Georgia Tech team and collector of football memorabilia. An erroneous statement in this work to the effect that the Spalding Football Guide was first published in 1887 helped give rise to much subsequent bibliographical confusion.

6-6 Grid Wars Rage through Seventy-Fifth Year. Lt. V. Farrell. 1944. Booklet.

  A review of great players, coaches, and games.

6-7 The Story of Football in Text and Pictures. Lamont Buchanan. Vanguard Press. 1947, 1952. Clothbound.

  An informal illustrated history.

6-8 History of American Football. Allison Danzig. Prentice-Hall. 1956. Clothbound.

  Evolution and development, yearly highlights, rankings, team records. Great coaches and teams.

6-9 Football's Unforgettable Games. Harold Claasen. Ronald Press. 1963. Clothbound.

  Accounts of 100 games. Photos.

6-10 The Story of Football. Robert Leckie. Random House. 1965. Clothbound.

  A general history for the younger reader. Photos.

6-11 Football's Greatest Games. Jim Koger. Morrow Publishing Co. 1966. Clothbound.

  Summaries of 60 great games as selected by a panel of sportswriters.

6-12 Football. Earl S. Miers. Grosset & Dunlap. 1967, 1969, reissue. Clothbound.

  A narrative history of college and pro football. Development, the early pros, great stars, and games. Photos.

6-13 The Game of Football. Jack Newcombe. Garrard Publishing

General Histories

Professional Titles

6P-1   Pro Football, Its "Ups" and "Downs." Dr. Harry A. March. J.B. Lyon Co. 1934, 1939. Clothbound.

> The 1934 edition was the first pro football publication. Informal history, lineups and accounts of important games, yearly standings, photos. Valuable information on the game prior to the formation of the National Football League.

6P-2   The Story of Pro Football. Howard Roberts. Rand McNally & Co. 1953. Clothbound.

> A narrative history of the game and its teams. Player index.

6P-3   The History of Professional Football. Harold (Spike) Claassen. Prentice-Hall. 1963. Clothbound.

> A narrative history of the game. Historical sketches, coaches, rosters, all-star players, and all-time scores of each team. Championship game accounts, lineups and statistics. All-Star Game results, yearly standings, other data.

6P-4   Pro Football. Robert Smith. Doubleday & Co. 1963. Clothbound.

> A narrative history of the game and its great players.

6P-5   The Game. Tex Maule. Random House. 1963, 1964, 1967. Clothbound.

> A pictorial history of the National Football League. Historical background, team histories, chronology, all-time records, color photos.

6P-6   The $400,000 Quarterback. Robert Curran. Macmillan Co. 1965. Clothbound. Signet. 1969, reissue. Paperbound.

> The story of the first five years of the American Football League. History of each team and of the league as a whole.

6P-7   Touchdown! George Sullivan. G.P. Putnam's Sons. 1967. Clothbound.

> A pictorial history of the American Football League. A sketch of each team, all-star players, all-time records, yearly standings, coaches.

6P-8   We Came of Age. Jack Orr. Lion Press. 1969. Clothbound.

> An illustrated history of the American Football League.

General Histories

> An historical sketch of each team. Statistics and records.

6P-9   <u>The Other League.</u> Jack Horrigan and Mike Rathet. National Football League Properties; Follett Publishing Co. 1970. Clothbound.

> A pictorial history of the American Football League. Player index, records.

6P-10   <u>Best Pro Football Games.</u> Bob Curran. Essandess Special Editions. 1967. Paperbound.

> Descriptions of 25 top games of 1966 as selected by the coaches. Photos.

6P-11   <u>Pro Football's Unforgettable Games.</u> George Sullivan. G.P. Putnam's Sons. 1967. Clothbound.

> Accounts of 12 outstanding games, from the 1925 Giants-Bears to the 1963 Jets-Bills.

6P-12   <u>Remember the Time.</u> Waltham Watch Co. National Football League Properties. 1967. Booklet.

> Sketches of Jim Thorpe and Sammy Baugh. Accounts of great games.

6P-13   <u>Half a Century.</u> Kimberly-Clark. NFL Properties. 1969. Magazine.

> Historical captioned photos.

6P-14   <u>The Mighty Ones.</u> Stanley Grosshandler. Vantage Press. 1969. Clothbound.

> Notes on the history of pro football. Great teams and players, yearly player records.

6P-15   <u>The First Fifty Years.</u> National Football League Properties. Ridge Press; Simon & Schuster. 1969-to date. Clothbound.

> An illustrated history of the National Football League.

6P-16   <u>Pro Football Hall of Fame Fact Book.</u> National Football League Properties. 1969. Booklet.

> An historical sketch of pro football.

6P-17   <u>Great Moments in Pro Football.</u> Phil Berger. Julian Messner, Inc. 1969. Clothbound. Tempo Books. 1970, reissue. Paperbound.

> Profiles of great teams, players and games.

6P-18   <u>Great Moments in Pro Football.</u> Zander Hollander, ed. Random

General Histories

House. 1969. Clothbound. Scholastic Book Services. 1971, reissue. Paperbound.

> Punt, Pass and Kick Library. Twelve chapters by various writers on great games and players.

6P-19 The Pro Season. Tex Maule. Doubleday & Co. 1970. Clothbound.

> A chronicle of the 1969 season.

6P-20 Illustrated History of Pro Football. Robert Smith. Grosset & Dunlap. 1970, 1972. Clothbound.

> A narrative history of the game. Development of football, the early pro teams, the evolution of the modern game.

6P-21 Pro Football in the Days of Rockne. Emil Klosinski. Carlton Press. 1970. Clothbound.

6P-22 Professional Football's Greatest Games. Paul Michael. Prentice-Hall. 1972. Clothbound.

> Accounts of 23 games as selected through a poll of sports writers. Statistics, photos.

6P-23 Great Upsets of the NFL. Richard Kaplan. Random House. 1972. Clothbound.

> Punt, Pass and Kick Library. Accounts of ten games. Photos.

6P-24 Pro Football's Greatest Upsets. George Sullivan. Garrard Publishing Co. 1972. Clothbound.

> Accounts of four games. For young readers.

7. Team Histories

7-1 Michigan on the Gridiron, 1904. Wagner & Co. The Richmond & Backus Co. 1904. Paperbound.

    Scores of University of Michigan games since 1892. Schedules for Michigan, Chicago, Minnesota, Northwestern, and Wisconsin. Rules, photos.

7-2 Three Years of Football at Dartmouth. Louis P. Benezet. 1904. Clothbound.

    Accounts and lineups of games played in 1901, 1902, and 1903. Notes, comments, summaries of each season.

7-3 A Brief History of Intercollegiate Football at the United States Military Academy. Lt. T.W. Hammond. Army Athletic Council. 1914. Paperbound.

    History since 1889. Yearly review of games, statistics, other data.

7-4 Gridiron Grenadiers. Tim Cohane. G.P. Putnam's Sons. 1948. Clothbound.

    A narrative history of football at the U.S. Military Academy.

7-5 The Black Knights of West Point. James Edson. Bradbury, Sayles, O'Neill. 1954. Clothbound.

    The history of football at the U.S. Military Academy since 1890. Lineups and account of every game. Yearly scores, team photos, All-American players, rosters, scores against each opponent.

7-6 Gangway for Navy. Morris Bealle. Columbia Publishing Co. 1951. Clothbound.

    The history of football at the U.S. Naval Academy since 1879. Yearly review, roster, scores. Player index, photos. Accounts of players' war heroics, players who became admirals and generals.

Team Histories

7-7   The Army-Navy Football Story. Zander Hollander. Phillies Cigars. 1959. Booklet.

         Reviews of past games and a preview of the coming one. Scores, rosters, player sketches, photos.

7-8   Army vs. Navy. Jack Clary. Ronald Press. 1965. Clothbound.

         Game accounts, background stories, photos.

7-9   The Army-Navy Game. Gene Schoor. Dodd, Mead & Co. 1967. Clothbound.

         Reprints of articles describing great moments, games, and players. Recollections by players and coaches. Lineups, All-America players, index.

7-10   Army vs. Notre Dame. Jim Beach and Daniel Moore. Random House. 1948. Cover title: The Big Game. Clothbound.

         History since 1913. Account and summary of each game. Rosters, statistics.

7-11   Football at Minnesota. Minnesota Alumni Weekly. General Alumni Association of the University of Minnesota. 1914. Clothbound and Paperbound.

         General history, yearly game accounts, rosters, scores. Sketches of past and present players.

7-12   History of Minnesota Football. Martin Newell. General Alumni Association of the University of Minnesota. 1928. Paperbound.

         Revised edition of 7-11, bringing the record up to 1926. Chronology, game accounts, sketches of players and coaches.

7-13   Minnesota Football History. University of Minnesota. 1963. Booklet.

         All-time scores by opponents. Series summaries.

7-14   Twenty-Five Years of Football at Washington and Jefferson College. R.M. Murphy. Ward Printing Co. 1914. Paperbound.

         History since 1890. Records, scores, rosters.

7-15   She Produces All-Americans. Lee North. Ward Printing Co. 1947. Paperbound.

         The history of football at Washington and Jefferson College.

7-16   California Football History. Clinton R. (Brick) Morse. 1924, 1937. Clothbound.

         University of California history since 1882. Season-by-season rosters, scores, photos, game accounts.

7-17   University of California Football Records. S. Dan Brodie. 1949.

Team Histories

Clothbound.
> Detailed statistics and records since 1882. Game summaries, rosters.

7-18 Sixty-Six Years on the California Gridiron. S. Dan Brodie. Olympic Publishing Co. 1949. Clothbound.
> The history of football at the University of California since 1882. Lineups, statistics, accounts of important games. All-America players, award winners. All-time team and individual records. Yearly rosters, scores, attendance figures. Photos.

7-19 Historical Sketch of the Oneida Football Club of Boston, 1862-1865. Winthrop S. Scudder. 1926. Paperbound.
> First organized Rugby Football Club in the United States, founded by Gerrit S. Miller. Reprint of the newspaper account of the game played on November 9, 1863, photos of living members and the Oneida Football Monument on the Boston Common.

7-20 Forty-Two Years on the Tiger Gridiron. H. Warren Taylor. Otto Claitor. 1936. Clothbound.
> The history of football at Louisiana State University since 1893. Yearly rosters, scores, review. Anecdotes, photos, all-time records.

7-21 The Fighting Tigers. Peter Finney. Louisiana State University Press. 1968. Clothbound.
> A yearly narrative history of football at Louisiana State University. Scores, records, rosters, photos.

7-22 The History of Springfield College Football. H.S. DeGroat. 1936. Cover title: Springfield Football. Paperbound.
> Yearly summaries and scores, series summaries and scores, all-time teams, photos.

7-23 On Carolina's Gridiron. Smith Barrier. Seeman Printery, Inc. 1937. Clothbound.
> A narrative history of football at the University of North Carolina. All-time scores, records, roster. Accounts of every game played since 1888. Photos.

7-24 Fifty Years of Vanderbilt Football. Fred Russell and Maxwell Benson. 1938. Clothbound. Supplemental insert, 1941.
> History since 1890. Yearly review, scores, team photos.

7-25 Fifty Years of Football at Syracuse University. Arthur L. Evans. Syracuse University Football Committee. 1939. Clothbound.
> Yearly review and record. Lineups and accounts of

Team Histories

                outstanding games, all-time roster, team photos. Songs, lore, reminiscences.

7-26   Fifty Years of Colgate Football. Dr. Ellery C. Huntington. Colgate Athletic Council. 1940. Clothbound.

                Yearly history. Scores, rosters, all-time selections.

7-27   Fifty Years of Football. Frederick Ware. Omaha World Herald. 1940. Paperbound.

                A narrative history of football at the University of Nebraska. Accounts of famous games, scores, records, photos.

7-28   Spotlighting the Husker Greats of Yesterday and Today. University of Nebraska. Alumni N Club. 1951. Paperbound.

                A review of great Nebraska games and players. Records, photos.

7-29   Go, Big Red. Hollis J. Limprecht, James Denney, and Howard S. Silber. Kratville Publications. 1966, 1967. Clothbound.

                An informal history of University of Nebraska football. Roster, scores, All-America players, photos.

7-30   Alabama's Crimson Tide. James Edson. Paragon Press. 1946. Clothbound.

                The history of football at the University of Alabama since 1892. Game scores, conference results, all-time roster. An account of every game played, including bowls. Photos.

7-31   The Crimson Tide: A Story of Alabama Football. Clyde Bolton. Strode Publishers. 1972. Clothbound.

                A narrative, anecdotal history. Scores, all-time roster.

7-32   The Road to the Top. Tom Little. L & M Corp. 1965. Paperbound.

                A pictorial history of football at the University of Alabama. Highlights, facts from each coaching era.

7-33   The Georgetown Hoyas. Morris Bealle. Columbia Publishing Co. 1947. Clothbound.

                History since 1874. Yearly review, scores, roster. Reprints of newspaper accounts, photos.

7-34   The History of Football at Harvard. Morris Bealle. Columbia Publishing Co. 1948. Clothbound.

Team Histories

Yearly review and scores, lineups and accounts of games, all-time teams. Coaches and captains, rosters.

7-35   <u>What's the Matter with Harvard Football</u>. Harold Kaese. Boston Globe. 1950. Booklet.

> A reprint of newspaper articles criticizing the Harvard University football program and suggesting remedies.

7-36   <u>What's Right Now with Harvard Football</u>. Harold Kaese. Boston Globe. 1951. Booklet.

> A follow-up to 7-35.

7-37   <u>Oklahoma Kickoff</u>. Harold Keith. Vail-Ballou Press. 1948. Clothbound.

> A narrative history of football at the University of Oklahoma covering the first 25 years of football at the University of Oklahoma (1895-1920). Photos.

7-38   <u>Thirteen Years of Winning Oklahoma Football</u>. Volney Meece and Bill Bryan. Globe Color Press. 1960. Paperbound.

> Scores, rosters, and game summaries, 1947-59. Photos.

7-39   <u>Leading a Bulldog's Life</u>. Jack Troy. Foote and Davies. 1948. Clothbound.

> An informal history of football at the University of Georgia since 1892. All-time teams, scores, captains.

7-40   <u>I've Seen 'em All</u>. Charles Martin. McGregor Co. 1961. Paperbound.

> A narrative history of football at the University of Georgia. Scores, all-time teams.

7-41   <u>Bulldogs with a Bite</u>. Tom Little. L & M Corp. 1966. Paperbound.

> A pictorial history of football at the University of Georgia. Highlights, facts from each coaching era.

7-42   <u>The Ghosts of Herty Field</u>. Joan Stegeman. University of Georgia Press. 1966. Clothbound.

> The history of University of Georgia football from 1891-1916. Lineups, scores, photos.

7-43   <u>Who's Who in Iowa Football</u>. Tait Cummins. Stamats Publishing Co. 1948. Paperbound.

> University of Iowa yearly history, rosters, scores. Photos.

Team Histories

7-44   <u>Football in the Gay Nineties.</u> W.C. Edson. c1950. Booklet.

         A description of early football in Iowa and the University of Iowa.

7-45   <u>University Football through the Years.</u> William J. Petersen, ed. State Historical Society of Iowa. 1957. Paperbound. <u>The Palimpsest.</u> Vol. 38, no. 10.

         Articles by various authors on the history of Iowa University football. Iowa in the Big Ten, coaches, great teams, and players, the Rose Bowl. Statistical records.

7-46   <u>Seventy-Five Years with the Fighting Hawkeyes.</u> Richard M. Lamb and Bert McGrane. William C. Brown. 1964. Clothbound.

         Yearly history of football at the University of Iowa. Yearly scores, lettermen, coaches, honor-winning players. Best-of-decade selections.

7-47   <u>Football at the University of Richmond.</u> John Wendell Bailey. Williams Printing Co. 1949. Clothbound and Paperbound.

         History since 1878. Yearly summaries, coaches' records, yearly roster, record against each opponent. Reprints of newspaper articles.

7-47A   <u>Football at the University of Richmond.</u> John Wendell Bailey. Williams Printing Co. 1958. Booklet.

         Supplement to 7-47 covering 1949-58.

7-48   <u>Ten Top Trojan Football Thrillers.</u> Braven Dyer. Houlgate House. 1949. Clothbound.

         Accounts of ten famous University of Southern California games. Reprints of newspaper articles.

7-49   <u>The Notre Dame Story.</u> Francis Wallace. Rinehart & Co. 1949. Clothbound.

         An informal anecdotal history.

7-50   <u>With Rockne at Notre Dame.</u> Eugene (Scrapiron) Young. G.P. Putnam's Sons. 1951. Clothbound.

         An account of football and athletics at Notre Dame during and after the Rockne era, by the Notre Dame athletic trainer.

7-51   <u>Notre Dame Football.</u> Jim Beach. Sport Magazine. McFadden-Bartell. 1962. Paperbound.

         A narrative history. All-America players.

Team Histories

7-52 A Treasury of Notre Dame Football. Gene Schoor, ed. Funk & Wagnalls. 1962. Clothbound.

    An anthology by various writers on Notre Dame's football history, great players, coaches and games. All-time roster, scores.

7-53 Notre Dame, from Rockne to Parseghian. Francis Wallace. David McKay Co. 1966, 1967. Clothbound.

    A study of seven coaches and their campaigns at Notre Dame: Frank Leahy, Hunk Anderson, Elmer Layden, Terry Brennan, Joe Kuharich, Hugh Devore, and Ara Parseghian. A narrative account of football at Notre Dame from 1918 to 1965.

7-54 Before Rockne at Notre Dame. Chet Grant. Dujarie Press. 1968.

    A personal narrative of football at Notre Dame from 1902-1909.

7-55 A Salute to Notre Dame. Associates Investment Co. 1969. Booklet.

    Sketches of Notre Dame coaches.

7-56 The Glory of Notre Dame. Fred Katz, ed. Bartholomew House. 1972. Clothbound.

    Twenty-two stories by various authors about Notre Dame football.

7-57 The Volunteers. Tom Siler. Archer & Smith Printing Co. 1950. Paperbound.

    An informal history of football at the University of Tennessee since 1890. Lineups and accounts of outstanding games. Records, photos.

7-58 Tennessee, Football's Greatest Dynasty. Tom Siler. 1961, 1962. Holston Printing Co. Paperbound.

    History since 1926. Anecdotes, records, photos.

7-59 Tennessee's Dazzling Decade. Tom Siler. Hodge Printing Co. 1970. Paperbound.

    A narrative history of football at the University of Tennessee from 1960-70. Scores, records, photos.

7-60 From T to T at UT. Ed Harris. Knoxville Journal. 1964. Paperbound. Supplemental insert, 1966.

    The history of football at the University of Tennessee. Also contains a reprint of 8-60. Photos.

7-61 The Story of Football at the University of Texas. Wilbur Evans.

Team Histories

Texas Heritage Foundation. 1951. Paperbound.

> History since 1893. Yearly summaries, scores, photos.

7-62 Football at Texas. University of Texas. 1964. Booklet.

> A photographic review of University of Texas football under Darrell Royal.

7-63 Here Come the Texas Longhorns. Lou Maysel. Stadium Publishing Co. 1970. Clothbound.

> A yearly history of football at the University of Texas. Scores, rosters, records, photos.

7-64 Game of the Century. J. Neal Blanton. Jenkins Publishing Co. 1970. Clothbound.

> The story of the 1969 Texas-Arkansas game, which decided the 1969 national championship, and which was won by Texas.

7-65 The Fabulous Redmen. John S. Steckbeck. J. Horace McFarland Co. 1951. Clothbound.

> Yearly history of the Carlisle Indians from 1892-1918. Game scores, coaches, records, rosters.

7-66 The Yale Football Story. Tim Cohane. G.P. Putnam's Sons. 1951. Clothbound.

> A narrative history since 1872. Rosters, scores.

7-67 Of Tigers and Touchdowns. B. Peter Carry. Daily Princetonian. 1964. Booklet.

> A brief history of Princeton football.

7-68 Four Decades of Yale-Princeton Football. Joseph H. Bearns. Princeton Herald. 1938, 1941. Paperbound.

> General accounts, scores of each game since 1873. Photos.

7-69 Six Decades of Yale-Princeton Football. Joseph H. Bearns. Princeton Herald. 1946, 1949. Paperbound.

> Expanded editions of 7-68.

7-70 Hell for Leather. D. Shortridge. 1951. Booklet.

> The history of football at Purdue University since 1887.

7-71 The Route of the Boilermakers. Gerald E. Harlan. 1958. Paperbound.

Team Histories

Record book of Purdue University football since 1887.

7-72   The Golden Hurricane. Robert Rutland. Tulsa Quarterback Club. 1952. Clothbound.

    A narrative history of football at the University of Tulsa from 1895-1945. Scores, photos.

7-73   Kings of American Football. Morris Bealle. Columbia Publishing Co. 1952. Clothbound.

    Yearly history of football at the University of Maryland since 1890. Scores, rosters, yearly summaries, series scores, photos.

7-74   War Eagle. James Edson. Auburn Alumni Association. 1952. Clothbound.

    The history of football at Auburn University since 1892. Game-by-game line-ups and summaries. Team photos, season summaries.

7-75   Soaring Eagles. Tom Little. L & M Corp. 1965. Paperbound.

    A pictorial history of football at Auburn University. Highlights, facts from each coaching era.

7-76   All-Time History of the Battling Buckeyes. Tom Thomson. Thomson Publishing Co. 1952. Magazine.

    An account of football at Ohio State University. Great games, coaches' sketches, great players. All-time scores and series summaries. Sketches of current players, photos.

7-77   Three Yards and a Cloud of Dust. Bill Levy. World Publishing Co. 1966. Clothbound.

    A narrative history of football at Ohio State University. Records, scores, photos.

7-78   Columbus Discovers Football. Dick Johnson. All American Archives. 1972. Clothbound.

    A narrative sketch of football at Ohio State University from 1890-1921. Scores, photos.

7-79   History of Football at the University of Delaware. T. Elbert Chance. 1955. Paperbound.

    History, scores, lettermen, highlights for each season since 1889.

7-80   A Brief History of Football at the University of Delaware. T. Elbert Chance and John Garvick. University of Delaware. 1963. Paperbound. Supplemental inserts by J.M. Morris. 1963-65. Pa-

Team Histories

7-81   perbound.
Revised edition of 7-79.

Pigskin Parade at Trinity. Robert S. Morris. Trustees of Trinity College. 1955. Clothbound.

> The history of football at Trinity College. Yearly review, scores, roster. Coaches' records. Record against each opponent, all-time roster.

7-82   **Cavalcade.** Dan Endsley, ed. Stanford University. 1959. Magazine.

> Articles by various writers on Stanford football since 1919. Player sketches, photos.

7-83   **The Grizzly Gridiron.** Bob Gilluly. Montana State University Press. 1960. Paperbound.

> The history of football at Montana State University since 1897. Anecdotes, records, photos, yearly review, and rosters, scores.

7-84   **Villanova University Football.** Michael J. O'Connell. Villanova University Press. 1964. Clothbound.

> Yearly rosters, scores, team photos. Freshman, junior varsity, and 150-pound football. Coaching records, summaries against each opponent, all-time team, and player records.

7-85   **Go, Gators.** Arthur Cobb. Sunshine Publishing Co. 1966, 1967. Clothbound.

> University of Florida football history since 1906. Greatest teams, players, games. Articles by various coaches.

7-86   **The Wearers of the "T".** Tom Little. L & M Corp. 1966. Paperbound.

> A pictorial history of football at Georgia Tech. Highlights, facts from each coaching era.

7-87   **The Carolina-Clemson Game.** Don Barton. Carolina-Clemson Football Game Book, Inc. 1967. Clothbound.

> A yearly account of the games between the University of South Carolina and Clemson University since 1896. Game summaries, lineups, all-time rosters. Sketches of coaches, all-star players, yearly summaries.

7-88   **Waynesburg College Football Records.** Waynesburg College. 1967. Paperbound.

> Team and player records, photos.

Team Histories

7-89   <u>Mountaineer Football.</u> Tony Constantine and Dan Miller. West Virginia University. 1969. Paperbound.

         A yearly history of football at the University of West Virginia. Scores, records, roster.

7-90   <u>The History of Football at Dickinson College.</u> Wilbur J. Gobrecht. Kerr Printing Co. 1971. Clothbound.

         A yearly review. Scores, scoring plays, rosters, photos. Written by the present head coach.

7-91   <u>Football, CU-Style.</u> Fred Casotti. Pruett Publishing Co. 1972. Clothbound.

         A narrative history of football at the University of Colorado since 1947.

7-92   <u>Football at Rutgers.</u> Larry Pitt. Rutgers University. 1972. Paperbound.

         A narrative history. Yearly rosters, scores.

7-93   <u>The Big Game.</u> Fred Russell. Packard Motor Car Co. 1952. Booklet.

         Reviews of Harvard-Yale, Army-Navy, California-Stanford, Tulane-Louisiana State University and traditional series.

7-94   <u>Football's Iron Men Teams.</u> Sec Taylor. Packard Motor Car Co. 1953. Booklet.

         Reviews of great teams and players. Statistics.

7-95   <u>National Champions.</u> Jim Koger. Atlantic Publishing Co. 1970. Clothbound.

         A sketch of the first-ranked national collegiate football team for each year since 1900. Scores, rosters, records of other outstanding teams for each year.

Collegiate Athletic Histories

General athletic histories of individual colleges, with football coverage.

7-96   <u>A History of Yale Athletics.</u> Richard M. Hurd. Tuttle, Morehouse & Taylor. 1888, 1892. Cover title: <u>Yale Athletics.</u> Clothbound.

         The 1892 edition bears an 1888 copyright date. It

Team Histories

is identical to the first volume except for an appendix covering the years 1888-92.

7-97   Yale, Her Campus, Classrooms, and Athletics. Walter Camp and L.S. Welch. L.C. Page & Co. 1899. Clothbound.

7-98   Dartmouth Athletics. John H. Bartlett and John P. Gifford. Dartmouth College. 1893. Clothbound.

7-99   Athletics at Dartmouth. Horace G. Pender and Raymond M. McPartlin. Dartmouth College Athletic Council. 1923. Clothbound.

7-100   A History of Athletics at Pennsylvania. George W. Orton. Athletic Association, University of Pennsylvania. 1896. Clothbound.

7-101   The History of Athletics at the University of Pennsylvania. Edward R. Bushnell. Athletic Association, University of Pennsylvania. 1909. Clothbound.

7-102   Harvard Teams. W.B. Wheelwright and A.M. Goodridge. O.B. Graves. 1899. Clothbound.

7-103   Ten Years Athletics at Harvard. W.S. Cooledge. 1901. Booklet.

7-104   The H Book of Harvard Athletics. John A. Blanchard. Harvard Varsity Club. 1923. Clothbound.

7-105   The Second H Book of Harvard Athletics. Geoffrey H. Movius. Harvard Varsity Club. 1964. Clothbound.

7-106   The Games of California and Stanford. Jack F. Sheehan and Louis Honig. Commercial Publishing Co. 1900. Clothbound.

7-107   Fifty Years on the Quad. Norris E. James. Stanford Alumni Association. 1938. Clothbound.

7-108   Great Moments in Stanford Sports. Pete Grothe. Pacific Books. 1952. Paperbound.

7-109   Athletics at Princeton. Frank Presbry and James H. Moffat. Frank Presbry Co. 1901. Clothbound.

7-110   Cornell University, a History. Waterman T. Hewett. University Publishing Society. 1905. Vol. 3. Clothbound.

7-111   Athletics at Lafayette College. Francis A. March, Jr. Lafayette College. 1926. Clothbound.

7-112   Athletics in the University of North Carolina. Central Alumni Office. 1927. Paperbound.

7-113   The M Book of Athletics, Mississippi A & M College. John W. Bailey. Curtiss Printing Co. 1930. Clothbound.

7-114   The M Book of Athletics, Mississippi State College. John W. Bailey. Williams Printing Co. 1947. Clothbound.

7-115   A Glance at Amherst Athletics. W.L. Tower. 1935. Paperbound.

7-116   One Hundred Years of Athletics, the University of Michigan. Phil Pack. Michigan M Club. 1937. Paperbound.

7-117   Memorable Moments in Michigan Sports. Sigma Delta Chi. Kays Press. 1953. Paperbound.

7-118   Michigan's All-Time Athletic Record. University of Michigan. 1953. Title page: Athletic Record of the University of Michigan. Booklet.

7-119   Michigan All-Time Athletic Record Book. University of Michigan. 1968. Paperbound.

7-120   Athletics at Wesleyan. Frank W. Nicolson. Wesleyan University Alumni Council. 1938. Clothbound and Paperbound.

7-121   Who's Who in Minnesota Athletics. Richard C. Fisher and Peter W. DeGrote. Who's Who in Minnesota Athletics. 1941. Clothbound.

7-122   A Sports History of the University of the South. Sewanee Alumni News. Alumni Association of The University of the South. 1949. Paperbound.

7-123   University of Southern California Athletics. Greater Alumni Association. 1950. Paperbound.

7-124   The Tale of the Wildcats. Walter Paulison. Northwestern University Alumni Association. 1951. Clothbound.

7-125   Ohio State Athletics. James E. Pollard. Ohio State University. 1959. Clothbound and Paperbound.

7-126   History of Athletics at Maryville College. Ken D. Kribbs. Mangrum Printers. 1969. Clothbound.

7-127   Varsity Athletic Record Book, University of Maine. Stuart P. Haskell, Jr., ed. University of Maine. 1970. Paperbound.

7-128   Spartan Saga. Lyman L. Frimodig and Fred W. Stabley. Michigan State University. 1971. Paperbound.

7-129   The Gladiators. John McCallum. Pacific Lutheran University

Team Histories

Press. 1972. Clothbound.

Professional Titles

7P-1 History of the Duluth Eskimos. Ole Haugsrud. c 1943. Paperbound.

    A privately-printed narrative account of the Duluth, Minnesota, team which played in the National Football League from 1921-29. Written by the team's secretary-treasurer.

7P-2 The Green Bay Packers. Arch Ward. G.P. Putnam's Sons. 1946. Clothbound.

    An informal history. All-time scores, big games.

7P-3 The Green Bay Packers. Chuck Johnson. Thomas Nelson & Sons. 1961, 1963. Clothbound.

    A narrative history with emphasis on the 1960 championship season. Rosters, records.

7P-4 Packers of the Past. Milwaukee Journal. 1966. Booklet.

    Reprints of articles appearing in the Journal from September-December 1965. Sketches of Green Bay Packer stars such as Hutson, Blood, Goldenberg, Rote, Dilweg, Asbell, others.

7P-5 The Lombardi Era of the Green Bay Packers. Art Daley and Jack Yuenger. Inland Press. 1968. Cover title: The Lombardi Era and the Green Bay Packers. Magazine.

    A statistical review of the 1959-67 seasons. Statistics, line scores, photos. Articles by various writers.

7P-6 Packer Dynasty. Phil Bengston and Todd Hunt. Doubleday & Co. 1968. Clothbound.

    An account of the Green Bay Packer years during the coaching reign of Vince Lombardi. Bengston was an assistant coach during those years and succeeded Lombardi as head coach in 1968.

7P-7 The Fabulous Green Bay Packers. Chuck Johnson. Milwaukee Journal. 1968. Magazine.

    Reprints of articles recounting Green Bay Packer championship games in 1965, 1966, and 1967. Statistics, photos.

7P-8 Fifty Years of Professional Football. Hank Lefebvre and Ray Wanek. Green Bay Packer Alumni Associates. 1968. Magazine.

A photographic history of the Green Bay Packers.

7P-9 The Chicago Bears. Howard Roberts. G.P. Putnam's Sons. 1947. Clothbound.

A narrative yearly history. Scores against each opponent.

7P-10 My Life with the Redskins. Corinne Griffith. A.S. Barnes & Co. 1947. Clothbound.

The story of the Boston and Washington Redskins, by a former movie star and ex-wife of George Preston Marshall, the team's owner. An account of each season from 1936-46, yearly scores, team records. Behind-the-scene accounts, anecdotes.

7P-11 The Redskins. Morris Bealle. Columbia Publishing Co. 1959. Clothbound.

Yearly history of the Washington Redskins from 1937-58, and the Boston Redskins from 1932-36. An account of sandlot and semi-pro football in Washington from 1888-1940. Scores, rosters, photos.

7P-12 Historical and Statistical Data on the Redskins. The Washington Redskins. 1949, 1950. Paperbound.

Player sketches, statistical summaries of all previous games played between the Redskins and each of their 1949 opponents. Game accounts, scores, records.

7P-13 Maroon Football Team 50th Anniversary. Arrangements Committee. 1956. Paperbound.

Issued to commemorate the celebration of the Toledo Maroons' 50th anniversary. Reprints of newspaper articles covering the team's games of 1915 and 1916. Photos.

7P-14 The Los Angeles Rams. Bob Oates. Murray & Gee. 1955. Clothbound.

An informal history. Accounts of famous games. Records, scores, photos.

7P-15 The Baltimore Colts Story. John Steadman. Press Box Publishers. 1958. Clothbound.

The history of the team in the All-America Football Conference and National Football League. Background of the franchise loss in 1950 and return to the NFL in 1953. Memorable moments, all-time roster, photos.

Team Histories

7P-16 Football's Miracle Men. John Steadman. Pennington Press. 1959. Clothbound.

    Revised edition of 7P-15, with an account of the 1958 championship game between Baltimore and New York.

7P-17 The Baltimore Colts. George Wright. Hawkins Associates. 1962. Booklet.

    Player sketches in comic book form.

7P-18 The San Francisco 49ers. Dan McGuire. Coward-McCann. 1960. Clothbound.

    History of the team in the All-America Football Conference and National Football League. Team and player records, rosters, photos.

7P-19 All-Time Records of the San Francisco Forty-Niners. S. Dan Brodie. 1959. Paperbound.

    Individual and team records. Long plays.

7P-20 The New York Giants. Don Smith. Coward-McCann. 1960. Clothbound.

    History, records, rosters, photos.

7P-21 The Giants of New York. Barry Gottehrer. G.P. Putnam's Sons. 1963. Clothbound.

    A narrative history of the New York Giants. All-time records.

7P-22 Pottsville Maroons Testimonial and Reunion. Joseph Zacko. 1962, 1963. Magazine.

    Issued in connection with a reunion of the Pottsville National Football League team, held in Pottsville, Pennsylvania, June 27-29, 1963. The franchise existed from 1925-28 and eventually evolved into the Washington Redskins. The team won the championship in 1925, but it was later declared forfeited by the commissioner in a decision still being hotly disputed. History of the team, scores, player sketches, articles, photos.

7P-23 Statistical Records of the Oakland Raiders. S. Dan Brodie. 1961. Booklet.

    Team and player statistics and records.

7P-24 Return to Glory. Bill Levy. World Publishing Co. 1965. Clothbound.

Team Histories

>A narrative history of the Cleveland Browns. All-time roster, scores, player, and team records.

7P-25   <u>Twenty Years with the Cleveland Browns.</u> Varo Cerbaro. 1966. Paperbound.

>History, great players, and games. All-time scores, photos.

7P-26   <u>A Decade at the Met: The Twins and Vikings.</u> Minneapolis Chamber of Commerce. 1966. Magazine.

>The development of Metropolitan Stadium in Bloomington, Minnesota, and a review of the Minnesota Vikings.

7P-27   <u>True Hearts and Purple Heads.</u> Jim Klobuchar. Ross and Haines. 1970. Paperbound.

>A narrative history of the Minnesota Vikings.

7P-28   <u>Sunday at the Met.</u> Jim Klobuchar and Skip Heine. Twin City Federal Savings and Loan. 1971. Magazine.

>A photographic review of the Minnesota Vikings.

7P-29   <u>Broadway Joe and His Super Jets.</u> Larry Fox. Coward-McCann. 1969. Clothbound.

>A history of the New York Jets.

7P-30   <u>The Long Pass.</u> Lou Sahadi. World Publishing Co. 1969. Clothbound. Bantam Books. 1969, reissue. Paperbound.

>A narrative history of the New York Jets.

7P-31   <u>The Dallas Cowboys and the NFL.</u> Donald Chipman, Randolph Campbell, and Robert Calvert. University of Oklahoma Press. 1970. Clothbound.

>A study of the planning, organization, development, and operation of a pro football team. An examination of the various business and financial aspects of pro football, and an account of the organizational battles between the American and National Football Leagues.

7P-32   <u>The Dallas Cowboys: Pro or Con?</u> Sam Blair. Doubleday & Co. 1970. Clothbound.

>A history of the Cowboys. Statistics, anecdotes, photos.

7P-33   <u>We Love You, Cowboys.</u> Bob St. John. Sport Magazine Press. 1972. Clothbound.

Team Histories

A narrative history of the Dallas Cowboys. Records.

7P-34 Winning It All. Joe McGuff. Doubleday & Co. 1970. Clothbound.

    A history of the Kansas City Chiefs. Team and player statistics.

7P-35 Promises to Keep: The Miami Dolphins Story. Bill Braucher. Dodd, Mead & Co. 1972. Clothbound.

    A narrative history of the team.

7P-36 The Miami Dolphins. Morris T. McLemore. Doubleday & Co. 1972. Clothbound.

    A yearly history. Scores, records.

7P-37 Miracle in Miami. Lou Sahadi. Henry Regnery Co. 1972. Clothbound.

    The story of the Miami Dolphins. Records, statistics.

7P-38 Chargers. Sports Pictorial. No date. Paperbound.

    A pictorial review of the San Diego Chargers.

7P-39 The Great Teams of Pro Football. Robert Smith. Dell Publishing Co. 1964. Paperbound.

    Historical sketches of the fourteen National Football League teams.

7P-40 Championship Teams of the NFL. Phil Berger. Random House. 1968. Clothbound.

    Punt, Pass and Kick Library. Sketches of six teams.

8. Biographies

8-1   Marshall Newell, a Memorial. Gerrish Newell. Lamson Wolfe & Co. 1898. Clothbound.

            A privately-printed biography of a four-time All-American.

8-2   Gerrit Smith Miller. Winthrop Scudder. The Noble and Greenough School. 1924. Paperbound.

            A sketch of the organizer of the Oneida Football Club, the first U.S. Rugby Football team, founded in 1862.

8-3   A Resolution Adopted by the Intercollegiate Football Rules Committee on the Death of Walter Camp. Intercollegiate Football Rules Committee. 1925. Paperbound.

            With an account of his career by Parke Davis.

8-4   Walter Camp. Harford Powell, Jr. Little, Brown & Co. 1926. Clothbound. Books for Libraries Press. 1970, reissue. Clothbound.

            A biography of "The Father of American Football." Development of football, Camp's All-America teams, the Camp Memorial.

8-5   Touchdown! Amos Alonzo Stagg and Wesley W. Stout. Longmans, Green & Co. 1927. Clothbound.

            An autobiographical account of Stagg's playing and coaching career. Photos.

8-6   Amos Alonzo Stagg. W. Watson and E. Parker. 1933. Booklet.

            A pictorial biography.

8-7   A.A. Stagg, Grand Old Man of Football. The Sporting News. 1946. Paperbound.

            Predecessor to 2P-3. A biography of Stagg, favorite plays of famous coaches, greatest grid thrills. Pro football rules.

Biographies

8-8 The Unreconstructed Amateur. Bob Considine. Amos Alonzo Stagg Foundation, Inc. 1962. Clothbound.

    A pictorial biography of Amos Alonzo Stagg.

8-9 Mr. Football: Amos Alonzo Stagg. Ellis Lucia. A.S. Barnes & Co. 1970. Clothbound.

    The biography of a pioneer coach and innovator, who was one of those chiefly responsible for the development of college football.

8-10 The Autobiography of Knute K. Rockne. Bonnie Skiles Rockne (Mrs. Knute K.), ed. Bobbs Merrill. 1930, 1931, reissue. Clothbound.

    1930 edition (Notre Dame edition) limited to 2,400 copies. Introduction and postscript by Father John Cavanaugh, president of Notre Dame University. Rockne's autobiography, coaching philosophy, insights into the game. Photos.

8-11 A Football Classic. Wonder Publications. 1931. Magazine.

    An illustrated biography of Knute Rockne.

8-12 Knute Rockne's Career. Modern Magazines. 1931. Magazine.

    A sketch of Rockne's life and coaching career. Famous Notre Dame stars, famous plays, Rockne's football strategy.

8-13 The Uncensored Truth about Rockne's Strange Death. Graphic Arts Co. 1931. Magazine.

    Details of the plane crash which caused Knute Rockne's death. Biographical sketch, photos.

8-14 The Life of Knute Rockne. P.L. Trussell. Wonder Publications, Inc. 1931. Magazine.

    A narrative sketch of Rockne's coaching career. Photos.

8-15 Goals, the Life of Knute Rockne. Huber W. Hurt. Murray Book Corp. 1931. Clothbound.

    Famous plays and players, records.

8-16 Knute Kenneth Rockne. Parke Davis. 1931. Booklet.

    A posthumous tribute written for the American Football Coaches Association.

8-17 Knute Rockne, Man Builder. Harry Stuhldreher. Macrae-Smith. 1931. Clothbound. Grosset & Dunlap. Reissue. Clothbound.

Biographies

By a former member of the "Four Horsemen." Rockne as a coach, a man, and as the public knew him.

8-18　Rockne. Warren Brown. Reilly & Lee. 1931. Clothbound.

　　Includes yearly records, players coached by Rockne. Photos.

8-19　Rockne, Idol of American Football. Robert Harron. A.L. Burt Co. 1931. Clothbound.

　　Includes yearly scores, lineups, tributes to Rockne by notables.

8-20　Rockne of Notre Dame. Delos W. Lovelace. G.P. Putnam's Sons. 1931, 1931, revised. Clothbound.

　　Rockne's life and career. Game scores and rosters.

8-21　Rockne of Notre Dame. Rockne Memorial Association, Inc. 1931. Paperbound.

　　A eulogy. Description of the Rockne Memorial.

8-22　Salesman from the Sidelines. McCready Huston. Ray Long and Richard R. Smith. 1932. Clothbound.

　　An account of Knute Rockne's business career and association with the Studebaker Corp.

8-23　Knute Rockne, Football Wizard of Notre Dame. Arthur Daley. P.J. Kennedy & Sons. 1960. Clothbound.

　　For teenagers.

8-24　Knute Rockne. Francis Wallace. Doubleday & Co. 1960. Clothbound.

　　A biographical account by a newspaperman who was a close friend of Rockne's.

8-25　King of Coaches. Brother Daniel Bengert. Dujare Press. 1965. Clothbound.

　　A biography of Knute Rockne for young readers.

8-26　Knute Rockne: Notre Dame's Football Great. George Sullivan. Garrard Publishing Co. 1970. Clothbound.

　　A biography for younger readers.

8-27　Zuppke of Illinois. Harold (Red) Grange. A.L. Glaser. 1937. Clothbound.

　　Limited edition. An account of Zuppke's coaching career. Famous games, Zuppke's football philosophy,

Biographies

football at the University of Illinois. A chapter on the Grange era at Illinois. Photos.

8-28   **Dr. Henry L. Williams.** Stan W. Carlson. 1938. Clothbound.

     A biography of the coach at Minnesota University from 1900-21. Season summaries, rosters.

8-29   **Forty Years of Football.** Donald Herring. Carlyle House. 1940. Clothbound.

     The autobiography of a member of the Princeton football team, 1904-06, later assistant coach. Princeton football through the years, great players. A brief historical sketch of the game.

8-30   **Frank Leahy and the Fighting Irish.** Arch Ward. G.P. Putnam's Sons. 1944, 1947. Clothbound.

     A biography of Notre Dame's great coach and the story of football at Notre Dame during his career.

8-31   **This Is Harry Gilmer.** Edwin Bragg. 1947. Paperbound.

     A sketch of the University of Alabama All-American. Photos.

8-32   **"Hurry Up" Yost in Story and Song.** J. Fred Lawton. J.W. Edwards. 1947. Clothbound.

     Reminiscences of and verse about all-time great coach Fielding H. Yost by a life-long friend.

8-33   **Fielding H. Yost, Football Immortal.** Chester W. Cleveland and Hugh Collett, eds. The Magazine of Sigma Chi. January 1948. Paperbound.

     Memorial tributes by various coaches, writers, and national figures. Photos.

8-34   **Fielding Yost's Legacy to the University of Michigan.** John Behee. Uhlrich's Books. 1971. Clothbound.

     An in-depth biography of a football pioneer, with an account of the development of the University of Michigan's athletic program.

8-35   **Alexander of Georgia Tech.** Edwin Camp. Georgia Institute of Technology. 1950. Clothbound.

     The story of W.A. Alexander, head coach from 1919-46.

8-36   **Doak Walker, Three-Time All American.** Dorothy Bracken and Doak Walker. Steck Co. 1950. Clothbound.

Biographies

A biography of the three-time All American at Southern Methodist University.

8-37　　The Jim Thorpe Story. Gene Schoor and Henry Gilfond. Julian Messner, Inc. 1951. Clothbound. Archway. 1967, reissue. Paperbound.

A biography of the immortal athlete. Career, records.

8-38　　Thorpe of Carlisle. James Peterson. Hinckley and Schmidt. 1955. Clothbound.

A narrative sketch of the all-time great halfback. Photos.

8-39　　Thorpe. Carlisle Jaycees. 1969. Booklet.

A tribute to Jim Thorpe issued in connection with a commemoration held at Carlisle, Pennsylvania, as part of an effort to have Thorpe's Olympic medals restored.

8-40　　Jim Thorpe. Donald Clifford Snow (pseudonym Thomas Fall). Thomas Y. Crowell Co. 1970. Clothbound.

A sketch for young readers.

8-41　　Jim Thorpe, All-Around Athlete. George Sullivan. Garrard Publishing Co. 1971. Clothbound.

A biographical sketch for young readers.

8-42　　Red Grange, Football's Greatest Halfback. Gene Schoor and Henry Gilfond. Julian Messner, Inc. 1952. Clothbound.

Includes playing records.

8-43　　The Red Grange Story. Harold (Red) Grange and Ira Norton. G.P. Putnam's Sons. 1953. Clothbound.

Grange's autobiography covering his career from high school through college and professional football. Includes college statistics.

8-44　　Seventy-Seven Grange of Illinois. James Peterson. Hinckley & Schmidt. 1956. Clothbound.

A narrative account of Grange's college career. Photos.

8-45　　Bob Mathias, Champion of Champions. Jim Scott. Prentice-Hall. 1952. Clothbound. T.S. Denison & Co. 1963. Clothbound.

A biography of the star college football halfback and Olympic track great.

8-46　　Gipp of Notre Dame. James Peterson. Hinckley & Schmidt.

Biographies

1954. Clothbound.

> A narrative sketch of George Gipp, Notre Dame's legendary halfback. Photos.

8-47   This Was Football. W.W. (Pudge) Heffelfinger and John McCallum. A.S. Barnes & Co. 1954. Clothbound.

> The autobiography of an all-time All-American. An account of a fifty-year playing career and observations on football through the years. Photos.

8-48   Jock Sutherland, Architect of Men. Harry Scott. Exposition Press. 1954. Clothbound.

> An in-depth biography of an all-time great college and pro coach. Career coaching record, scores, rosters.

8-49   Coach Tommy of the Crimson, Tide. Naylor Stone. Vulcan Press. 1954. Clothbound and Paperbound.

> The biography of Frank Thomas, star quarterback at Notre Dame and coach of Alabama University from 1931-46. Season summaries, photos.

8-50   Alan Ameche. University of Wisconsin. 1955. Booklet.

> Records, career highlights, and honors won by the star Wisconsin University fullback.

8-51   Terry Brennan of Notre Dame. Dave Warner. Newman Press. 1956. Clothbound.

> A biography of the Notre Dame player and coach. Records.

8-52   Eckersall of Chicago. James Peterson. Hinckley & Schmidt. 1957. Clothbound.

> The narrative sketch of all-time great quarterback Walter Eckersall. The story of football at the University of Chicago and in the Western Conference from 1894-1906. Photos.

8-53   Slater of Iowa. James Peterson. Hinckley & Schmidt. 1958. Clothbound.

> A narrative sketch of Fred (Duke) Slater, Negro All-America tackle, 1918-21, and member of the Football Hall of Fame. Photos.

8-54   Choo Choo: The Charlie Justice Story. Bob Quincy and Julian Scheer. Bentley Publishing Co. 1958. Clothbound.

> A narrative account of Justice's career at the Univer-

Biographies

sity of North Carolina. Records, lineups.

8-55   You Have to Pay the Price. Earl (Red) Blaik and Tim Cohane. Holt, Rinehart and Winston. 1960. Clothbound.

          An autobiography of the coach at Dartmouth University and the U.S. Military Academy. Scores, rosters.

8-56   No Ifs, No Ands, a Lot of Butts. Edward Thilenius and Jim Koger. Foote & Davies, Inc. 1960. Clothbound.

          The story of Wally Butts, University of Georgia coach. A 21-year account of Georgia football. Records, All-Americans.

8-57   Joe Bellino. Cynthia L. and William D. Barone. Winchester Publishers. 1961. Clothbound.

          A pictorial biography of a star high school and college player.

8-58   Joe Boland, Notre Dame Man. Peg Boland. NSP Publishing Co. 1962. Clothbound.

          Stories by friends of Boland during his playing, coaching, and broadcasting days.

8-59   The Way the Ball Bounces. Byron Gentry. Naylor Co. 1962. Clothbound.

          An autobiographical account of the football experiences of a former college and pro star and present-day lawyer. War experiences, essays on law and mores.

8-60   Bob Neyland, 37 Years a Volunteer. Ed Harris. Knoxville Journal. 1962. Paperbound.

          A pictorial biography of the long-time coach at the University of Tennessee.

8-61   Bob Suffridge, Football beyond Coaching. Raymond Edmunds. Bob Suffridge and Raymond Edmunds. 1963. Paperbound.

          An anecdotal biography of an all-time University of Tennessee guard.

8-62   Many a Saturday Afternoon. Mary Stuhldreher. David McKay Co. 1964. Clothbound.

          An autobiography by the wife of Harry Stuhldreher, member of Notre Dame's "Four Horsemen" and long-time college coach. An inside look into life as a football coach's wife, with anecdotes and amusing incidents.

Biographies

8-63   Winning Isn't Everything.   Benny Marshall.   Parthenon Press.   1965. Clothbound.

          The biography of Paul (Bear) Bryant, most successful present-day college football coach. Yearly scores, great games.

8-64   Borleske, Never Far from Hope.   Jack Hewins.   Superior Publishing Co.   1966.   Clothbound.

          The biography of R.V. Borleske, long-time football coach at Whitman College.

8-65   The Legend of Hobey Baker.   John Davies.   Little, Brown & Co. 1966.   Clothbound.

          The biography of a star halfback and legendary figure of his day.

8-66   Calling Life's Signals.   Steve Sloan and James Hefley.   Zondervan Publishing House.   1967.   Clothbound and Paperbound.

          The autobiography of a former star college quarterback. Advice for youth on spiritual, mental, and physical preparations for adulthood.

8-67   It's Always Too Soon to Quit.   Mel Larson.   Zondervan Publishing House.   1968.   Clothbound and Paperbound.

          The story of star college quarterback Steve Spurrier.

8-68   It Was a Different Game.   Elmer Layden and Ed Snyder.   Prentice-Hall.   1969.   Clothbound.

          The autobiography of a member of Notre Dame's "Four Horsemen."

8-69   Ernie Nevers, Football Hero.   Jim Scott.   T.S. Denison & Co. 1969.   Men of Achievement Series.   Clothbound.

          The biography of an all-time great college and pro player and coach.

8-70   Coach Tom Cahill.   Gordon White and Mervin Hyman.   Macmillan Co.   1969.   Clothbound.

          The biography of the West Point coach.

8-71   Andy Kerr, a Man Who Served.   Russell Speirs.   Salina Press. 1969.   Clothbound.

          A privately-printed tribute to the long-time Colgate University coach.

8-72   Jake Gaither: Winning Coach.   Wyatt Blassingame.   Garrard Publishing Co.   1969.   Americans All Series.   Clothbound.

Biographies

The biography of a successful Negro college coach, written for young readers.

8-73 Rebel Coach. John Vaught. Memphis State University Press. 1971. Clothbound.

Vaught's autobiography and the story of football at the University of Mississippi from 1946-70, by the head coach who built their successful football program.

8-74 I Play to Win. Fred Steinmark. Little, Brown & Co. 1971. Clothbound.

Biography of a University of Texas football player who developed cancer during his senior year.

8-75 My Little Brother's Coming Tomorrow. Bruce Bahrenburg. G.P. Putnam's Sons. 1971. Clothbound.

The account of a white football player, Jim Gregory, at Grambling College, a black southern school.

8-76 Joe Paterno: Football My Way. Mervin Hyman and Gordon White, Jr. Macmillan Co. 1971. Clothbound.

A profile of Paterno, the highly successful Penn State coach. His philosophy of football and life.

8-77 Football Thrills. Harold (Red) Grange. Approved Comics, Inc. 1951, 1952. Booklet.

Cartoon stories of Grange, Thorpe, Nagurski, others.

8-78 Famous Football Players. Robert Shoemaker. Thomas Y. Crowell Co. 1953. Clothbound.

Sketches of Thorpe, Camp, Booth, Grange, the Four Horsemen, Blanchard, and Davis, seven others.

8-79 The Four Horsemen of Notre Dame. James Peterson. Hinckley & Schmidt. 1959. Clothbound.

Sketches of Crowley, Layden, Stuhldreher, and Miller. An account of Notre Dame football during their careers. Photos.

8-80 Football Immortals. Alexander Weyand. Macmillan Co. 1962. Clothbound.

Sixty-four all-time players, by position. Great pros; presidents and football.

8-81 Football Y Men. Albert B. Crawford. Yale University. 1963. Three volumes: 1872-1919. 1920-39. 1940-60. Men of Yale Series. Clothbound.

Biographies

Biographical sketches of Yale football lettermen. Summaries of types of occupations, war records, service to Yale.

8-82   The Glory Runners. Al Hirshberg. G.P. Putnam's Sons. 1968. Clothbound.

         Sketches of 22 collegiate running backs.

8-83   Black Champions of the Gridiron. Andrew S. (Doc) Young. Harcourt, Brace & World. 1969. Clothbound.

         Biographies of star halfbacks. O.J. Simpson and Leroy Keyes.

8-84   Buttonhooks to Bombs! Tel Ra Productions. 1971. Booklet.

         Sketches of famous collegiate passers and receivers.

8-85   The Perfect Football Coach. Edwin Pope. Packard Motor Car Co. 1955. Booklet.

         Sketches of great coaches. Records, data.

8-86   Football's Greatest Coaches. Edwin Pope, ed. Tupper & Love. 1955, 1956. Clothbound.

         Sketches of 28 immortals, as selected by a panel of sportswriters.

8-87   Football's Medicine Men. Mal Mallette. Packard Motor Car Co. 1956. Booklet.

         Sketches of outstanding coaches.

8-88   Yea, Coach! Guernsey Van Riper, Jr. Garrard Publishing Co. 1966. Clothbound.

         Sketches of Warner, Heisman, and Rockne.

Professional Titles

8P-1   Life and Football History of Harold (Red) Grange. Charles C. Pyle. Bentley, Murray & Co. 1926. Magazine.

         Biographical sketch, photos. Issued as promotional device for the American Football League, organized by Pyle, with Grange as the star attraction.

8P-2   Luckman at Quarterback. Sid Luckman. Ziff-Davis. 1949. Clothbound.

         The autobiography of an all-time great quarterback. Football as a sport and as a career. Action photos.

Biographies

8P-3 The Frank Gifford Story. Don Smith. G.P. Putnam's Sons. 1960. Clothbound.

   The biography of a high school, college, and pro star. Playing records.

8P-4 Frank Gifford: The Golden Year, 1956. William Wallace. Prentice-Hall. 1969. Clothbound.

   An account of Gifford's 1956 season as a New York Giant halfback.

8P-5 The Rick Casares Story. M. Kallis Co. 1960. Booklet.

   Issued in conjunction with a testimonial dinner. An account of Casares' career with the Chicago Bears. Photos.

8P-6 Always on Sunday. Bobby Layne and Bob Drum. Prentice-Hall. 1962. Clothbound.

   An account of the playing career and off-field exploits of an all-time great pro quarterback.

8P-7 Confessions of a Gypsy Quarterback. George Ratterman and Robert Deindorfer. Coward-McCann. 1962. Clothbound.

   A humorous autobiographical account of a substitute pro quarterback. Amusing insights and anecdotes.

8P-8 They Pay Me to Catch Footballs. Tommy McDonald and Ed Richter. Chilton Co. 1962. Clothbound and Paperbound. Scholastic Book Services. 1964, reissue. Paperbound.

   The autobiography of a star pro pass receiver. Photos.

8P-9 The Johnny Unitas Story. Lee Greene. G.P. Putnam's Sons. 1962. Clothbound.

   The biography of an all-time great quarterback.

8P-10 Pro Quarterback: My Own Story. John Unitas and Ed Fitzgerald. Simon & Schuster. 1965. Clothbound.

   The autobiography of an all-time great quarterback. Playing tips, strategy, technical aspects of passing and quarterbacking.

8P-10A The Johnny Unitas Story. John Unitas and Ed Fitzgerald. Tempo Books. 1968, reissue. Paperbound.

   Reissue of 8P-10.

8P-11 Johnny Unitas and the Long Pass. Julian May Dikty (pseudonym Julian May). Crestwood House. 1972. Clothbound.

   A biography for young readers.

Biographies

8P-12   Fourth and One. Lee Grosscup. Harper & Row. 1963. Clothbound.

        A day-by-day account of Grosscup's quarterbacking experiences with the New York Giants, Minnesota Vikings, and New York Titans during the 1962 season.

8P-13   Backseat Quarterback. Perian Conerly. Doubleday & Co. 1963. Clothbound.

        An account of life in professional football by the wife of Charlie Conerly, star pro quarterback. Inside views of the game and behind-the-scene anecdotes.

8P-14   I Pass! Y.A. Tittle and Don Smith. Franklin Watts. 1964, 1966. Clothbound.

        The autobiography of an all-time great pro quarterback. Viewpoints on the game and its techniques.

8P-15   The Jimmy Brown Story. James P. Terzian and Jim Benagh. Julian Messner, Inc. 1964. Clothbound.

        The biography of an all-time great fullback.

8P-16   Off My Chest. Jimmy Brown and Myron Cope. Doubleday & Co. 1964. Clothbound.

        The autobiography of an all-time great fullback. Views on the game, the race question, and other players.

8P-17   Jim Brown, The Running Back. Larry Klein. G.P. Putnam's Sons. 1965. Clothbound.

        An account of Brown's career from high school through professional football. Great games, behind-the-scene insights.

8P-18   Jim Brown, the Golden Year. Stan Issacs. Prentice-Hall. 1970. Clothbound.

        An account of Brown's 1964 season in which his running led the Cleveland Browns to the NFL Championship.

8P-19   Jim. James Toback. Doubleday & Co. 1971. Clothbound. Signet. 1972, reissue. Paperbound.

        An intimate account of Toback's experiences while conducting an extended interview with former football great Jim Brown.

8P-20   Jim Brown Runs with the Ball. Julian May Dikty (pseudonym Julian May). Crestwood House. 1972. Clothbound.

Biographies

A biography for young readers.

8P-21   The Public Calls It Sport. Harry Wismer. Prentice-Hall. 1965. Clothbound.

         An account of the author's turbulent career as the owner of the American Football League New York Jets.

8P-22   Football and the Single Man. Paul Hornung and Al Silverman. Doubleday & Co. 1965. Clothbound.

         An autobiography of the Green Bay star and controversial figure.

8P-23   Footsteps of a Giant. Emlen Tunnell and William Gleason. Doubleday & Co. 1966. Clothbound.

         The autobiography of a star defensive back and first Negro to play for the New York Giants. Views on football and life.

8P-24   Get in the Game. Bill Glass. Word Books. 1965. Clothbound and Paperbound.

         The autobiography of a pro linebacker. A declaration of the principles of upright living.

8P-25   My Greatest Challenge. Bill Glass. Word Books. 1968. Clothbound.

         Observations and recollections on the game by a star pro linebacker. A statement of his religious beliefs.

8P-26   Paper Lion. George Plimpton. Harper & Row. 1966. Clothbound. Pocket Books. 1967, reissue, 1972, reissue. Paperbound.

         Experiences of a writer as a Detroit Lion quarterback during summer training and in an exhibition game. An inside look at the game and its players.

8P-27   Violence Every Sunday. Mike Holovak and Bill McSweeny. Coward-McCann. 1967. Clothbound.

         The autobiography of a pro football coach, by the 1966 American Football League Coach of the Year. Views and thoughts on the game.

8P-28   No Time for Losing. Fran Tarkenton. Fleming H. Revell Co. 1967. Clothbound.

         An autobiography of the quarterback who introduced the "scrambling" roll-out type offense to the pro game. Illustrated instructions on quarterbacking.

8P-29   Better Scramble than Lose. Fran Tarkenton and Jack Olsen. Four

Biographies

8P-30 Winds Press. 1969. Clothbound. Scholastic Books. 1971, re-issue. Paperbound.

Tarkenton's account of his career as a pro quarterback.

Fran Tarkenton: The Scrambler. Bill Libby. G.P. Putnam's Sons. 1970. Clothbound.

The biography of a star pro quarterback.

8P-31 Broken Patterns. Fran Tarkenton and Brock Yates. Simon & Schuster. 1971. Clothbound.

A frank autobiography of a star pro quarterback.

8P-32 Bart Starr. John Devaney. Scholastic Book Services. 1967. Paperbound.

The biography of a star pro quarterback.

8P-33 Bart Starr, The Cool Quarterback. George Sullivan. G.P. Putnam's Sons. 1970. Clothbound.

The biography of a star quarterback.

8P-34 A Perspective on Victory. Bart Starr and John Weibusch. Follett Publishing Co. 1972. Clothbound.

The autobiography of a star pro quarterback, with insights on the game.

8P-35 Joe Namath, a Football Legend. David Lipman. G.P. Putnam's Sons. 1968. Clothbound.

The biography of a star quarterback.

8P-36 Joe Namath, Superstar. Robert Jackson. Henry Z. Walck. 1968. Clothbound.

A biography of the star quarterback for young readers.

8P-37 Joe Namath: Maverick Quarterback. Phil Berger. Cowles Book Co. 1969. Clothbound.

A biography of the star pro quarterback.

8P-38 Joe Namath's Sportin' Life. Maury Allen. Paperback Library. 1969. Paperbound.

The on-and off-field biography of a star pro quarterback and renowned playboy.

8P-39 Super Joe Namath. Stanley Weston. Rostam Publishing. 1969. Magazine.

Articles on the star pro quarterback. Photos.

Biographies

8P-40   SuperJoe: The Joe Namath Story. Larry Bortstein. Grosset & Dunlap. 1969. Clothbound. Tempo Books. 1969, reissue. Paperbound.

    A biography of the star quarterback.

8P-41   I Can't Wait Until Tomorrow. Joe Namath and Dick Schaap. Random House. 1969. Clothbound.

    The autobiography of Joe Namath, star quarterback and playboy.

8P-42   Sports Hero Joe Namath. Marshall and Sue Burchard. G.P. Putnam's Sons. 1971. Clothbound.

    A biographical sketch for young readers.

8P-43   Instant Replay: The Green Bay Diary of Jerry Kramer. Jerrry Kramer and Dick Schaap. World Publishing Co. 1968. Clothbound. Signet. 1969, reissue. Paperbound.

    The diary of a star Green Bay Packer lineman, covering the 1967 season. Inside views of the game.

8P-44   Jerry Kramer's Farewell to Football. Jerry Kramer and Dick Schaap. World Publishing Co. 1969. Clothbound. Bantam Books. 1970, reissue. Paperbound.

    Kramer's autobiography and account of his last season as a football player.

8P-45   Always a Winner. Don Shinnick and James Hefley. Zondervan Publishing House. 1969. Clothbound. 1971, reissue. 1972, reissue. Paperbound.

    The autobiography of a star NFL linebacker.

8P-46   Carroll Dale Scores Again! Dan Harman. Warner Press. 1969. Paperbound.

    The biography of a star pro receiver.

8P-47   The Dick Bass Story. Bill Libby. Julian Messner, Inc. 1969. Clothbound.

    The biography of a star college and pro halfback. Records.

8P-48   In the Pocket: My Life as a Pro Quarterback. Earl Morrall and George Sullivan. Grosset & Dunlap. 1969. Clothbound.

    The story of a much-travelled quarterback who in the late stages of his career became a starter for the Baltimore Colts, who won the 1969 NFL Championship.

8P-49   The Earl Morrall Story: Comeback Quarterback. Earl Morrall

Biographies

and George Sullivan. Tempo Books. 1971. Paperbound. Revised edition of 8P-48. Includes the 1970 Baltimore Colts Super Bowl championship season.

8P-50   Coach: A Season with Lombardi. Tom Dowling. W.W. Norton & Co. 1970. Clothbound. Popular Library. 1971, reissue. Paperbound.

An account of and insights into Vince Lombardi's 1969 season as coach of the Washington Redskins.

8P-51   Lombardi. Al Silverman. Macfadden-Bartell. 1970. Magazine.

A biographical sketch of Vince Lombardi. Interviews with players and coaches.

8P-52   Lombardi -- His Life and Times. Robert W. Wells. Wisconsin House, Ltd. 1971. Clothbound.

A narrative sketch of Vince Lombardi with accounts of outstanding games he coached, and a review of each season.

8P-53   Lombardi: Winning Is the Only Thing. Jerry Kramer, ed. World Publishing Co. 1970. Clothbound. Pocket Books. 1971, reissue. Paperbound.

Comments about all-time coaching great Vince Lombardi, by former college teammates, coaching associates, and players coached by him in college and pro football.

8P-54   Lombardi. John Wiebusch, ed. Follett Publishing Co. 1971. Clothbound.

Recollections about Vince Lombardi by his family, players, friends and associates. Photos.

8P-55   The Vince Lombardi Story. Dave Klein. Lion Press. 1971. Clothbound.

An account of the teams and players coached by Lombardi.

8P-56   Vincent Lombardi, Young Football Coach. Hortense Myers and Ruth Burnett. Bobbs, Merrill. 1971. Clothbound.

A biographical sketch for young readers.

8P-57   The 41st Packer. Dan Eckstein. Jacobs Press. 1970. Clothbound.

The diary of a rookie's attempt to make the Green Bay Packer team in 1969, and, after being the last man cut, his experiences in Canadian football.

Biographies

8P-58 I Am Third. Gale Sayers and Al Silverman. Viking Press. 1970. Clothbound.

> Autobiography of the star running back of the Chicago Bears.

8P-59 Len Dawson: Superbowl Quarterback. Larry Bortstein. Grosset & Dunlap. 1970. Clothbound. Tempo Books. 1970, reissue. Paperbound.

> The biography of a star quarterback.

8P-60 Len Dawson, Pressure Quarterback. Len Dawson and Lou Sahadi. Cowles Book Co. 1970. Clothbound.

> The biography of a star quarterback.

8P-61 Life in the Pit: The Deacon Jones Story. Bill Libby. Doubleday & Co. 1970. Clothbound.

> The biography of an all-time great pro defensive end.

8P-62 O.J.: The Education of a Rich Rookie. O.J. Simpson and Pete Axthelm. Macmillan Co. 1970. Clothbound.

> The story of Simpson's first year in pro football after starring as a college halfback and winning the Heisman Trophy.

8P-63 Player of the Year. Roman Gabriel and Bob Oates. World Publishing Co. 1970. Clothbound.

> A diary of the 1969 season as kept by Los Angeles Rams' quarterback Roman Gabriel.

8P-64 Confessions of a Dirty Ballplayer. Johnny Sample, Fred Hamilton and Sonny Schwartz. Dial Press. 1970. Clothbound. Dell Publishing Co. 1971, reissue. Paperbound.

> The autobiography of a controversial pro defensive halfback.

8P-65 Brian Piccolo: A Short Season. Jeannie Morris. Rand McNally. 1971. Clothbound.

> A biography of the Chicago Bears' running back, who died of cancer at age 26.

8P-66 Brian's Song. William Blinn. Bantam Books. 1972. Paperbound.

> A television screenplay on the life of Brian Piccolo.

8P-67 Bump and Run. Marty Domres and Robert Smith. Bantam Books. 1971. Paperbound.

> A frank autobiographical account of Domres' career as

Biographies

a college and pro quarterback. An inside look at pro football.

8P-68 From Football to Finance: The Story of Brady Keys, Jr. Eric B. Roberts. Harcourt, Brace & World. 1971. Clothbound.

The biography of a star college and pro player who organized and built the first black-owned national franchise operation.

8P-69 George Halas and the Chicago Bears. George Vass. Henry Regnery Co. 1971. Clothbound.

The biography of a National Football League pioneer and all-time great coach, and a history of the Chicago Bears.

8P-70 High for the Game. Chip Oliver and Ron Rapoport. William Morrow & Co. 1971. Clothbound.

The autobiography of a pro football linebacker who dropped out to become a hippie. Oliver later made an unsuccessful attempt at a comeback.

8P-71 On God's Squad. Norm Evans, Ray Didinger, and Sonny Schwartz. Creation House. 1971. Clothbound.

The autobiography of a star pro lineman and a statement of his religious beliefs.

8P-72 Out of Their League. Dave Meggyesy. Ramparts Press. 1971. Clothbound. Paperback Library. 1971, reissue. Paperbound.

The autobiography of a pro football linebacker who quit at the height of his career because of his dissatisfaction with the administration of the game. A critical inside look at pro football.

8P-73 The Speed King: Bob Hayes of the Dallas Cowboys. David Lipman and Ed Wilks. G.P. Putnam's Sons. 1971. Clothbound.

A biography of the track athlete who was the first man to run 100 yards in 9.1 seconds and who made a successful transition to pro football.

8P-74 Stop-Action. Dick Butkus and Robert W. Billings. E.P. Dutton & Co. 1972. Clothbound.

A diary of the last two games of the Chicago Bears' 1971 season, by their star linebacker.

8P-75 When All the Laughter Died in Sorrow. Lance Rentzel. Saturday Review Press. 1972. Clothbound.

The autobiography of a star college and pro football player who was indicted on a morals charge.

Biographies

8P-76   Blanda, Alive and Kicking. Wells Twombly. Nash Publishing Corp. 1972. Clothbound.

         The biography of George Blanda, still active as a pro quarterback and kicker at the age of 44.

8P-77   The Future Is Now. William Gildea and Kenneth Turan. Houghton Mifflin Co. 1972. Clothbound.

         The biography of outstanding pro coach George Allen.

8P-78   What a Pro Football Coach Does. Roy Hoopes. John Day. 1972. Clothbound.

         An illustrated account of the activities of Washington Redskins coach George Allen.

8P-79   Keep Off My Turf. Mike Curtis and Bill Gilbert. J.B. Lippincott Co. 1972. Clothbound.

         An account of the Baltimore Colts' 1971 season by their star linebacker. Outspoken opinions about the game and other players.

8P-80   Goal to Go. Weeb Ewbank and Neil Roiter. Hawthorn Books. 1972. Clothbound.

         Accounts of Ewbank's ten greatest coaching victories.

8P-81   Somebody Called "Doc". Zola Levitt. Creation House. 1972. Clothbound.

         The story of Ira Eshleman, a pro football chaplain.

8P-82   Pioneer in Pro Football. Jack Cusack. No date. Paperbound.

         Experiences and recollections of the manager of the Canton Bulldogs from 1912 - 1917 and the Cleveland Indians in 1921.

8P-83   The Quarterbacks. Don Smith. Franklin Watts. 1963. Clothbound. J. Lowell Pratt. 1964, reissue. Paperbound.

         Sketches of ten past and present stars.

8P-84   Great Quarterbacks of the NFL. Dave Anderson. Random House. 1965. Punt, Pass and Kick Library. Clothbound.

         Sketches of ten past and present stars of the National Football League. Photos.

8P-85   The Pro Quarterbacks. John Devaney. G.P. Putnam's Sons. 1967. Clothbound.

         Sketches of outstanding players. For younger readers.

8P-86   Pass to Win. George Sullivan. Garrard Publishing Co. 1968.

Biographies

	Clothbound.
	Sketches of Baugh, Graham, and Hutson.
8P-87	Greatest Pro Quarterbacks. Maury Allen. Scholastic Book Services. 1969. Paperbound.
	Sketches of ten modern stars.
8P-88	Star Quarterbacks of the NFL. Bill Libby. Random House. 1970. Punt, Pass and Kick Library. Clothbound.
	Sketches of ten modern stars.
8P-89	The Pro Quarterbacks. Milton J. Shapiro. Julian Messner, Inc. 1971. Clothbound.
	Sketches of six modern stars. Records.
8P-90	The Gamemakers. George Sullivan. G.P. Putnam's Sons. 1971. Clothbound.
	Profiles of 17 star quarterbacks from Baugh to Namath.
8P-91	Pro Football's Passing Game. George Sullivan. Dodd, Mead & Co. 1972. Clothbound.
	Profiles of star passers and receivers.
8P-92	Great Pro Quarterbacks. Lud Duroska. Grosset & Dunlap. 1972. Clothbound.
	Sketches of 14 stars. Records.
8P-93	Pro Quarterback Handbook. R.J. Drazkowski. Pro Football Weekly. 1972. Paperbound.
	Sketches, statistics, records of past and present quarterbacks.
8P-94	Great Quarterbacks Series. Bill Gutman. Tempo Books. 1972. Paperbound.
	Vol. 1 covers Staubach, Griese, Plunkett, Gabriel. Sketches, statistics.
8P-95	Great Running Backs of the NFL. Jack Hand. Random House. 1966. Punt, Pass and Kick Library. Clothbound.
	Sketches of 11 past and present stars of the National Football League. Photos.
8P-96	The Running Backs. Murray Olderman. Prentice-Hall. 1969. Clothbound.
	The evolution of the pro running game. Techniques, styles, requirements. Sketches, statistics, photos of 75 stars.

Biographies

8P-97 AFL Dream Backfield. Howard Liss. Cowles Book Co. 1969. Clothbound.
Sketches of Dawson, Alworth, Gilchrist, and Haynes.

8P-98 Great Running Backs in Pro Football. Phil Berger. Julian Messner, Inc. 1970. Clothbound.
Sketches of 15 stars.

8P-99 Star Running Backs of the NFL. Bill Libby. Random House. 1971. Punt, Pass and Kick Library. Clothbound.
Sketches of outstanding halfbacks and fullbacks.

8P-100 The Great Running Backs. George Sullivan. G.P. Putnam's Sons. 1972. Clothbound.
Sketches of outstanding pro runners. Career records.

8P-101 Great Pass Receivers of the NFL. Dave Anderson. Random House. 1966. Punt, Pass and Kick Library. Clothbound.
Sketches of 11 past and present stars of the National Football League. Photos.

8P-102 Great Pass Catchers in Pro Football. Howard Coan. Julian Messner, Inc. 1971. Clothbound.
Sketches of 13 modern receivers.

8P-103 Star Pass Receivers of the NFL. John Devaney. Random House. 1972. Punt, Pass and Kick Library. Clothbound.
Sketches of nine players. Photos.

8P-104 Great Defensive Players of the NFL. Dave Anderson. Random House. 1967. Punt, Pass and Kick Library. Clothbound.
Sketches of Huff, W. Davis, L. Wilson, Nobis, Marchetti, Lilly, Schmidt, D. Jones, Bednarik, H. Jordan, Lane, Butkus. Photos.

8P-105 Great Linebackers of the NFL. Richard Kaplan. Random House. 1970. Punt, Pass and Kick Library. Clothbound.
Sketches of ten stars.

8P-106 The Front Four. Howard Liss. Lion Press. 1971. Clothbound.
The development of the defensive line in pro football. Sketches of outstanding linemen.

8P-107 Golden Toes: Football's Greatest Kickers. Don Kowet. St. Martin's Press. 1972. Clothbound.
Sketches of outstanding pro punters and place kickers. Instructions on kicking.

8P-108 Football Stars of (year). Pyramid Books. 1963-to date. Barry Gottehrer. 1963, 1964. Berry Stainback. 1965-68. Larry

Biographies

                Bortstein. 1969-71. Ben Olan and Hal Brock. 1972. Paperbound.

                Sketches of players and coaches. Playing records.

8P-109   Heroes of the NFL. Jack Hand. Random House. 1965. Punt, Pass and Kick Library. Clothbound.

                Sketches of ten players who overcame obstacles to become stars in the National Football League. Photos.

8P-110   NFL Rookies to Watch. Norman Miller. Brown and Williamson Tobacco Corp. 1966. Booklet.

                Sketches, photos.

8P-111   Famous Pro Football Stars. William Heuman. Dodd, Mead & Co. 1967. Clothbound.

                Sketches of Thorpe, Nevers, Hubbard, Grange, Clark, Nagurski, Hein, Hutson, Baugh, Luckman, Waterfield, Graham, Tittle, Unitas, Brown.

8P-112   Pro Football Heroes. Steve Gelman. Scholastic Book Services. 1968. Paperbound.

                Sketches of ten stars.

8P-113   Pacemakers in Football. Mac Davis. World Publishing Co. 1968. Clothbound.

                Sketches of 30 stars.

8P-114   The Greatest Packers of Them All. Chuck Johnson. G.P. Putnam's Sons. 1968. Clothbound.

                Sketches of past and present Green Bay Packer stars.

8P-115   Everybody's Big Game: Professional Football. NFL Properties. 1970. Booklet.

                An advertising supplement containing sketches and photos of coaches and players.

8P-116   The Dallas Cowboys' Super Wives. Bobbi Field. Shoal Creek Publishers, Inc. 1972. Clothbound.

                Sketches of the players' wives. Recipes, an explanation of the game.

8P-117   NFL Man of the Year Award. Vitalis. 1970-to date. Booklet.

                A press guide containing sketches of the NFL Players nominated for the award.

8P-118   Sport Magazine Biographical Series. Bartholomew House. Paperbound.

Biographies

8P-118A Johnny Unitas. Ed Fitzgerald. 1961. Thomas Nelson. 1961, reissue. Clothbound.

8P-118B Football's Greatest Quarterbacks. Booton Herndon. 1962.

8P-118C Paul Hornung. Dick Schaap. 1962.

LAMAR DODGING THE YALE TACKLERS.

9. Instructionals

General

9-1 <u>Football</u>. Carl M. Johanson. Mills Brothers. 1893. Paperbound.

> The author was the captain of the Cornell University team in 1891 and 1892. The play of each position, training, signals, plays, rules.

9-2 <u>How to Play Football</u>. Walter Camp, ed. A.G. Spalding & Brothers. 1894, 1900, 1902-32. Camp listed as editor through 1926. Paperbound.

> The 1894 edition contained playing instructions by Camp; training instructions; a review of the season at Harvard, Princeton, and University of Pennsylvania; rosters of these teams; instructions on giving signals and instructions by college coaches and players. Later editions contained articles on position play by college stars. All-America teams, schedules, rule changes and the Football Code. The editions from 1914 on were enlarged.

9-3 <u>A Primer of College Football</u>. W.H. Lewis. Harper & Brothers. 1896. Paperbound.

> Fundamentals, the play of each position, offense, defense, training. Photos.

9-4 <u>Ingersoll's Football Tactics</u>. Robert H. Ingersoll and Brothers. c 1900. Booklet.

> Organizing a team, the value of football, explanation of the game, tactics, the play of each position, rules.

9-5 <u>Modern Football, How to Play the Game</u>. Walter E. McCornack. 1902. Booklet.

> Coaching, captaining, the play of each position. Offense, defense, rushing.

Instructionals

9-6	Football, How to Play the Game. William H. Bannard. R.K. Fox. 1905. Paperbound.
	Descriptions of the Rugby and Association games, rules, plays, signals.
9-7	The Story of a Football Season. George Brooke. J.B. Lippincott Co. 1907. Clothbound.
	A fictionalized account of a season's activities and games, with playing instructions.
9-8	Football Rudiments. Walter Lillard. Andover Press. 1911. Booklet.
	Basic techniques, training rules. Photos.
9-9	Letters from Brother Bill, Varsity Sub, to Tad, Captain of the Beechville High School Eleven. Walter Towers. Thomas Y. Crowell Co. 1915. Clothbound.
	Instructions through fictionalized accounts of games and practices. Photos.
9-10	Wilson Instructional Series. Thomas E. Wilson & Co. Paperbound.
9-10A	Thirty Selected Trick Football Plays. John R. Bender. 1922.
	Running and passing diagrams.
9-10B	Football Defense. John L. Griffith and George (Potsy) Clark. 1923.
9-10C	Football Offense. John L. Griffith and George (Potsy) Clark. 1923.
9-10D	Forward Passing. John L. Griffith and George (Potsy) Clark. 1923.
9-10E	Fundamentals, Tackling, Blocking, etc. John L. Griffith and George (Potsy) Clark. 1923.
9-10F	Fundamentals of Football Training. John L. Griffith and George (Potsy) Clark. 1923.
9-10G	Hints to Coaches. John L. Griffith and George (Potsy) Clark. 1923.
9-10H	How to Play Quarterback and Other Football Positions. John L. Griffith and George (Potsy) Clark. 1923.
9-11	Players' Football Manual and Notebook. Homer Smothers. 1929. Paperbound.

Instructionals

> Fundamentals, duties of each position, qualities needed to be a good athlete. Illustrations, blank pages for chalk talks and plays.

9-12 How to Play Football. Walter Eckersall. 1923. Paperbound.

> The play of each position, punting, tackling, blocking. Passing, generalship, information for spectators. Play diagrams.

9-13 Hip-Pocket Football. Steck Co. 1933. Booklet.

> Playing hints.

9-14 Ditto Practice Lessons in Football. M. Kent. Ditto, Inc. 1935. Paperbound.

> Fundamentals, play diagrams.

9-15 How I Play My Position. Albert Richard Co. 1935. Booklet.

> Instructions by the 1934 All-American team. Photos of players modeling clothing.

9-16 How to Play Football. Bernie Bierman. Heffelfinger Publications. 1936. Booklet.

> Training, playing, new rules. Watching and understanding the game.

9-17 How to Play Plain and Fancy Football. Coaches Exchange. c 1940. Booklet.

> Psychology, strategy, fundamentals.

9-18 How to Play Football. Charles (Bud) Wilkinson. 1940. Booklet.

> All phases of the game.

9-19 Football. Office of the Chief of Naval Operations. U.S. Naval Institute. 1943, 1950. Clothbound.

> Naval aviation physical training manual. The 1950 edition was published under the auspices of the V-5 Association of America. Background, football in the Navy. How to teach the game, fundamentals, individual skills, and execution. Formations and signals.

9-20 U.S. Rubber Co. Instructional Series. Booklet.

9-20A Football, the T Formation. Frank Leahy. 1944.

9-20B Football, Blocking and Tackling. Frank Leahy. 1944.

9-20C Football, Punting and Passing. Frank Leahy. 1944.

Instructionals

9-20D	Football. Frank Leahy. 1945.
9-21	Quaker Oats Instructional Series. Quaker Oats Co. Booklet.
9-21A	How to Play Winning Football. Herbert O. (Fritz) Crisler. 1943. Drills, blocking, tackling, kicking, the play of each position.
9-21B	Touchdown Plays. Herbert O. (Fritz) Crisler, ed. 1946. Diagrams and descriptions of key plays from important games, described by eight coaches.
9-21C	How to Star in Football. Herbert O. (Fritz) Crisler. 1948. Advice from 13 coaches.
9-21D	Championship Football. Herbert O. (Fritz) Crisler. 1948.
9-21E	How to Play Football. Charles Caldwell. 1952.
9-21F	How to Play Football. Charles (Bud) Wilkinson. 1954. Reissue.
9-22	Inside Football. A.G. Spalding & Brothers. 1947. Booklet. Instructions in cartoon form. Kicking, passing, receiving.
9-23	How Champions Play Football. Street & Smith. 1948. Magazine. Pictorial instructions. Ten best plays of 1947. Other sports covered.
9-24	Football Techniques Illustrated. Jim Moore and Tyler Micholeau. A.S. Barnes & Co. 1951, 1962. Clothbound. Rushing, passing, catching, kicking. Fumble recoveries, blocking, defense. Formations, strategy, tactics, glossary.
9-25	Play Football Safely. George E. Koontz. William-Frederick Press. 1952. Paperbound. Fundamentals and mechanics of blocking, tackling, punting, and passing. For players, coaches, and parents.
9-26	Athletic Leadership. Lloyd H. Helgeson. 1960. Paperbound. A manual for team captains and quarterbacks.
9-27	Football. J.R. Otto. Creative Educational Society. 1961, 1962. Clothbound. The evolution and growth of the game. Fundamental

Instructionals

techniques, plays, and play situations. Photos of game action.

9-28 **Learning How: Football.** J.R. Otto. Creative Educational Society. 1964. Paperbound.

Fundamental techniques, questions and answers, game photos.

9-29 **How to Play Football.** Rawlings Manufacturing Co. 1963. Booklet.

Various phases outlined by different coaches.

9-30 **Football Skills Test Manual.** David K. Brace. American Association for Health, Physical Education and Recreation. 1965. Paperbound.

9-31 **Illustrated Football Techniques.** No date. Paperbound.

Offense, defense, the play of each position, kicking. Diagrams.

9-32 **American Football for Women.** Jack Spaulding. A.G. Spalding & Brothers. 1939. Clothbound.

Playing instructions, rule explanations.

Coaching

9-33 **Football, How to Coach a Team.** Walter Camp. Wright & Ditson. 1886. Booklet.

Selection of players, the play of each position. Reprinted in 2-2C.

9-34 **The Football Calendar.** Walter Camp. 1916. Clothbound.

A football-shaped weekly calendar with verses and advice on various subjects for players and coaches.

9-35 **Football Without a Coach.** Walter Camp. D. Appleton & Co. 1920. Clothbound. Finch Press. 1972, reissue. Clothbound.

General discussion, instructions, practice, plays, strategy. Proper player's attitude toward the game.

9-36 **Haughton Instructional Series.** Percy Haughton. c 1900. Booklet.

Instructions by a future immortal coach at the beginning of his coaching career.

9-36A **Play of the Backs.**

Instructionals

9-36B	Play of the Quarterback.
9-36C	Tackle Play.
9-36D	Generalship.
9-36E	A Manual of Punting.
9-37	A Course in Football for Players and Coaches. Glenn S. Warner. 1908, 1912, reissue. Clothbound.

    Practice, generalship, the play of each position. Blocking, passing, catching, kicking. Defense, tackling, signals. Outfitting, training apparatus. Each section was also published separately as a correspondence course.

9-38	Football for Coaches and Players. Glenn S. Warner. 1927. Clothbound.

    Revised edition of 9-37.

9-39	A Course in Football Tactics for 1911. John S. Peoples. 1911. Paperbound.
9-40	Inside Dope on Football Coaching. John Richards. Thomas E. Wilson & Co. 1917, 1918. Cover title: Football Book. Paperbound.

    Plays, rules, formations, elements of playing.

9-41	Inside Football. Frank Cavanaugh. Small, Maynard & Co. 1919. Clothbound.

    General instructions, plays.

9-42	Modern Football for Players and Coaches. Mark M. Banks. 1919. Paperbound.

    Covering all standpoints of the game. Fundamentals, defense against running, passing, and kicking. Offensive play, conditioning, training.

9-43	Winning Football. William Roper. Dodd, Mead & Co. 1920. Clothbound.

    A general discussion of the game, the importance of spirit and ingenuity. Practice, training the quarterback, running the team, kicking. Game day preparations, scheduling factors. Full-page photos of game action.

9-44	American Football. Charles Daly. Harper & Brothers. 1921. Clothbound.

Instructionals

Playing instructions, play diagrams. Photos of prominent players and coaches.

9-45 **Football Technique and Tactics.** Robert Zuppke. Bailey & Himes. 1922, 1924. Clothbound.

Fundamentals, tackling, blocking, line play, and backfield play. Offense, defense, punting, passing, kickoffs, fair catches. Generalship, signals, team development.

9-46 **Coaching Football.** Robert Zuppke and Milton Olander. Bailey & Himes. 1930. Clothbound.

Pre-season preparation, the season's regimen, fundamentals. Offense, defense, kicking, passing. Strategy, scouting.

9-47 **How to Coach and Play Football.** Howard Jones and Alfred Wesson. Clio Press. 1923. Clothbound.

Running, passing, kicking. Offensive system, defensive line, generalship, signals. Conditioning, psychology, ethics, sportsmanship. The benefits of football.

9-48 **Football.** John W. Wilce. Charles Scribner's Sons. 1923. Clothbound.

General instructions, fundamentals, offense, defense. Practice, training, photos, diagrams of plays that won games.

9-49 **Football Notes.** Fielding H. Yost, George Little, and Elton E. Wieman. 1924. Paperbound.

Taken from lectures to classes in football at the University of Michigan. History, planning the season, fundamentals. Offense, defense, kicking, passing. Generalship, coaching, essentials of winning football.

9-50 **Coaching.** Knute Rockne. Devin-Adair Co. 1925, 1928, reissue, 1929, reissue. Clothbound. Grove Press. 1970, reissue. Clothbound.

Offense, passing, shifts, the play of each position. Signals, scouting, training, equipment. Mental aspects, the season's campaign, questions and answers.

9-51 **Coaching, the Way of the Winner.** Knute Rockne. Devin-Adair Co. 1930, 1931, reissue. Clothbound.

Revised edition of 9-50.

9-52 **Rockne's Football Problems.** Knute Rockne. 1926, 1927, reissue. Paperbound.

Instructionals

Questions and answers based on the text of 9-50.

9-53   <u>Football Notes.</u> Knute Rockne. 1926. Paperbound.

             Detailed, behind-the-scenes viewpoints on coaching. Psychology, offensive and defensive strategy, duties of each player.

9-54   <u>Knute Rockne on Football.</u> Knute Rockne. Individual Publications. 1931. Magazine.

             Rockne's views on various phases of the game. Techniques, philosophy. All-America teams, photos.

9-55   <u>Practical Football and How to Teach It.</u> Guy Lowman. A.S. Barnes & Co. 1927. Clothbound.

             Training and conditioning, equipment. General fundamentals, passing, kicking, centering. Backfield and line fundamentals, offense, defense, the play of each position. Team play and coaching, tactics. The treatment of injuries, scouting.

9-56   <u>Football Fundamentals.</u> Frank A. Faulkenberry. Methodist Publishing House. 1930. Clothbound.

             History and development. Changes through the years in rules and style of play. Analysis of the stance for each position. Photos.

9-57   <u>Football Techniques.</u> Elton E. Wieman. 1932. Paperbound.

9-58   <u>The Rainy Day Coach.</u> Heartly (Hunk) Anderson, Noble Kizer and H.E. (Suz) Sayger. Sayger Sports Syndicate. 1933. Clothbound.

             Illustrated general playing instructions. Plays, defenses.

9-58A   <u>The Rainy Day Coach Supplement.</u> Harry Kipke. 1934. Paperbound.

9-59   <u>Practical Football.</u> Herbert O. Crisler and Elton E. Wieman. McGraw-Hill. 1934. Clothbound.

             History and development. Planning the season, general instructions for offense and defense. Formations, scouting, organization, problems in coaching.

9-60   <u>Manual for Functional Football.</u> John Da Grosa. American Football Institute. 1935. Paperbound.

             A textbook of questions and answers. Each book was also published separately.

9-60A   <u>Book I. Offensive Fundamentals.</u>

Instructionals

9-60B   Book II. Defensive Fundamentals.

9-60C   Book III. Offense.

9-60D   Book IV. Defense.

9-60E   Book V. Coaching.

9-61   Functional Football. John Da Grosa. A.S. Barnes & Co. 1936, 1937, reissue, 1942, 1946. Clothbound.

         A condensation of 9-60 in narrative form.

9-62   Winning Football. B.W. (Bernie) Bierman and Frank Mayer. McGraw-Hill. 1937. Clothbound.

         Strategy, psychology, techniques. Full-page photos of game action.

9-63   Possibilities in Coaching Football. Frank Wilton, Jr. Oxford Printing Co. 1937. Paperbound.

         A consideration of football's educational values for the player. The football program, the player and the game, coaching methods. Football as an educational activity, ideals and beliefs in relation to football. Instructional opportunities in coaching, personality development through football.

9-64   Football. W. Glenn Killinger. A.S. Barnes & Co. 1939. Clothbound.

         For players, coaches, and spectators. Plays, strategy, diagrams.

9-65   Championship Football. Dana X. Bible. Prentice-Hall. 1947. Clothbound.

         General instructions, play diagrams. A guide for players, coaches, and fans.

9-66   Progressive and Fundamental Football. Harold C. Ave and F.A. Beau. School-Aid Co. 1948. Clothbound.

         Fundamentals, general instructions. Pre-season planning, offense and defense. Game tactics and generalship. Diagrams.

9-67   Pigskin Tactics. Vince DiFrancesca, F.A. Beau and Harold C. Ave. School-Aid Co. 1953. Clothbound.

         Revised edition of 9-66. A streamlined approach to football fundamentals. Plays, diagrams, photos.

9-68   Modern Football. Herbert O. Crisler. Whittlesey House. 1949.

Instructionals

Clothbound.

> General instructions, offense, defense, play diagrams, photos of game action.

9-69 American Football Coaches Association: Lectures Delivered at the Football Clinics. American Football Coaches Association. 1949-53. Booklet.

> Talks given by prominent coaches covering plays, systems, other topics. Diagrams.

9-70 American Football Coaches Association: Summer Manual. American Football Coaches Association. 1954-to date. Booklet.

> Lectures given at coaching clinics.

9-71 How to Play Football. Lynn Waldorf. Little Technical Library. 1942. Clothbound.

> Equipment, fundamentals, offense, defense, signals. How to watch, game photos.

9-72 This Game of Football. Lynn Waldorf. McGraw-Hill. 1952. Clothbound.

> Offense, defense, kicking, training, and conditioning. Team foundations, fundamentals, practice organization. Functions of a coach, appraisal of American football. Personal recollections, photos.

9-73 Revolutionary Football. Herbert Phillips, ed. University of Georgia. 1953. Paperbound.

> A collection of essays by Dobby Dodd, Jake Gaither, Jim Tatum, Wally Butts, Tom Nugent, and other coaches on new and unusual formations, such as the "double T," "Y," "I," and "dissolving T."

9-74 Bobby Dodd on Football. Robert Dodd. Prentice-Hall. 1954. Clothbound.

> The evolution of football, an analysis of coaching, failures. Offense, defense, quarterbacking, kicking. Preparation, organization, scouting, training.

9-75 Encyclopedia of Football Drills. George H. Allen. Prentice-Hall. 1954. Clothbound.

> Different drills for each phase of the game. Diagrams, photos.

9-76 Complete Book of Winning Football Drills. George H. Allen. Prentice-Hall. 1959. Clothbound.

> Revised and enlarged edition of 9-75.

Instructionals

9-77 Inside Football. George H. Allen and Don Weiskopf. Allyn & Bacon. 1969. Clothbound.

Fundamentals, strategy, and tactics of high school, college and pro football. Stop-action photos.

9-78 The Contributions Sixteen Millimeter Cinematographic Techniques Make to Coaching Football. Francis P. Harrison. University of Michigan. University Microfilms. 1954. Paperbound.

College thesis.

9-79 Football at Ohio State. Wayne (Woody) Hayes. 1957. Clothbound.

Offensive strategy, the running game, passing. Split-T play series, drills, quarterbacks training. Defense, kicking, scouting, the statistical system. Organization and planning, coach-player relationships.

9-80 Football Fundamentals. John Bateman and Paul Governali. McGraw-Hill. 1957. Clothbound.

Strategy, teaching methods, offense, defense, plays. Sequence photos.

9-81 Fundamental Football. James Houlgate. A.S. Barnes & Co. 1958. Clothbound.

General discussion, player requisites. Offensive and defensive line play fundamentals, backfield fundamentals. Punting, passing, quarterbacking.

9-82 How to Be a Successful Coach. James Bonder. Prentice-Hall. 1960. Clothbound.

All phases of coaching techniques.

9-83 Organization for Successful Football Coaching. Robert E. Walker. Prentice-Hall. 1960. Clothbound.

Staffing, practice, the player's notebook. Scouting, game day procedure, plays. Road trips, audiovisual aids.

9-84 How to Coach Winning Football. Otto Unruh. Prentice-Hall. 1960. Clothbound.

The basis of sound coaching, preparations for the season, practice. The day of the game, handling players, the power of suggestion. Offense, defense, passing, kicking, generalship, game strategy.

9-85 Building a Championship Football Team. Paul Bryant. Prentice-Hall. 1960. Clothbound.

Instructionals

Quarterbacking, kicking, defense. Organization, planning, molding an efficient coaching staff.

9-86   First and Ten. Hugh (Duffy) Daugherty and Clifford Wilson. William C. Brown. 1961, 1970. Clothbound.

A step-by-step analysis of techniques and strategy. Offensive fundamentals, team strategy, individual play. Kicking, defense, scouting, administration.

9-87   How to Organize and Conduct Football Practice. George Katchmer. Prentice-Hall. 1962. Clothbound.

Planning, the manual, conditioning, and training. Junior high, high school and college programs.

9-88   Football; Principles and Play. David Nelson. Ronald Press. 1962. Clothbound.

Defense, offense, kicking, organization.

9-89   Missouri Power Football. Dan Devine and Al Onofrio. Lucas Brothers. 1962, 1967. Paperbound.

Offensive and defensive fundamentals, drills, plays.

9-90   Championship Football by Twelve Great Coaches. Tom Ecker and Paul Jones, eds. Prentice-Hall. 1962. Clothbound.

Playing instructions and philosophy by Broyles, Bryant, Curtice, Dodd, Engle, Faurot, Nelson, Nugent, Owens, Royal, Warmath, and Wyatt.

9-91   Darrell Royal Talks Football. Darrell Royal and Blackie Sherrod. Prentice-Hall. 1963. Clothbound.

A coach's view of the game. The science of football, game accounts, anecdotes.

9-92   The Football Coach's Complete Handbook. Bill Hammer. Prentice-Hall. 1963. Paperbound.

Philosophy, psychology, team development. Practice, fundamentals, offense, defense, kicking. Drills, scouting, film analysis.

9-93   Championship Football Drills. Don Fuoss. Prentice-Hall. 1965. Clothbound.

The teaching of offensive and defensive fundamentals and techniques.

9-94   Pre-Game Football. George A. Katchmer, ed. Prentice-Hall. 1965. Clothbound.

Chapters by various coaches on game preparation and

Instructionals

strategy. Preparing for various situations and types of opponents.

9-95   Football Coaching. John McKay. Ronald Press. 1966. Clothbound.

The complete University of Southern California system. Running and passing plays, line play, pass coverage. Reaction football, kicking. Training, scouting, public relations. Diagrams.

9-96   Best of Football from the Coaching Clinic. Editors of Coaching Clinic. Parker Publishing Co. 1967. Clothbound.

Reprints, from a monthly magazine, of articles, grouped by general topic, by college and high school coaches.

9-97   Illustrated Guide to Championship Football. Frank Kapral. Parker Publishing Co. 1967. Clothbound.

Offensive and defensive fundamentals and techniques. Plays, drills. Diagrams, photos.

9-98   Organizational Keys and Checklists for Successful Football Coaching. Jack Olcott. Parker Publishing Co. 1968. Clothbound.

Foundation, organization, checklists.

9-99   Techniques of Football Coaching. Harry Larche. A.S. Barnes & Co. 1969. Clothbound.

Administration, organization, offense, defense, kicking, conditioning, psychology.

9-100   Coaching Today's Athlete: A Football Textbook. John Ralston, Mike White and Stanley Wilson. National Press Books. 1971. Paperbound.

Philosophy of coaching, responsibilities, coach-player relationships, staff, practice, clinics, offense, defense, passing, position play, kicking, scouting, training.

9-101   Coaching Football. Paul Dietzel. Ronald Press. 1971. Clothbound.

Organization, off-season preparation, fundamentals, game preparation, kicking, offense, defense, scouting.

9-102   University of Arkansas Football Clinic. University of Arkansas. 1971. Paperbound.

Drills, plays, formations, offense, defense.

9-103   Parseghian and Notre Dame Football. Ara Parseghian and Tom Pagna. Men-In-Motion. 1971. Clothbound.

Instructionals

Organization, defense, offense, passing, kicking, scouting, glossary.

Offense

9-104   Football Offense. Andrew L. Smith. Flint, Douglas Printing Co. 1924. Booklet.

     Mental qualifications, coaching, generalship. Kicking, punting, passing, interference, the play of each position, plays.

9-105   Michigan State Multiple Offense. Clarence (Biggy) Munn. Prentice-Hall. 1953. Clothbound.

     Evolution, numbering system, organization. Offensive line and backfield play, running, passing, kicking.

9-106   The Fundamentals of an Original System of Offensive Play in Football. Robert D. Hoff. State University of Iowa. University Microfilms. 1957. Paperbound.

     College thesis.

9-107   Offensive Football. Jordan Olivar. Ronald Press. 1958. Clothbound.

     The "belly series." Philosophy, personnel, numbering system, variations. Passing, quarterback training, play calling. Integration with other series.

9-108   Football Offense in Revolution. Calvin A. Walden. Pageant Press. 1960. Clothbound.

     The bifocal attack. Modern defense, strategic offense, patterns, stances. Backfield and line techniques, signals, personnel.

9-109   The Complete Book of Backfield Play. Robert E. Walker. Prentice-Hall. 1962. Clothbound.

     Technique, formations, running, blocking, passing, kicking.

9-110   Ray Graves' Guide to Modern Football Offense. Ray Graves. Parker Publishing Co. 1967. Clothbound.

     Offensive trends, policies, procedures. Personnel, general offensive system. Running, passing, backfield, and line play. Protection, play calling, practice, organization.

9-111   Springfield College Football Team Offense. Edward T. Dunn.

Instructionals

Springfield College. 1967. Paperbound.

> Theory, fundamentals, drills.

9-112   Sports Illustrated Football: Offense. Charles (Bud) Wilkinson. J.B. Lippincott Co. 1972. Paperbound.

> Conditioning, receiving, quarterbacking, line play, formations, fundamentals, strategy.

Plays

9-113   Twenty Modern Football Plays. George Levene. 1911. Paperbound.

> Kicking, running and passing plays.

9-113A   Twenty Football Plays for 1912. George Levene. 1912. Paperbound.

> Continuation of 9-113.

9-114   The All-American Football Coaching Course. William G. Kline. 1929. Paperbound.

> Play diagrams and descriptions.

9-115   The Varsity Football Play Set. William G. Kline. Coaches Institute. 1933. Paperbound.

> Diagrams and discussions of offensive plays.

9-116   Selected Football Plays from Nine Standard Formations. Lysle K. Butler and M.K. Kiracofe. 1934. Paperbound.

> Individual play diagrams with descriptive notes for each.

9-117   Fifty Football Plays by Fifty Great Coaches. Arthur J. (Dutch) Bergman, ed. A.S. Barnes & Co. 1936. Paperbound.

> Contributed by Allison, Anderson, Owen, Sutherland, Warner, Da Grosa, others. Diagrams.

9-118   Crucial Games and the Plays That Won Them. Albert Richard Co. 1936. Booklet.

> Stories by the 1935 All-Americans. Photos, play diagrams, other data.

9-119   Headwork Wins Football Games. Albert Richard Co. 1937. Booklet.

> Important plays in games of the 1936 season as related by members of the All-American team.

Instructionals

9-120   New 1948 Plays: Football. American Football Coaches Association. Wells Publishing Co. 1948. Paperbound.

        Fundamentals, strategy, generalship. Passing, running, kicking, play diagrams. Favorite plays of various college coaches.

9-121   Winning Football Plays. Dave Camerer, ed. Ronald Press. 1954, 1962, 1966. Clothbound.

        Discussions and diagrams by Blaik, Brennan, Caldwell, Evashevski, Erdelatz, Tatum, Wilkinson, others. Thirty-four outstanding plays discussed and analyzed. Illustrations.

Quarterbacking

9-122   Quarterback Strategy. Lowell Dawson. 1932. Paperbound.

        Requisites, play sequences, game preparations. Plays, do's and don'ts.

9-123   Quarterback Generalship and Strategy. Don Fuoss. Prentice-Hall. 1958. Clothbound.

        Selection of personnel, teaching, training. Offense, defense, running, passing, kicking. Zones, manual, generalship.

9-124   How to Train the Quarterback. George H. Allen. Prentice-Hall. 1960. Clothbound.

        History of quarterbacking, selecting the quarterback, laws of generalship. Drills, signals, forms, and charts. Running, passing, kicking, defense. Generalship, effects of score and time.

9-125   Coaching the Quarterback. Jack Olcott. Parker Publishing Co. 1972. Clothbound.

        Selection, ball handling, game preparations, strategy, fundamentals, play calling, passing, punting.

Passing

9-126   The Forward Pass in Football. Elmer Berry. A.S. Barnes & Co. 1921. Booklet.

        Development of the pass, passing rules, techniques, fundamentals, formations, and plays, defense.

Instructionals

9-127 **The Lateral Pass Technique and Strategy.** Joseph A. Pipal. 1927, 1934. Booklet.

    History, training, fundamentals, and fine points. Throwing, plays, strategy, defense. Forward pass technique and strategy was outlined in the 1934 edition.

9-128 **The Forward Pass and Its Defense.** Charles (Gus) Dorais. Athletic Book Co. 1931. Clothbound.

    By Knute Rockne's teammate, later a coach. History of the pass, varieties, uses, execution. Defense, drills, diagrams.

9-129 **History and Strategy of the Forward Pass.** Flem Hall. Packard Motor Car Co. 1951. Booklet.

9-130 **The Passing Game.** Ray Pelfrey and Steve Owens. William C. Brown. 1956. Clothbound.

    Offense, defense, pass patterns, quarterback instructional aids. For coaches and players.

9-131 **The Passing Game in Football.** Jack Curtice. Ronald Press. 1961. Clothbound.

    Fundamentals, play patterns, strategy.

9-132 **The Passing and Kicking Game.** Tim Timerario. 1964. Paperbound.

    Diagrammed instructions for boys, high school and college players.

9-133 **Coaching an Explosive Passing Offense.** Douglas Gerhart. Parker Publishing Co. 1969. Clothbound.

    Key factors, techniques, strategy.

9-134 **Forward Passing.** Andy Kerr. Ken-Wel Sporting Goods Co. No date. Booklet.

    Execution, technique, practice.

Formations

9-135 **Analysis of "T" Formation with Man-in-Motion.** Bob Hall and John Da Grosa. 1941. Paperbound.

    Formations, plays, defense. Action photos.

9-136 **Modern T Formation with Man-in-Motion.** Clark Shaughnessy,

Instructionals

Ralph Jones, and George Halas. 1946. Paperbound.

Principles, backfield and line play. Signals, strategy, running, passing.

9-137 Coaching the T Formation. Forrest England. Arkansas State College Press. 1948. Clothbound.

Philosophy, offensive line, backfield play, quarterback strategy, defense.

9-138 The T Formation from A to Z. Forrest England. School Aid Co. 1952. Clothbound.

Philosophy, backfield and line play, play series. Defense, drills, strategy.

9-139 Notre Dame Football, the T Formation. Frank Leahy. Prentice-Hall. 1949. Clothbound.

Plays, instructions covering each position.

9-140 Football, Secrets of the Split-T Formation. Don Faurot. Prentice-Hall. 1950. Clothbound.

By the developer of the split-T. Reasoning behind, plays, formations, blocking, passing. Defense, kicking, strategy, glossary.

9-141 The Operation of the T-Formation in Football at North Texas State University. Odus Mitchell. North Texas State University. 1951. Paperbound.

Running, passing, kicking, the play of each position, development of the formation. By the North Texas State coach.

9-142 Oklahoma Split-T Football. Charles (Bud) Wilkinson. Prentice-Hall. 1952. Clothbound.

Theory, techniques, formations, signals, plays, passes, strategy.

9-143 Coaching Football and the Split-T Formation. Jim Tatum and Warren Giese. William C. Brown. 1953. Paperbound.

√

Background and development of football and coaching. Training, conditioning, offensive formations, defense. Coaching the split-T, glossary.

9-144 Split-Line T Offense. A.S. (Jake) Gaither. Prentice-Hall. 1963. Clothbound.

Evolution and development, quarterback strategy, blocking, offensive series. Running, passing, pass protection, kicking, drills.

Instructionals

9-145   <u>Fundamentals of the T Formation.</u> James Bonder. William C. Brown. 1956. Paperbound.

         Coaching, practice, skills. Blocking, line and backfield play, pass defense, kicking, game planning.

9-146   <u>Fly-T Football.</u> Hampton Pool, Joe Nordmann, Al Hunt, John Sanders, and John Trump. Prentice-Hall. 1957. Clothbound.

         Evolution, variations, formations, plays. Passes, counter plays, play series, scouting.

9-147   <u>The Winged T.</u> Forrest Evashevski and David Nelson. William C. Brown. 1957. Title page: <u>Scoring Power with the Winged T Offense.</u> Clothbound.

         Background, development, and philosophy of a new offense combining features of the single wing, split T, and tight T. Fundamentals, backfield and line techniques, play series. Diagrams, action photos.

9-148   <u>The Modern Winged T Play Book.</u> David Nelson and Forrest Evashevski. William C. Brown. 1961. Paperbound.

         Numbering system, formations, plays.

9-149   <u>Wing-T and the Chinese Bandits.</u> Paul Dietzel. Chinese Bandits. 1959. Paperbound.

         Morale, organization, training, and game preparation at Louisiana State University. Offense, defense, play diagrams. Technical aspects of Louisiana State University's 1958 season.

9-150   <u>Ben Martin's Flexible T Offense.</u> Ben Martin. Prentice-Hall. 1961. Clothbound.

         Personnel, signals, the quarterback. Plays, passing, running.

9-151   <u>Slot T Football.</u> Max R. Spilsbury. Prentice-Hall. 1961. Clothbound.

         Coaching, backfield and line play, blocking. Quarterbacking, rushing, passing, kicking. Scouting, psychology, intrinsic values of football.

9-152   <u>The Explosive Short-T.</u> Homer Rice. Prentice-Hall. 1963. Clothbound.

         Evolution, description, technique. Running and passing series, formations.

9-153   <u>The Unbalanced Line Open End T Offense.</u> Edward L. Teague, Jr. Prentice-Hall. 1964. Clothbound.

Instructionals

Building the offense, developing and organizing the attack. Training the quarterback, drills, analysis.

9-154 Football's Multiple Spread T Offense. Robert Swanson. Parker Publishing Co. 1966. Clothbound.

Concepts, basic formation. Running, passing, play sequence. The play of each position, blocking.

9-155 Power T Football. Dee Andros and Rowland (Red) Smith. Parker Publishing Co. 1971. Clothbound.

Running, passing, techniques, training, play sequences.

9-156 Modern Single Wing Football. Charles Caldwell, Jr. J.B. Lippincott Co. 1951. Clothbound.

The human equation, fundamentals, running and passing, the quarterback. Glossary, photos.

9-157 Simplified Single Wing Football. Kenneth W. Keuffel. Prentice-Hall. 1952. Clothbound.

Organization, individual techniques, drills. Running, passing, offensive strategy.

9-158 Spread Formation Football. Leo R. (Dutch) Meyer. Prentice-Hall. 1952. Clothbound.

Fundamentals, passing, strategy, the play of each position.

9-159 The Modern Short Punt: A Winning Formation. Lou Howard. Prentice-Hall. 1959, 1963. Clothbound.

Advantages, personnel, numbering system. Blocking technique, running and passing plays, pass defense. Psychology, spirit, philosophy.

9-160 Swing-End Offense. Robert E. Walker. Prentice-Hall. 1964. Clothbound.

A system designed to exploit defensive adjustments. Development, formations, methods of attacking, quarterbacking.

9-161 The Modern Notre Dame Formation. Charles Bachman. 1969. Paperbound.

Development of the Notre Dame formation. Plays, blocking. Recollections of Knute Rockne and Notre Dame football. By a retired college coach.

Instructionals

Line Play

9-162 The Line Man's Bible. Ernest Graves. 1921. Clothbound.
Offense, defense, coaching.

9-163 Line Coaching. Thomas Lieb. Athletic Supply Co., Inc. 1927. Clothbound. Thomas J. Lieb. 1930, 1947. Clothbound.
Equipment, training, fundamentals. Offense, defense, the play of each position. Photos.

9-164 Football Line Play for Players and Coaches. Bernard Oakes. A.S. Barnes & Co. 1932, 1948. Clothbound.
Training, coaching, stances, blocking. Offense, defense, the play of each lineman, tackling.

9-165 The Five-Man Line Defense. John Da Grosa. American Football Institute. 1937. Booklet.
History, reasoning behind, values of. Diagrams, individual assignments. By the originator of the formation.

9-166 How to Meet the Five-Man Line Shifting and Changing Defenses. John Da Grosa. American Football Institute. 1938. Booklet.
Diagrams, charts, signal calling, play construction.

9-167 Fundamental Line Drills for Line Skills in the T Formation. Jim Bonder. William C. Brown. 1952. Paperbound.
Basic principles, practice, skills. Blocking, centering, the line as a unit, defensive play.

9-168 Football, Straight Line Philosophy. Charles F. Lappenbusch. 1952. Paperbound.
Book I. Offense. Book II. Kill the T.

9-169 A Study of Linemen Stances and Body Alignments and Their Relationship to Starting Speed in Football. Robert E. Fitch. Indiana University. Northern Engraving and Manufacturing Co. 1957. Paperbound.
College thesis.

9-170 Effect of Variations in Hand and Foot Spacing on Movement Time and on Force of Charge. Jack A. Owens. University Microfilms. 1957. Paperbound.
College thesis.

9-171 Offensive and Defensive Line Play. Gomer Jones. Prentice-Hall.

Instructionals

 1961. Clothbound.

 Essentials of line play, drills, selection of personnel. Fundamentals, techniques, signals, theory.

9-172 Football End Play. Ben Martin. Ronald Press. 1961. Clothbound.

 Stance, blocking, pass routes, receiving, covering kicks, defense.

9-173 The Coaching of Football Line Play. Victor Rowen. Charles E. Merrill Publishing Co. 1968. Paperbound.

 Offense and defense.

9-174 Coaching the Offensive and Defensive Line Game. Donald E. Fuoss. Parker Publishing Co. 1972. Clothbound.

 Practice, selecting personnel, fundamentals, techniques.

9-175 Coaching Linebackers and the Perimeter Defense. Gene Ellenson. Prentice-Hall. 1972. Clothbound.

 Selecting players, fundamentals, techniques, details of the perimeter defense.

Kicking

9-176 Kicking the American Football. Leroy Mills. G.P. Putnam's Sons. 1932, 1936, reissue. Clothbound.

 Teaching system, general instructions. Accounts of famous games decided by kicks, photos.

9-177 Michigan's Kicking Game. Harry Kipke and H.E. (Suz) Sayger. Sayger Sports Syndicate. 1934. Clothbound.

 Illustrated techniques for punting, place kicking, and drop kicking.

9-178 The Lost Art of Kicking. Charles Erb. Adohr Milk Farms. 1939, 1940, reissue. Paperbound.

 Importance, instructions, team spirit. Accounts of games in which a kick was the turning point.

9-179 The Complete Kicking Game. Don Fuoss. Prentice-Hall. 1959. Clothbound.

 Strategy, personnel, fundamentals, technique, factors. Centering protecting, coverage, blocking. Scouting, practice, rules.

Instructionals

9-180   Secrets of Kicking the Football. Dr. Edward Storey. G.P. Putnam's Sons. 1971. Clothbound.

    Step-by-step instructions for learning and improving the football kick.

Defense

9-181   Defensive Football. Frank Leahy. Prentice-Hall. 1951. Clothbound.

    Formations, defense against each main type of offensive lineup.

9-182   Umbrella Defenses. Jack C. Mitchell and Bernard A. Taylor. William C. Brown. 1956. Paperbound.

    Variations, pass defenses. Defenses against spread and single wing formations, goal line defenses, strategy, drills.

9-183   Modern Defensive Football. Gomer Jones and Charles (Bud) Wilkinson. Prentice-Hall. 1957. Clothbound.

    Objectives, theory, fundamentals. Strategy, unit play, types of defenses.

9-184   Simplified Multiple Defense. George Katchmer. Prentice-Hall. 1958. Clothbound.

    Reasons for multiple defenses, combatting modern offenses, types of defenses. Defense against running, passing, and kicking. Scouting methods.

9-185   Jericho. Dewayne King. Prentice-Hall. 1963. Clothbound.

    A modern system of pass defense. Philosophy, theory, psychology. Basic principles, formations, coaching, practice.

9-186   Football Coach's Guide to Secondary Defense. Billy R. Hughes. Parker Publishing Co. 1964. Clothbound.

    Principles, alignments versus different running and passing plays, adjustments.

9-187   Ray Graves' Guide to Modern Football Defense. Ray Graves. Prentice-Hall. 1966. Clothbound and Paperbound.

    Philosophy, alignments, responsibilities. Defensive formations, teaching, organization.

9-188   Defense Spartan Style. Hugh (Duffy) Daugherty. Four Winds

Instructionals

Press. 1967. Clothbound.

Defense as taught at Michigan State University. Philosophy, theory, strategy. The defensive line, linebackers, end play, the secondary. Goal-line defense, developing players.

9-189   Springfield College Football Team Defense. Edward T. Dunn. Springfield College. 1967. Paperbound.

Terminology, theory, fundamentals, drills. The play of each position, the kicking game.

9-190   Defense: The Winning Difference in Football. Edward Knecht. Parker Publishing Co. 1968. Clothbound.

How to develop an overpowering defense.

9-191   Pass Defense Drills. George H. Allen. Addison-Wesley. 1968. Clothbound.

Drills for various phases of the defensive game.

9-192   Football Coach's Guide to Successful Pass Defense. Jack Olcott. Parker Publishing Co. 1970. Clothbound.

Teaching, calls, defensive alignments, practice, drills.

9-193   Complete Guide to the Split-Pro Defense. Gailord Bellamy. Prentice-Hall. 1971. Clothbound.

Evolution, coaching techniques.

9-194   How to Coach Football's Forty-Four Stack Defense. Tom Simonton. Parker Publishing Co. 1972. Clothbound.

Alignment, personnel, numbering system, coaching, game situations, signals, drills.

Professional Titles

General

9P-1   Football. George (Potsy) Clark. Rand McNally. 1935. Paperbound.

First instructional devoted to the professional game. General playing instructions, the play of each position, strategy, defensive formations. Diagrams and explanations of favorite plays of each team.

9P-2   Football As Champions Play It. Homer Rice. Pennsylvania Rubber Co. 1948. Booklet.

Instructionals

Playing instructions demonstrated through illustrations of Cleveland Browns players.

9P-3	Union Oil Instructional Series. Union Oil Co. 1958. Booklet.
9P-3A	Fine Points of Ball Carrying. Frank Gifford.
9P-3B	Fine Points of Football Defense. Les Richter.
9P-3C	Fine Points of Football Offense. Elroy Hirsch.
9P-3D	Fine Points of Line Play. Pete Elliott.
9P-3E	Fine Points of Pass Receiving. Elroy Hirsch.
9P-3F	Fine Points of Passing, Running and Kicking. Frank Albert.
9P-3G	Fine Points of Playing Quarterback. Y.A. Tittle.
9P-3H	Fine Points of Playing Quarterback. Bob Waterfield.

9P-4   The Book of Football. Sports Illustrated. J.B. Lippincott Co. 1960. Clothbound.

            Playing instructions by star players. The T formation by Tittle, the offensive end by Berry, place kicking by Groza, line play by Robustelli, others. Diagrams, photos.

9P-5   Tips on How to Punt, Pass and Kick. Ford Motor Co. 1962. Booklet.

            Illustrated instructions by Yale Lary, Johnny Unitas, and Paul Hornung.

9P-6   How the Pros Play Football. Robert Smith and William Dudley. Doubleday & Co. 1964. Clothbound.

            The play of each position. Offense, defense, kicking, pass receiving, strategy, plays.

9P-7   How to Pass, Kick, Run, Block. Bart Starr, Lou Groza, and Yale Lary. North American Philips Co. 1965. Paperbound.

            Techniques of pro football by star players. Illustrations, diagrams. Season previews.

9P-8   How to Punt, Pass and Kick. Richard Pickens. Random House. 1965. Punt, Pass and Kick Library. Clothbound.

            An elementary guide with tips from Lary, Starr, and Groza. Photos, index.

9P-9   On Any Given Sunday. Kimberly-Clark. 1965. Magazine.

Instructionals

An explanation of the play of each position as practiced by the pros. Photos.

9P-10 The Specialist in Pro Football. Al Silverman. Random House. 1966. Clothbound.

Reprinted from a series in Sport Magazine. The play of seventeen positions and specialities as explained by pro stars.

9P-11 Pro Football Playbook. Gary Knafelc. Sports Reports. 1967. Paperbound.

Offensive and defensive tactics explained by a former player. Illustrations.

9P-12 Poised for Action. Prudential Insurance Co. 1967, 1968. Booklet.

Conditioning and playing pointers by NFL players. NFL team reviews.

9P-13 Pro Football, U.S.A. Hal Higdon. G.P. Putnam's Sons. 1968. Clothbound.

The play of each position as told by 40 pro stars.

9P-13A Inside Pro Football. Hal Higdon. Tempo Books. 1970. Paperbound.

Abridged edition of 9P-13.

9P-14 The Making of a Rookie. Howard Liss. Random House. 1968. Punt, Pass and Kick Library. Clothbound.

The development and training of a first year pro player. Playing instructions.

9P-15 How the Pros Play Football. Berry Stainback. Random House. 1970. Clothbound.

Strategies, techniques, and philosophy as outlined by 16 star players.

Offense

9P-16 Backfield Play. Charlie Trippi. Ziff-Davis. 1948. Clothbound and Paperbound.

Formations, signals, ball-carrying, blocking, kicking, tackling. Action photos. By a star halfback.

9P-17 Offensive Football. Bob Griese, Gayle Sayers and Bill Bondur-

Instructionals

ant. Atheneum. 1972. Clothbound.

Passing, running, kicking. By a star pro quarterback and halfback.

Plays

9P-18   Jock Sutherland's 20 Winning Football Plays. Jock Sutherland. West Disinfecting Co. 1940. Booklet.

By an immortal pro and college coach.

9P-19   Pro Football Plays in Pictures. George Sullivan. Grosset & Dunlap. 1971. Paperbound.

Formations, plays, patterns.

Passing

9P-20   The Passing Game. Benny Friedman. Steinfeld, Inc. 1931. Paperbound.

General discussion and instructions, using game situations. Sequence photos, diagrams. By a star quarterback.

9P-21   Passing and Kicking. Sammy Baugh. 1940. Booklet.

Playing tips by an all-time great quarterback.

9P-22   Passing for Touchdowns. Sid Luckman. Ziff-Davis. 1948. Clothbound and Paperbound.

By an all-time great quarterback. Reasons for passing, development of the passing game, types of passes. Defense, pass protection, receiving. Luckman's pro football records.

9P-23   Tricks in Passing. Paul Christman. Ziff-Davis. 1948. Clothbound and Paperbound.

Fine points of passing strategy. By a star quarterback.

9P-24   The Forward Pass. Charles Conerly and Tom Meany. E.P. Dutton & Co. 1960. Clothbound.

General discussion and instructions by a star pro quarterback. Examples drawn from game situations. Personal recollections. Diagrams, illustrations.

Instructionals

Quarterbacking

9P-25   Otto Graham - T Quarterback. Otto Graham. Prentice-Hall. 1953. Clothbound.

               The techniques of quarterbacking the T formation, by an all-time great quarterback.

9P-25A   T-Formation Tips. Otto Graham. Thomas E. Wilson & Co. 1954. Booklet.

               Reprinted sections from 9P-25.

9P-26   The Making of a Pro Quarterback. Ed Richter. Chilton Books. 1963. Clothbound. Tempo Books. 1967, reissue. Paperbound.

               The transition from college to pro football. Plays, passing, strategy, defenses. Photos.

9P-27   How to Become a Quarterback. Bart Starr. 1963. Booklet.

               Illustrated playing instructions by a star quarterback.

9P-28   Quarterbacking. Bart Starr and Mark Cox. Prentice-Hall. 1967. Clothbound.

               By a star quarterback. Historical sketch of the Green Bay Packers, biographical sketch of Starr. Drills, qualifications of the quarterback, mechanics. Art of passing, formations, patterns, rules of passing. Pass protection, pass defense, kicking. Game plan, plays, descriptions of the 1966 championship games, examples drawn from game experiences. Photos.

9P-29   Winning Football. Bart Starr. Sport Specials. 1970. Paperbound.

               Quarterbacking techniques and strategy by a star pro quarterback.

9P-30   Quarterbacking to Win. Y.A. Tittle and Howard Liss. Argonaut, Inc. 1964. Clothbound.

               By an all-time great quarterback. Passing, running, game preparation.

9P-31   Inside Quarterbacking. Len Dawson and Bob Billings. Henry Regnery Co. 1972. Clothbound and Paperbound.

               Techniques, formations, strategy, and conditioning by a star pro quarterback.

Line Play

9P-32 **Playing the Line.** Clyde (Bulldog) Turner. Ziff-Davis. 1948. Clothbound and Paperbound.

    Fundamentals and fine points. By a star lineman.

Kicking

9P-33 **Football Kicking Techniques.** Ken Strong and Emil Brodbeck. McGraw-Hill. 1950. Clothbound.

    Players' guide to punting, place kicking, and drop kicking. By a star kicker.

9P-34 **Kicking to Win.** Pat Summerall and John Chanin. Viking Press. 1968. Clothbound.

    A comprehensive analysis of punting and place-kicking by a former pro kicking star.

9P-35 **Kicking the Football Soccer Style.** Pete Gogolak and Ray Siegener. Atheneum. 1972. Clothbound.

    Techniques by a pro football kicker.

Defense

9P-36 **Defensive Football.** Sam Huff and Don Smith. Ronald Press. 1963. Clothbound.

    Instructions by a star pro linebacker. Tackling techniques, defenses against various formations, photos.

9P-37 **Inside Defensive Football.** Dick Butkus and Robert W. Billings. Henry Regnery Co. 1971. Clothbound and Paperbound.

    Illustrated instructions by a star pro linebacker. Fundamentals, techniques, philosophy.

Coaching

9P-38 **My Kind of Football.** Steve Owen and Joe King. David McKay Co. 1952. Clothbound.

    Offensive and defensive formations and plays. Autobiographical account of Owen's playing and coaching career, anecdotes.

Instructionals

9P-39   We Play to Win! Raymond (Buddy) Parker. Prentice-Hall. 1955. Clothbound.

             A discussion of the principles and theories of pro football as practiced by the Detroit Lions. Selecting the coaching staff, the quarterback, signals. Offense, defense, plays, kicking, scouting.

9P-40   Norman Van Brocklin's Football Book. Norman Van Brocklin and Hugh Brown. Ronald Press. 1961. Clothbound.

             Various aspects of passing, punting, and quarterbacking. Analysis of the opponent, glossary, personal recollections.

9P-41   Run to Daylight. Vince Lombardi and W.C. Heinz. Prentice-Hall. 1963. Clothbound. Grosset & Dunlap. 1967, reissue. Clothbound. Tempo Books. 1968, reissue. Paperbound.

             An account of seven days in Lombardi's life as he prepared the Green Bay Packers for the October 7, 1962, game against the Detroit Lions. Behind-the-scenes details of practice, strategy, and game preparations. A detailed account of the game from Lombardi's viewpoint.

9P-42   Allie Sherman's Book of Football. J.F. Dreyspool, ed. Doubleday & Co. 1963. Clothbound.

             The play of each position, formations, techniques. Running, passing, kicking, drills. Photos.

10. Anthologies

10-1   Famous Feats of Football. Stanley Woodward, ed. 1925. Paperbound.

Reprint of a newspaper series. Forty-seven accounts of thrilling plays that won games, as told by the winning coaches.

10-2   Football Digest. Herbert Simons, ed. Simons Publications. 1947-52. Paperbound.

A collection of the year's best feature stories on college and pro football. Scores, schedules, ratings.

10-3   Kickoff! Ed Fitzgerald, ed. Bantam Books. 1948. Paperbound.

An anthology of newspaper and magazine articles and book excerpts.

10-4   My Greatest Day in Football. Murray Goodman and Leonard Lewin, eds. A.S. Barnes & Co. 1948. Clothbound. Bantam Books. 1949, reissue. Paperbound. Grosset & Dunlap. 1971, reissue. Clothbound.

Thirty-seven accounts by all-time college and pro greats from Stagg to Waterfield. Game lineups.

10-5   Kickoff. Phyllis Fenner, ed. Alfred A. Knopf, Inc. 1960. Clothbound.

An anthology of non-fiction and fiction stories for boys.

10-6   The Fireside Book of Football. Jack Newcombe, ed. Simon & Schuster. 1964. Clothbound.

An anthology of newspaper and magazine articles on college and pro football. Great games, players and coaches. Photos, cartoons.

Anthologies

Professional Titles

10P-1   <u>Pro, Pro, Pro.</u> John Lowell Pratt, ed. Franklin Watts. 1963. Clothbound. J. Lowell Pratt. 1964, reissue. Paperbound.

             Stories by various authors. Great players and games.

10P-2   <u>My Sunday Best.</u> Jack Fleischer, ed. Grosset & Dunlap. 1971. Clothbound. Tempo Books. 1972, reissue. Paperbound.

             Descriptions by 14 pro coaches of the most exciting games they have coached. Coaching philosophies and tactics.

11. Periodicals

11-1 The Football World. J.D. Fetzer. Football World Publishing Co. September-December 1921. Magazine.

Monthly. Articles, schedules, photos. Succeeded in January 1922, by the The Athletic World, which contained extensive football coverage in 1922 and 1923.

11-2 What's What in Football. H.A. Marple. What's What Publishing Co. 1937-41. Paperbound.

Ten weekly issues during September, October, and November. Ratings, scores, statistics, schedules. Some pro coverage.

11-3 Football Form and Digest. Deke Houlgate. Seven-Up Bottling Co. 1938-45. Newspaper.

Weekly during the season. Articles, previews, scores, other data. College and pro coverage.

11-3A Football Digest. Bill Schroeder. Seven-Up Bottling Co. 1946-to date. Newspaper.

Continuation of 11-3.

11-4 The Football News. Detroit. September 14, 1939-to date. Newspaper.

Weekly during the season. Scores, photos, reviews, previews, feature articles, statistics. Emphasis on college football, some pro coverage.

11-5 Mobil Pigskin Prophet. L.B. Chapman and Sam Hayes. Mobil Oil Corp. 1940, 1941. Newspaper.

Forecasts, schedules, reviews. College and pro coverage.

11-5A Mobil Touchdown Tips. L.B. Chapman and Sam Hayes. Mobil Oil Corp. 1946-48. Newspaper.

Continuation of 11-5.

Periodicals

11-6   Football Figures Weekly. Dan Zimmerman. September 29, 1941-December 1941. Newspaper.

Statistical review, facts, photos. Some pro coverage.

11-7   Gridiron Weekly. Athletic Publications. 1944-46. Newspaper.

Eleven issues during the season. Statistics, predictions.

11-8   Football Alibis and Postmortems. Athletic Publications. 1944-46. Booklet.

Weekly during the season. Analyses, predictions, statistics.

11-8A   Weekly Gridiron Record. Athletic Publications. 1947-62. Booklet.

Continuation of 11-8. Issued twice-weekly during the season.

11-9   Football Form. Leonard Yormark. October 14, 1945-December 1, 1945. Magazine.

Weekly during the season. Articles, photos. High school, college, and pro coverage.

11-10   Fluor Football Forecaster. Deke Houlgate. Fluor Corp. September 21, 1946-January 1, 1949. Newspaper.

Illustrated review issued weekly during the season. Statistics, records.

11-11   The Quarterback. The Sporting News. October 5, 1946-January 12, 1947. Newspaper.

Twelve weekly issues during the season. Scores, articles, photos.

11-12   The Football Review. Northern Collegiate Sports. 1950. Newspaper.

Weekly from September through December.

11-13   Football Newsletter. National Sports Bureau. 1954-56. Booklet.

Twelve issues per year, September through January. Team previews and reviews, ratings, predictions. College and pro coverage.

11-14   Nation-Wide Football. 1961-to date. Paperbound.

Twelve weekly issues during the season. College and pro scores, statistics, schedules, predictions.

11-15   The 5th Down. Bert McGrane. Football Writers Association of

Periodicals

America. 1964-to date. Paperbound.

Six monthly issues, August through January. News items, articles.

11-16 Weekly Football Guide. 1967. Paperbound.

Twelve weekly issues during the season. Team ratings, statistics, schedules, scores, predictions.

11-17 Sportscasters Bulletin. Sportscasters, Inc. 1967. Paperbound.

Eleven weekly issues during the season. Schedules, statistics, features, predictions.

11-18 Chris Schenkel's Sportscene: Football. American Equity Press. 1970-to date. Magazine.

Monthly, September-February. College and pro coverage. Articles, statistics.

11-19 Gridiron. Bert Sugar, ed. Champion Sports Publishing Co. September 1971-to date. Newspaper.

Weekly from September-January, monthly during off-season. College and pro coverage.

Professional Titles

11P-1 The Football Graphic. National Football League. 1954. Newspaper.

Nine weekly issues published. Articles, photos, game summaries, statistics.

11P-2 Pro News. Vic Wilmot, ed. Pro News Publishing Co. 1957-58. Paperbound.

Weekly during the season.

11P-3 Pro Pigskin. 1961. Paperbound.

Weekly during the season.

11P-4 Pro Football Illustrated. Ted Elbert, ed. August 1961-November 2, 1963; December 7, 1963-October 10, 1964. Newspaper.

Weekly during the season, monthly during the off-season. Articles, team reviews, rosters. Individual and team statistics and records for each game and for the season.

11P-5 Pro Football Newsletter. 1965. Paperbound.

Twenty-six issues. Articles on each team.

Periodicals

11P-6   **Pro Football Weekly.** Pro Football Weekly, Inc. August 1967-to date. Newspaper.

         Weekly August-February, monthly during off-season. Articles on teams and players. Game summaries, statistics.

11P-7   **Pro Football Digest.** David J. Chapin, ed. Digest Publishing Corp. December 1967-January-February 1969. Paperbound.

         Six issues yearly. Reprints of newspaper and magazine articles, plus original features.

11P-8   **Quarterback.** Quarterback Publishing Co. October 1969-October 1970. Magazine.

         Ten monthly issues. Articles, features, team previews.

11P-8A   **Pro Quarterback.** SCH Publications. November 1970-to date. Magazine.

         Continuation of 11P-8.

11P-9   **Pro Football Exclusive.** Fritz Van. Fritz Van Enterprises. 1969. Newspaper.

         Monthly. Team reviews, statistics, photos.

11P-10   **The Huddle.** Tom Gorman, ed. Baltimore Football, Inc. 1969, 1970. Magazine.

         Published nine times in 1969, 13 times in 1970. Official magazine of the Baltimore Colts. Interviews, articles.

11P-11   **Pro Football Guide.** Gridiron Publications, Inc. Goldwin Publications, Inc. 1969-to date. Newspaper.

         Weekly, September-January. Monthly, February-August. Articles on a variety of topics.

11P-12   **Football Digest.** John Kuenster, ed. Century Publishing Co. September 1971-to date. Paperbound.

         Issued ten times per year. Articles on pro football by various authors. Statistics, features.

Team Newspapers

Issued usually monthly, to fans. Dates are approximate.

11P-13   **Packer Football News.** Green Bay Packers. 1938-47.

Periodicals

11P-13A	Packer Hi-Lites.	Green Bay Packers. 1948-to date.
11P-14	Bear News.	Chicago Bears. 1947-to date.
11P-15	Ram News.	Los Angeles Rams. 1948-to date.
11P-16	Giant Touchdown.	New York Giants. 1948-to date.
11P-17	Detroit Lion Fanfare.	Detroit Lions. 1949-to date.
11P-18	Eagles Nest.	Philadelphia Eagles. 1950-to date.
11P-19	Big Red.	Chicago Cardinals. 1952-59.
11P-20	Baltimore Colts Roundup.	Baltimore Colts. 1955-to date.
11P-21	Block and Tackle.	Cleveland Browns. 1956-to date.
11P-22	Saints Signals.	New Orleans Saints. 1966-to date.
11P-23	Falcon Facts.	Atlanta Falcons. 1966-to date.
11P-24	Pro File.	Dallas Cowboys. 1968-to date.
11P-25	Chicago Rockets Tales.	Chicago Rockets. 1947, 1948.
11P-25A	Chicago Hornets Highlights.	Chicago Hornets. 1949.
11P-26	Forward Passes from the Football Dodgers.	Brooklyn Dodgers. 1947.
11P-26A	Punts and Dodger Passes.	Brooklyn Dodgers. 1948.
11P-27	Don Sidelines.	Los Angeles Dons. 1948, 1949.
11P-28	Buffalo Bills Bulletin.	Buffalo Bills. 1960-to date.
11P-29	War Whoops.	Kansas City Chiefs. 1965-to date.
11P-30	San Diego Chargers.	San Diego Chargers. 1968-to date.
11P-31	Broncos Corral.	Denver Broncos. 1969-to date.
11P-32	Miami Dolphins.	Miami Dolphins. 1969-to date.
11P-33	Jet Stream.	New York Jets. 1970-to date.

12. Fiction

12-1   MARK SEVERANCE

12-1A   <u>Hammersmith: His Harvard Days.</u> Houghton Mifflin Co. 1878. Clothbound.

               The first novel known to contain football coverage. One chapter describes a football match.

                           *   *   *

12-2   BURR MCINTOSH

12-2A   <u>Football and Love.</u> Popular Publishing Co. 1895, 1903, reissue. Paperbound.

               A novel centered around the 1894 Yale-Princeton game.

                           *   *   *

12-3   CHARLES R. TALBOT

12-3A   <u>The Imposter.</u> Lothrop Publishing Co. 1895. Clothbound.

               A football and college romance. With other stories for young people.

                           *   *   *

12-4   FRANCIS J. FINN, S.J.

12-4A   <u>That Football Game.</u> Benziger Brothers. 1897. Clothbound.

               A story of football at a Catholic prep school.

                           *   *   *

12-5   GILBERT PATTEN (*pseudonym Burt L. Standish)

12-5A   <u>*Frank Merriwell at Yale.</u> Street & Smith. 1897. Paperbound. David McKay Co. 1903, reissue. Clothbound.

Fiction

12-5B	*Frank Merriwell's Return to Yale. Street & Smith. 1897. Paperbound.	
12-5C	The Rockspur Eleven. Street & Smith. 1900. Paperbound. David McKay Co. 1901, reissue. Clothbound.	
12-5D	*Frank Merriwell as Coach. Street & Smith. 1901. Paperbound.	
12-5E	*Frank Merriwell's Champions. Street & Smith. 1904. Paperbound.	
12-5F	*Dick Merriwell's Way. Street & Smith. 1908. Paperbound.	
12-5G	*Dick Merriwell's Power. Street & Smith. 1909. Paperbound.	
12-5H	Boltwood of Yale. Barse & Hopkins. 1914. Clothbound.	
12-5I	On College Battlefields. Barse & Hopkins. 1917. Clothbound.	

* * *

12-6	RALPH HENRY BARBOUR	
12-6A	The Halfback. D. Appleton & Co. 1899. Clothbound. New York Book Co. 1904, reissue. Grosset & Dunlap. 1917, reissue.	
12-6B	For the Honor of the School. D. Appleton & Co. 1900. Clothbound.	
12-6C	Behind the Line. D. Appleton & Co. 1902. Clothbound.	
12-6D	The Crimson Sweater. D. Appleton & Co. 1906. Clothbound.	
12-6E	Forward Pass. D. Appleton & Co. 1908. Clothbound.	
12-6F	Kingsford, Quarter. Century Co. 1910. Clothbound.	
12-6G	Change Signals! D. Appleton & Co. 1912. Clothbound.	
12-6H	Around the End. D. Appleton & Co. 1913. Clothbound.	
12-6I	Left End Edwards. Dodd, Mead & Co. 1914. Clothbound.	
12-6J	Left Tackle Thayer. Dodd, Mead & Co. 1915. Clothbound. Grosset & Dunlap. 1916, reissue.	
12-6K	Danforth Plays the Game. D. Appleton & Co. 1915. Clothbound.	
12-6L	The Secret Play. D. Appleton & Co. 1915. Clothbound.	

Fiction

12-6M	Rivals for the Team.	D. Appleton & Co. 1916. Clothbound.
12-6N	Left Guard Gilbert.	Dodd, Mead & Co. 1916. Clothbound. Grosset & Dunlap. 1917, reissue.
12-6P	Hitting the Line.	D. Appleton & Co. 1917. Clothbound.
12-6Q	Center Rush Rowland.	Dodd, Mead & Co. 1917. Clothbound.
12-6R	Fullback Foster.	Dodd, Mead & Co. 1919. Clothbound. Grosset & Dunlap. 1920, reissue. Clothbound.
12-6S	The Play that Won.	D. Appleton & Co. 1919. Clothbound.
12-6T	Quarterback Bates.	Dodd, Mead & Co. 1920. Clothbound.
12-6U	Fourth Down.	D. Appleton & Co. 1920. Clothbound.
12-6V	Kick Formation.	D. Appleton & Co. 1921. Clothbound.
12-6W	Left Half Harmon.	Dodd, Mead & Co. 1921. Clothbound. Grosset & Dunlap. 1923, reissue. Clothbound.
12-6X	Right End Emerson.	Dodd, Mead & Co. 1922. Clothbound.
12-6Y	Right Guard Grant.	Dodd, Mead & Co. 1923. Clothbound.
12-6Z	For the Good of the Team.	D. Appleton & Co. 1923. Clothbound.
12-6AA	The Fighting Scrub.	D. Appleton & Co. 1924. Clothbound.
12-6BB	Follow the Ball.	D. Appleton & Co. 1924. Clothbound.
12-6CC	Right Tackle Todd.	Dodd, Mead & Co. 1924. Clothbound.
12-6DD	Right Half Rollins.	Dodd, Mead & Co. 1925. Clothbound. Grosset & Dunlap. 1927, reissue. Clothbound.
12-6EE	Barry Locke, Halfback.	Century Co. 1925. Clothbound.
12-6FF	Hold 'em Wyndham.	D. Appleton & Co. 1925. Clothbound.
12-6GG	The Last Play.	D. Appleton & Co. 1926. Clothbound.
12-6HH	The Long Pass.	D. Appleton & Co. 1927. Clothbound.
12-6II	Hunt Holds the Center.	D. Appleton & Co. 1928. Clothbound.
12-6JJ	Fortunes of the Team.	Houghton Mifflin Co. 1928. Clothbound.
12-6KK	Substitute Jimmy.	Century Co. 1928. Clothbound.

Fiction

12-6LL	Tod Hale on the Scrub.	Dodd, Mead & Co. 1928. Clothbound.
12-6MM	Candidate for the Line.	D. Appleton & Co. 1930. Clothbound.
12-6NN	The Fumbled Pass.	D. Appleton & Co. 1931. Clothbound.
12-6PP	Goal to Go.	D. Appleton-Century. 1933. Clothbound.
12-6QQ	The Scoring Play.	D. Appleton-Century. 1934. Clothbound.
12-6RR	Watch That Pass!	D. Appleton-Century. 1936. Clothbound.
12-6SS	The School That Didn't Care.	D. Appleton-Century. 1937. Clothbound.
12-6TT	Fighting Guard.	D. Appleton-Century. 1938. Clothbound.
12-6UU	The Last Quarter.	D. Appleton-Century. 1939. Clothbound.
12-6VV	Target Pass.	D. Appleton-Century. 1941. Clothbound.
12-6WW	Barclay Back.	D. Appleton-Century. 1942. Clothbound.

* * *

12-7   EUSTACE WILLIAMS

12-7A   The Substitute Quarterback. Diana Estes & Co. 1900. Clothbound.

* * *

12-8   LESLIE QUIRK

12-8A   Baby Elton, Quarterback. Century Co. 1902, 1904, reissue. Clothbound. Grosset & Dunlap. Reissue. Clothbound.

12-8B   Tackle, Quarterback and Other Stories. McLoughlin Brothers, Inc. 1912. Clothbound.

12-8C   The Fourth Down. Little, Brown & Co. 1912. Clothbound.

* * *

12-9   ALBERTUS TRUE DUDLEY

12-9A   Following the Ball. Lothrop, Lee & Shepard. 1903. Clothbound.

12-9B   In the Line. Lothrop, Lee & Shepard. 1905. Clothbound.

Fiction

12-9C	A Fullback Afloat.	Lothrop, Lee & Shepard. 1908. Clothbound.
12-9D	Unofficial Prefect.	Lothrop, Lee & Shepard. 1915. Clothbound.

* * *

12-10	MRS. CAROLYN S. CABOT
12-10A	Football Madness. Small, Maynard & Co. 1904. Paperbound.
12-10B	Football Grandma. Small, Maynard & Co. 1905. Paperbound.

* * *

12-11	ARTHUR PIER
12-11A	Boys of St. Timothy's. Charles Scribner's Sons. 1904. Clothbound.
12-11B	Harding of St. Timothy's. Houghton Mifflin Co. 1906. Clothbound.
12-11C	The New Boy. Houghton Mifflin Co. 1908. Clothbound.
12-11D	Friends and Rivals. Houghton Mifflin Co. 1925. Clothbound.
12-11E	The Coach. Penn Publishing Co. 1928. Clothbound.

* * *

12-12	WALTER L. SAWYER (*pseudonym Winn Standish)
12-12A	Captain Jack Lorimer. L.C. Page. 1906. Clothbound. A.L. Burt Co. Reissue. Clothbound.
12-12B	Jack Lorimer's Champions. L.C. Page. 1907. Clothbound. A.L. Burt Co. Reissue. Clothbound.
12-12C	Jack Lorimer's Holidays. L.C. Page. 1908. Clothbound.
12-12D	Jack Lorimer's Substitute. L.C. Page. 1909. Clothbound.
12-12E	Jack Lorimer, Freshman. L.C. Page. 1912. Clothbound. A.L. Burt Co. Reissue. Clothbound.

* * *

12-13	EDWARD STRATEMEYER (*pseudonym Lester Chadwick)
12-13A	Dave Porter's Return to School. Lothrop, Lee & Shepard. 1907. Clothbound.

Fiction

12-13B	The Football Boys of Lakeport.	Lothrop, Lee & Shepard. 1909. Clothbound.
12-13C	*A Quarterback's Pluck.	Cupples & Leon. 1910. Clothbound.
12-13D	*The Winning Touchdown.	Cupples & Leon. 1911. Clothbound.

* * *

12-14   T. TRUXTON HARE
 By a four-time All-American.

12-14A	Making the Freshman Team.	Penn Publishing Co. 1907. Clothbound. 1928, reissue. Clothbound.
12-14B	Sophomore Halfback.	Penn Publishing Co. 1908, 1936, reissue. Clothbound.
12-14C	A Junior in the Line.	Penn Publishing Co. 1909. Clothbound. 1925, reissue. Clothbound.
12-14D	Senior Quarterback.	Penn Publishing Co. 1910, 1938, reissue. Clothbound.
12-14E	A Graduate Coach.	Penn Publishing Co. 1911. Clothbound.
12-14F	Phillip Kent.	Penn Publishing Co. 1914. Clothbound.
12-14G	Phillip Kent in the Lower School.	Penn Publishing Co. 1916. Clothbound.
12-14H	Phillip Kent in the Upper School.	Penn Publishing Co. 1918. Clothbound.
12-14I	Kent of Malvern.	Penn Publishing Co. 1919. Clothbound.

* * *

12-15   BETH BRADFORD GILCHRIST (pseudonym John P. Earl)

12-15A	On the School Team.	Penn Publishing Co. 1908. Clothbound.
12-15B	Captain of the School Team.	Penn Publishing Co. 1938. Clothbound.

* * *

12-16   WALTER CAMP

12-16A	The Substitute.	D. Appleton & Co. 1908, 1909, reissue, 1910,

Fiction

reissue. Clothbound.

> Includes instructions on developing a team for the season's play, coaching, tactics, and details of individual play.

12-16B   Jack Hall at Yale. D. Appleton & Co. 1909, 1910, reissue. Clothbound.

12-16C   Danny the Freshman. D. Appleton & Co. 1921. Clothbound.

* * *

12-17   GEORGE FITCH

12-17A   The Big Strike at Siwash. Doubleday, Page. 1909. Clothbound.

> A humorous novel about a country bumpkin who becomes a college football player.

12-17B   At Good Old Siwash. Little, Brown & Co. 1910, 1911, reissue. Clothbound.

> Republication of 12-17A.

* * *

12-18   EVERETT TOMLINSON

12-18A   Captain Dan Richards. Griffith & Rowland Press. 1909. Clothbound.

12-18B   Carl Hall of Tait. Griffith & Rowland Press. 1912. Clothbound.

* * *

12-19   SAMUEL R. FULLER (pseudonym Norman Brainerd)

12-19A   Winning the Eagle Prize. Lothrop, Lee & Shepard. 1910. Clothbound.

* * *

12-20   HARRIE I. HANCOCK

12-20A   The High School Freshman. Henry Altemus Co. 1910. Clothbound.

12-20B   The High School Left End. Henry Altemus Co. 1910. Clothbound.

12-20C   The High School Captain of the Team. Henry Altemus Co. 1910. Clothbound.

Fiction

12-21   RALPH D. PAINE

12-21A   The Head Coach. Charles Scribner's Sons. 1910. Clothbound.

12-21B   First Down, Kentucky! Street & Smith. 1921. Clothbound. Grosset & Dunlap. 1923, reissue. Clothbound. Fictionalized story of "Bo" McMillin and the famous Centre College team of 1918-21.

                 *   *   *

12-22   ALDEN A. KNIPE

12-22A   Captain of the Eleven. Harper & Brothers. 1910. Clothbound.

12-22B   Bunny Plays the Game. Harper & Brothers. 1925. Clothbound.

                 *   *   *

12-23   MORGAN SCOTT

12-23A   Ben Stone at Oakdale. Hurst & Co. 1911. Clothbound.

                 *   *   *

12-24   RAYMOND STONE

12-24A   Tommy Tiptop and His Football Eleven. Graham & Matlack. 1912. Clothbound. Charles E. Graham & Co. Reissue. Clothbound.

                 *   *   *

12-25   JAMES M. HOPPER

12-25A   The Freshman. Moffat, Yard & Co. 1912. Clothbound.

                 *   *   *

12-26   HOWARD GARIS

12-26A   Dick Hamilton's Football Team. Grosset & Dunlap. 1912. Clothbound.

                 *   *   *

12-27   MATTHEW COLTON

12-27A   Frank Armstrong, Drop Kicker. Hurst & Co. 1912. Clothbound.

12-27B   Frank Armstrong at College. Hurst & Co. 1914. Clothbound.

Fiction

12-28	WILLIAM HEYLIGER (*pseudonym Hawley Williams)
12-28A	Bucking the Line. D. Appleton & Co. 1912. Clothbound.
12-28B	*Quarterback Reckless. D. Appleton & Co. 1912. Clothbound.
12-28C	*Five Yards to Go. D. Appleton & Co. 1913. Clothbound.
12-28D	Off Side. D. Appleton & Co. 1914. Clothbound.
12-28E	*Fair Play! D. Appleton & Co. 1915. Clothbound.
12-28F	*Straight Ahead! D. Appleton & Co. 1917. Clothbound.
12-28G	The Fighting Captain, and Other Stories. D. Appleton & Co. 1926. Clothbound.
12-28H	Quarterback Hothead. Grosset & Dunlap. 1931. Clothbound.
12-28I	Backfield Comet. D. Appleton-Century. 1934. Clothbound.
12-28J	Fighting Blood. Goldsmith Publishing Co. 1936. Clothbound.
12-28K	Stan Kent, Freshman Fullback. Goldsmith Publishing Co. 1936. Clothbound.
12-28L	Stan Kent, Varsity Man. Goldsmith Publishing Co. 1936. Clothbound.
12-28M	Backfield Play. D. Appleton-Century. 1938. Clothbound.
12-28N	Gridiron Glory. D. Appleton-Century. 1940. Clothbound.
12-28P	Top Lineman. D. Appleton-Century. 1943. Clothbound.

* * *

12-29	ALLEN CHAPMAN
12-29A	Fred Fenton in the Line. 1913. Clothbound.
12-29B	Tom Fairfield in Camp. Cupples & Leon. 1913. Clothbound.
12-29C	Tom Fairfield's Pluck and Luck. Cupples & Leon. 1913. Clothbound.

* * *

12-30	J.W. DUFFIELD
12-30A	Bert Wilson on the Gridiron. Sully & Kleinteich. 1914. Paperbound.

Fiction

12-31   ROY STOKES

12-31A   Andy at Yale. Sully & Kleinteich. 1914. Clothbound.

*   *   *

12-32   GEORGE BARTON

12-32A   The Bell Haven Eleven. John C. Winston Co. 1915. Clothbound.

*   *   *

12-33   GORDON BRADDOCK

12-33A   Rex Kingdon at Walcott Hall. Hurst & Co. 1915. Clothbound.

*   *   *

12-34   LAWRENCE PERRY

12-34A   The Fullback. Charles Scribner's Sons. 1916. Clothbound.

12-34B   Touchdowns. Charles Scribner's Sons. 1924. Clothbound.

*   *   *

12-35   SPENCER DAVENPORT

12-35A   The Rushton Boys at Rally Hall. Whitman Publishing Co. 1916. Clothbound.

*   *   *

12-36   BROOKS HENDERLEY

12-36A   Y.M.C.A. Boys at Football. Cupples & Leon. 1917. Clothbound.

*   *   *

12-37   MARK OVERTON

12-37A   Jack Winters' Gridiron Chums. New York Book Co. 1919. Clothbound.

*   *   *

12-38   HENRY G. HUNTING

12-38A   Touchdown and After. Macmillan Co. 1920. Clothbound.

Fiction

12-39   EARL REED SILVERS

12-39A   <u>Dick Arnold of Raritan College.</u> 1920. D. Appleton & Co. Clothbound.

12-39B   <u>Ned Beals, Freshman.</u> 1922. D. Appleton & Co. Clothbound.

12-39C   <u>Ned Beals Works His Way.</u> 1923. D. Appleton & Co. Clothbound.

12-39D   <u>Jackson of Hillsdale High.</u> 1923. D. Appleton & Co. Clothbound.

12-39E   <u>The Spirit of Menlo.</u> 1926. D. Appleton & Co. Clothbound.

12-39F   <u>Barry Goes to College.</u> 1928. D. Appleton & Co. Clothbound.

12-39G   <u>The Red-Headed Halfback.</u> 1929. D. Appleton & Co. Clothbound.

12-39H   <u>The Scarlet of Avalon.</u> 1930. D. Appleton & Co. Clothbound.

*   *   *

12-40   DAVID STONE

12-40A   <u>Yank Brown, Halfback.</u> Barse & Hopkins. 1921. Clothbound.

*   *   *

12-41   GEORGE PIERROT

12-41A   <u>Yea, Sheriton.</u> Doubleday, Page. 1925. Clothbound.

*   *   *

12-42   A. MAY HOLADAY

12-42A   <u>On the Sidelines.</u> Century Co. 1925.

*   *   *

12-43   KNUTE ROCKNE

12-43A   <u>The Four Winners.</u> Devin-Adair. 1925, 1946, reissue. Clothbound.

       By a famous coach.

*   *   *

Fiction

12-44   CHARLES E. PARKER

12-44A   The Whipper - Snapper. Frederick A. Stokes Co. 1926. Clothbound.

*   *   *

12-45   FITZHUGH GREEN

12-45A   Hold 'em Navy! D. Appleton & Co. 1926. Clothbound. Foreword by Richard Evelyn Byrd.

*   *   *

12-46   GRAHAM FORBES

12-46A   Frank Allen, Captain of the Team. Garden City Publishing Co. 1926. Clothbound.

*   *   *

12-47   JOHN R. UNIACK

12-47A   Making the Eleven at St. Michael's. Benziger Brothers. 1926. Clothbound.

*   *   *

12-48   ELMER DAWSON

12-48A   Gary Grayson's Hill St. Eleven. 1926. Grosset & Dunlap. Clothbound.

12-48B   Gary Grayson Football Rivals. 1926. Grosset & Dunlap. Clothbound.

12-48C   Gary Grayson at Lennox High. 1926. Grosset & Dunlap. Clothbound.

12-48D   Gary Grayson at Stanley Prep. 1927. Grosset & Dunlap. Clothbound.

12-48E   Gary Grayson Showing His Speed. 1927. Grosset & Dunlap. Clothbound.

12-48F   Gary Grayson's Winning Kick. 1928. Grosset & Dunlap. Clothbound.

12-48G   Gary Grayson Hitting the Line. 1929. Grosset & Dunlap. Clothbound.

Fiction

12-48H	Gary Grayson's Winning Touchdown. 1930. Grosset & Dunlap. Clothbound.	
12-48I	Gary Grayson's Double Signals. 1931. Grosset & Dunlap. Clothbound.	
12-48J	Gary Grayson's Forward Pass. 1932. Grosset & Dunlap. Clothbound.	

* * *

12-49	HAROLD M. SHERMAN
12-49A	One Minute to Play. Grosset & Dunlap. 1926. Clothbound. Novelization of a silent movie starring Red Grange.
12-49B	Fight 'em, Big Three. D. Appleton & Co. 1926. Grosset & Dunlap. 1929, reissue. Clothbound.
12-49C	Touchdown. Grosset & Dunlap. 1927. Clothbound.
12-49D	Block That Kick! Grosset & Dunlap. 1928. Clothbound.
12-49E	Over the Line. Goldsmith Publishing Co. 1929. Clothbound.
12-49F	Hold That Line! Grosset & Dunlap. 1930. Clothbound.
12-49G	Number 44, and Other Football Stories. Grosset & Dunlap. 1930. Clothbound.
12-49H	It's a Pass! Goldsmith Publishing Co. 1931. Clothbound.
12-49I	Goal to Go! Grosset & Dunlap. 1931. Clothbound.
12-49J	Interference, and Other Football Stories. Goldsmith Publishing Co. 1932. Clothbound. Books for Libraries Press. 1971, reissue.
12-49K	Crashing Through! Grosset & Dunlap. 1932. Clothbound.
12-49L	Captain of the Eleven. Goldsmith Publishing Co. 1933. Clothbound.

* * *

12-50	JOHN C. MELLETT (pseudonym Jonathan Brooks)
12-50A	Jimmy Makes the Varsity. Bobbs, Merrill. 1928. Grosset & Dunlap. Reissue. Clothbound.
12-50B	Pigskin Soldier. Doubleday, Doran & Co. 1931. Clothbound.

Fiction

12-50C	Varsity Jim. Bobbs, Merrill. 1939. Clothbound.

                        *   *   *

12-51	CHARLES FERGUSON
12-51A	Pigskin. Doubleday, Doran. 1929. Clothbound. A satirical romance concerning a college president.

                        *   *   *

12-52	JAMES M. NEVILLE
12-52A	Mud and Glory. J.W. Duffield & Co. 1929. Clothbound. A story of football at Princeton.

                        *   *   *

12-53	FRANCIS WALLACE
12-53A	Huddle! Farrar & Rinehart. 1930. Clothbound.
12-53B	O'Reilly of Notre Dame. Farrar & Rinehart. 1931. Clothbound.
12-53C	Stadium. Farrar & Rinehart. 1931. Clothbound.
12-53D	That's My Boy. Farrar & Rinehart. 1932. Clothbound.
12-53E	Big Game. Little, Brown & Co. 1936. Clothbound.
12-53F	Autumn Madness. Macrae-Smith. 1937. Clothbound.
12-53G	Razzle Dazzle. M.S. Mill Co. 1938. Clothbound.
12-53H	Front Man. Rinehart & Co. 1952. Clothbound. A novel of football and gambling.

                        *   *   *

12-54	COURTNEY FITZSIMMONS
12-54A	70,000 Witnesses. Robert M. McBride & Co. 1931. Clothbound. Grosset & Dunlap. 1931, reissue. Clothbound. A murder mystery.

                        *   *   *

12-55	JOHN S. STRANGE
12-55A	Murder on the Ten-Yard Line. Doubleday, Doran. 1931. Cloth-

Fiction

bound.

Crime Club series.

* * *

12-56   ALAN DRADY

12-56A   Red Morton, Waterboy. D. Appleton & Co. 1932. Clothbound.

* * *

12-57   REED FULTON

12-57A   Lardy the Great. Doubleday, Doran. 1932. Clothbound.

12-57B   Rookie Coach. Doubleday & Co. 1955. Clothbound.

* * *

12-58   JOEL SAYRE

12-58A   Rackety Rax. Alfred A. Knopf, Inc. 1932. Clothbound.
         The humorous story of a university founded by mobsters in order to field a football team composed of boxers and wrestlers.

* * *

12-59   WILLIAM LAMERS

12-59A   Joe McGuire, Freshman. Bruce Publishing Co. 1932. Clothbound.

* * *

12-60   THOMAS BALDWIN

12-60A   Kickoff! Goldsmith Publishing Co. 1932. Clothbound.

* * *

12-61   JACK WRIGHT

12-61A   On the Forty Yard Line. World Syndicate Publishing Co. 1932. Clothbound.

* * *

12-62   DICK HYLAND

12-62A   The Diary of a Line Smasher. A.C. McClurg & Co. 1932.

Fiction

Clothbound.

Adventures of a college football player, by a former All-American at Stanford University.

* * *

12-63   EDDIE DOOLEY

12-63A   Under the Goal Posts. J. Lowell Pratt. 1933. Clothbound. Grosset & Dunlap. Reissue. Clothbound.

By a former star player.

* * *

12-64   HARRY SYLVESTER

12-64A   Big Football Man. Farrar & Rinehart. 1933. Clothbound.

* * *

12-65   DONAL HAINES

12-65A   Triple Threat. Rinehart & Co. 1933. Clothbound.

12-65B   Blaine of the Backfield. Farrar & Rinehart. 1937. Clothbound.

* * *

12-66   RALPH CANNON

12-66A   Grid Star. Reilly & Lee. 1933. Clothbound.

12-66B   Out of Bounds. Reilly & Lee. 1937. Clothbound.

* * *

12-67   NOEL SAINSBURY (*pseudonym Charles Lawton)

12-67A   Gridiron Grit. Cupples & Leon. 1934. Clothbound.

12-67B   *Ros Hackney, Halfback. Cupples & Leon. 1937. Clothbound.

12-67C   *The Winning Forward Pass. Cupples & Leon. 1940. Clothbound.

12-67D   Touchdown to Victory. Cupples & Leon. 1942. Clothbound.

* * *

12-68   DR. RALPH Y. HOPTON and ANNE BALLIOL

12-68A   Pink Pants. Vanguard Press. 1935. Paperbound.

Fiction

A humorous novel concerning a female playing football at Harvard.

* * *

12-69	WILLIAM MEINCKE
12-69A	Rose Bowl. Robert Speller. 1936. Clothbound.

* * *

12-70	KENNEDY LYONS
12-70A	West Pointers on the Gridiron. Saalfield Publishing Co. 1936. Paperbound.

* * *

12-71	GRAHAM DEAN
12-71A	Herb Kent, West Point Fullback. Goldsmith Publishing Co. 1936. Clothbound.
12-71B	Herb Kent, West Point Cadet. Goldsmith Publishing Co. 1936. Clothbound.

* * *

12-72	GEORGE BRUCE
12-72A	Navy Blue and Gold. William Caslon Co. 1936. Clothbound.

* * *

12-73	ROY SNELL
12-73A	Red Dynamite. Reilly & Lee. 1936. Clothbound.
	A teen-age mystery.

* * *

12-74	EARL SCHENK MIERS
12-74A	The Backfield Feud. D. Appleton-Century. 1936. Clothbound.
12-74B	Career Coach. Westminster Press. 1941. Clothbound.
12-74C	Touchdown Trouble. World Publishing Co. 1953. Clothbound.

* * *

Fiction

12-75   B.J. CHUTE

12-75A   Blocking Back. Macmillan Co. 1938. Clothbound. E.P. Dutton & Co. 1966, reissue. Clothbound.

               A story of prep school football.

                       *   *   *

12-76   ROBERT PLAYFAIR

12-76A   The Crimson Road. Houghton Mifflin Co. 1938. Clothbound.

                       *   *   *

12-77   BERNIE BIERMAN

12-77A   Brick Barton and His Winning Eleven. E.P. Dutton & Co. 1938. Clothbound.

               By an outstanding coach.

                       *   *   *

12-78   BROTHER ERNEST, C.S.C.

12-78A   Captain Johnny Ford. Burkert-Walton Co. 1938. Clothbound.

                       *   *   *

12-79   ARTHUR SAMPSON

12-79A   The Two Quarterbacks. Houghton Mifflin Co. 1939. Clothbound.

12-79B   Football Coach. Houghton Mifflin Co. 1946. Clothbound.

               A fictionalized account of a season from the coach's viewpoint.

                       *   *   *

12-80   JOHN R. TUNIS

12-80A   Iron Duke. Harcourt, Brace. 1939. Clothbound.

12-80B   All-American. Harcourt, Brace. 1942. Clothbound.

12-80C   Go, Team, Go. William Morrow & Co. 1954. Clothbound.

12-80D   Buddy and His Old Pro. William Morrow & Co. 1955. Clothbound.

                       *   *   *

Fiction

12-81		RUSSELL G. EMERY
12-81A		Wings Over West Point. Macrae-Smith. 1940. Clothbound.
12-81B		T. Quarterback. Macrae-Smith. 1949. Clothbound.
12-81C		Gray Line and Gold. Macrae-Smith. 1951. Clothbound.

* * *

12-82		MARION RENICK (*Written with James L. Renick)
12-82A		*Tommy Carries the Ball. Charles Scribner's Sons. 1941. Clothbound.
12-82B		*David Cheers the Team. Charles Scribner's Sons. 1941. Clothbound.
12-82C		A Touchdown for Doc. Charles Scribner's Sons. 1948. Clothbound.
12-82D		Nicky's Football Team. Charles Scribner's Sons. 1951. Clothbound.
12-82E		Young Mr. Football. Charles Scribner's Sons. 1957. Clothbound.
12-82F		The Tail of the Terrible Tiger. Charles Scribner's Sons. 1959. Clothbound. Beginning readers' book.
12-82G		Football Boys. Charles Scribner's Sons. 1967. Clothbound.

* * *

12-83		JACKSON V. SCHOLZ
12-83A		Fighting Coach. William Morrow & Co. 1940. Clothbound. Pocket Books. 1949, reissue. Paperbound.
12-83B		Pigskin Warriors. William Morrow & Co. 1944. Clothbound.
12-83C		Goal to Go. William Morrow & Co. 1945. Clothbound.
12-83D		Gridiron Challenge. William Morrow & Co. 1947. Clothbound. Pocket Books. 1950, reissue. Paperbound.
12-83E		Johnny King, Quarterback. William Morrow & Co. 1949. Clothbound.
12-83F		Fullback for Sale. William Morrow & Co. 1951. Clothbound.

Fiction

	Pyramid Books. 1965, reissue. Paperbound.
12-83G	One-Man Team. William Morrow & Co. 1953. Clothbound.
12-83H	The End Zone. William Morrow & Co. 1954. Clothbound.
12-83I	Fighting Chance. William Morrow & Co. 1956. Clothbound.
12-83J	The Football Rebels. William Morrow & Co. 1960. Clothbound.
12-83K	Halfback on His Own. William Morrow & Co. 1962. Clothbound.
12-83L	Rookie Quarterback. William Morrow & Co. 1965. Clothbound.
12-83M	Backfield Buckaroo. William Morrow & Co. 1967. Clothbound.
12-83N	Fullback Fever. William Morrow & Co. 1969. Clothbound.
12-83P	Backfield Blues. William Morrow & Co. 1971. Clothbound.

* * *

12-84	CLINTON R. (BRICK) MORSE
12-84A	Jo Dunn, All-American. Christopher Publishing House. 1941. Clothbound.
	By a former star player.

* * *

12-85	CURTIS K. BISHOP
12-85A	Teamwork. Steck Co. 1942. Clothbound.
12-85B	Saturday Heroes. Steck Co. 1951. Clothbound.
12-85C	Football Fever. Steck Co. 1952. Clothbound.
12-85D	Hero at Halfback. Steck Co. 1953. Clothbound.
12-85E	Fighting Quarterback. Steck Co. 1954. Clothbound.
12-85F	Goal to Go. Steck Co. 1955. Clothbound.
12-85G	Half-Time Hero. Steck Co. 1956. Clothbound.
12-85H	The Lost Eleven. Steck Co. 1960. Clothbound.

Fiction

12-85I	<u>Sideline Quarterback</u>. J.B. Lippincott Co. 1960. Clothbound.
12-85J	<u>Lonesome End</u>. J.B. Lippincott Co. 1963. Clothbound.
12-85K	<u>Field Goal</u>. J.B. Lippincott Co. 1964. Clothbound.
12-85L	<u>Sideline Pass</u>. J.B. Lippincott Co. 1965. Clothbound.
12-85M	<u>Gridiron Glory</u>. J.B. Lippincott Co. 1966. Clothbound.
12-85N	<u>Hackberry Jones, Split End</u>. J.B. Lippincott Co. 1968. Clothbound.

* * *

12-86	DAVID JACKSON
12-86A	<u>Gridiron Gambler</u>. Dorrance & Co. 1943. Clothbound.

* * *

12-87	ADELAINE POWELL
12-87A	<u>Touchdown</u>. E.P. Dutton & Co. 1943. Clothbound.

* * *

12-88	CASPER BLACKBURN
12-88A	<u>Annapolis, Ahoy</u>. Macrae-Smith. 1945. Clothbound.

* * *

12-89	JAY DENDER
12-89A	<u>Tom Harmon and the Great Gridiron Plot</u>. Whitman Publishing Co. 1946. Clothbound.

* * *

12-90	HENRY FELSEN
12-90A	<u>Bertie Comes Through</u>. E.P. Dutton & Co. 1947. Clothbound. For boys.

* * *

12-91	JOE ARCHIBALD
12-91A	<u>Rebel Halfback</u>. Westminster Press. 1947. Clothbound.

Fiction

12-91B	Touchdown Glory. Westminster Press. 1949. Clothbound.
12-91C	Hold That Line! Macrae-Smith. 1950. Clothbound.
12-91D	Inside Tackle. Macrae-Smith. 1951. Clothbound.
12-91E	Block That Kick. Macrae-Smith. 1953. Clothbound.
12-91F	Fighting Coach. Macrae-Smith. 1954. Clothbound.
12-91G	Fullback Fury. Macrae-Smith. 1955. Clothbound.
12-91H	Go, Navy, Go. Macrae-Smith. 1956. Clothbound.
12-91I	Fight, Team, Fight. Macrae-Smith. 1958. Clothbound.
12-91J	Falcons to the Fight. Macrae-Smith. 1959. Clothbound. A story of football at the Air Force Academy.
12-91K	Backfield Twins. Macrae-Smith. 1960. Clothbound.
12-91L	Crazy Legs McBain. Macrae-Smith. 1961. Clothbound.
12-91M	Red-Dog Center. Macrae-Smith. 1962. Clothbound.
12-91N	Hard Nosed Halfback. Macrae-Smith. 1963. Clothbound.
12-91P	Quarterback and Son. Macrae-Smith. 1964. Clothbound.
12-91Q	West Point Wingback. Macrae-Smith. 1965. Clothbound.
12-91R	The Long Pass. Macrae-Smith. 1966. Clothbound.
12-91S	The Scrambler. Macrae-Smith. 1967. Clothbound.
12-91T	Power Back. Macrae-Smith. 1970. Clothbound.
12-91U	Phantom Blitz. Macrae-Smith. 1972. Clothbound.

* * *

12-92	PHILIP HARKINS
12-92A	Touchdown Twins. William Morrow & Co. 1947. Clothbound. Pocket Books. 1950, reissue. Paperbound.
12-92B	Punt Formation. William Morrow & Co. 1949. Clothbound.
12-92C	Son of the Coach. Holiday House. 1950. Clothbound.
12-92D	Breakaway Back. William Morrow & Co. 1959. Clothbound.

Fiction

12-92E	Fight Like a Falcon. William Morrow & Co. 1916. Clothbound.

* * *

12-93	C. PAUL JACKSON (*pseudonym Jack Paulson, **written with O.B. Jackson, ***written as Caary Jackson)
12-93A	All-Conference Tackle. Thomas Y. Crowell Co. 1947. Clothbound.
12-93B	Rose Bowl All-American. Thomas Y. Crowell Co. 1949. Clothbound.
12-93C	*Fourth Down Pass. J.C. Winston. 1950. Clothbound.
12-93D	Rose Bowl Linebacker. Thomas Y. Crowell Co. 1951. Clothbound.
12-93E	Shorty Carries the Ball. Wilcox & Follett. 1952. Clothbound.
12-93F	Dub, Halfback. Thomas Y. Crowell Co. 1952. Clothbound.
12-93G	Spice's Football. Thomas Y. Crowell Co. 1955. Clothbound.
12-93H	**Star Kicker. Whittlesey House. 1955. Clothbound.
12-93I	Buzzy Plays Midget League Football. Follett Publishing Co. 1956. Clothbound.
12-93J	Bud Plays Junior High Football. Hastings House. 1957. Clothbound.
12-93K	*Sideline Victory. Westminster Press. 1957. Clothbound.
12-93L	Bud Baker, T Quarterback. Hastings House. 1960. Clothbound.
12-93M	Chris Plays Small Fry Football. Hastings House. 1963. Clothbound.
12-93N	Fullback in the Large Fry League. Hastings House. 1965. Clothbound.
12-93P	No-Talent Letterman. McGraw-Hill. 1966. Clothbound.
12-93Q	Tim, the Football Nut. Hastings House. 1967. Clothbound.
12-93R	Hall of Fame Flankerback. Hastings House. 1968. Clothbound.
12-93S	***Haunted Halfback. Follett Publishing Co. 1969. Clothbound.

Fiction

12-93T	Rose Bowl Pro.	Hastings House. 1970. Clothbound.
12-93U	Pass Receiver.	Hastings House. 1970. Clothbound.
12-93V	Halfback!	Hastings House. 1971. Clothbound.
12-93W	Tom Mosely, Midget Leaguer.	Hastings House. 1971. Clothbound.
12-93X	Eric and Dud's Football Bargain.	Hastings House. 1972. Clothbound.

* * *

12-94   JULILLY KOHLER

12-94A   Football Trees. Children's Press. 1947. Story - Book Science Series. Clothbound.

* * *

12-95   HOWARD BRIER

12-95A   Phantom Backfield. Random House. 1948. Clothbound. Grosset & Dunlap. 1953, reissue. Clothbound.

* * *

12-96   CLAIR BEE

12-96A   Touchdown Pass. Grosset & Dunlap. 1948. Clothbound.

12-96B   A Pass and A Prayer. Grosset & Dunlap. 1951. Clothbound.

12-96C   Freshman Quarterback. Grosset & Dunlap. 1952. Clothbound.

12-96D   Ten Seconds to Play! Grosset & Dunlap. 1955. Clothbound.

12-96E   Fourth Down Showdown. Grosset & Dunlap. 1956. Clothbound.

12-96F   Triple Threat Trouble. Grosset & Dunlap. 1960. Clothbound.

* * *

12-97   MILLARD LAMPBELL

12-97A   The Hero. Julian Messner, Inc. 1949. Clothbound.

Fiction

12-98	EVERETT ALTON
12-98A	Gridiron Courage. Wilcox & Follett Co. 1949. Clothbound.

* * *

12-99	RAY MORSE
12-99A	Cadets at Kings Point. Aladdin Books. 1949. Clothbound.

* * *

12-100	LELAND SILLIMAN
12-100A	The Purple Tide. J.C. Winston. 1949. Clothbound.

* * *

12-101	WALTER R. BROOKS
12-101A	Freddy Plays Football. Alfred A. Knofp, Inc. 1949. Clothbound.
	A story about a football-playing pig.

* * *

12-102	ROBERT S. BOWEN (pseudonym J.R. Richard)
12-102A	Fourth Down. Lothrop, Lee & Shepard. 1949. Clothbound.
12-102B	Blocking Back. Lothrop, Lee & Shepard. 1950. Clothbound.
12-102C	Touchdown Kid. Lothrop, Lee & Shepard. 1951. Clothbound.
12-102D	*Fighting Halfback. Lothrop, Lee & Shepard. 1952. Clothbound.
12-102E	*Quarterback, All-American. Lothrop, Lee & Shepard. 1953. Clothbound.
12-102F	The Million Dollar Fumble. Lothrop, Lee & Shepard. 1954. Clothbound.
12-102G	The Last White Line. Lothrop, Lee & Shepard. 1955. Clothbound.

* * *

12-103	WILFRED MCCORMICK (*Bronc Burnett Series, **Rocky McCune Series)
12-103A	*Flying Tackle. G.P. Putnam's Sons. 1949. Clothbound.

Fiction

	Grosset & Dunlap. 1960, reissue.
12-103B	*Rambling Halfback. G.P. Putnam's Sons. 1950. Clothbound. Grosset & Dunlap. 1956, reissue. 1961, reissue.
12-103C	*Quick Kick. G.P. Putnam's Sons. 1951. Clothbound. Grosset & Dunlap. 1959, reissue. 1961, reissue.
12-103D	First and Ten. G.P. Putnam's Sons. 1952. Clothbound. Grosset & Dunlap. 1963, reissue.
12-103E	**The Captive Coach. David McKay Co. 1956. Clothbound. Grosset & Dunlap. 1963, reissue.
12-103F	**The Bigger Game. David McKay Co. 1958. Clothbound.
12-103G	**Five Yards to Glory. David McKay Co. 1959. Clothbound.
12-103H	*Stranger in the Backfield. David McKay Co. 1960. Clothbound. Grosset & Dunlap. 1961, reissue.
12-103I	*Man in Motion. David McKay Co. 1961. Clothbound. Grosset & Dunlap. 1964, reissue.
12-103J	*Too Late to Quit. David McKay Co. 1962. Clothbound. Grosset & Dunlap. 1963, reissue.
12-103K	*Rough Stuff. David McKay Co. 1963. Clothbound. Grosset & Dunlap. 1964, reissue.
12-103L	*The Right End Option. David McKay Co. 1964. Clothbound.
12-103M	*Seven in Front. David McKay Co. 1965. Clothbound.
12-103N	Touchdown for the Enemy. G.P. Putnam's Sons. 1965. Clothbound.
12-103P	Football in the Rough. Prentice-Hall. 1969. Clothbound.

* * *

12-104	ROGER TREAT
12-104A	Dick of the Bruins. Grosset & Dunlap. 1950. Clothbound.

* * *

12-105	ROBERT L. TAYLOR
12-105A	Professor Fodorski. Doubleday & Co. 1950. Clothbound.

Fiction

A politico-sporting romance.

* * *

12-106	BURGESS LEONARD
12-106A	Victory Pass. J.B. Lippincott Co. 1950.
12-106B	One-Man Backfield. J.B. Lippincott Co. 1953. Clothbound.

* * *

12-107	JOHN F. GARTNER
12-107A	Rock Taylor, Football Coach. Dodd, Mead & Co. 1951. Clothbound.

* * *

12-108	FRANK O'ROURKE
12-108A	Football Gravy Train. A.S. Barnes & Co. 1951. Clothbound.

* * *

12-109	DICK FRIENDLICH
12-109A	Goal Line Stand. Westminster Press. 1951. Clothbound.
12-109B	Line Smasher. Westminster Press. 1952. Scholastic Book Services. 1958, 1961, reissue. Paperbound.
12-109C	Left End Scott. Westminster Press. 1955. Clothbound.
12-109D	Gridiron Crusader. Westminster Press. 1958. Clothbound.
12-109E	Backfield Ace. Westminster Press. 1961. Clothbound.
12-109F	Touchdown Maker. Doubleday & Co. 1966. Clothbound.
12-109G	Fullback from Nowhere. Westminster Press. 1967. Clothbound.

* * *

12-110	GUERNSEY VAN RIPER
12-110A	Knute Rockne, Young Athlete. Bobbs, Merrill, 1952, 1959, reissue. Clothbound.

A fictionalized account of Rockne's boyhood.

Fiction

12-110B	Jim Thorpe, Indian Athlete. Bobbs, Merrill. 1956, 1961, re-issue. Clothbound.

        A fictionalized account of Thorpe's boyhood.

* * *

12-111	WILLIAM HEUMAN
12-111A	Junior Quarterback. William Morrow & Co. 1952. Clothbound and Paperbound.
12-111B	Rocky Malone. Steck Co. 1957. Clothbound.
12-111C	Left End Luisetti. Steck Co. 1958. Clothbound.
12-111D	Second String Hero. Steck Co. 1959. Clothbound.
12-111E	Horace Higby and the Field Goal Formula. Dodd, Mead & Co. 1965. Clothbound.
12-111F	Scrambling Quarterback. Dodd, Mead, & Co. 1967. Clothbound.
12-111G	Backup Quarterback. Steck-Vaughn. 1968. Clothbound.
12-111H	Gridiron Stranger. J.B. Lippincott Co. 1970. Clothbound.
12-111I	Horace Higby and the Gentle Fullback. Dodd, Mead & Co. 1970. Clothbound.

* * *

12-112	ROBERT SMITH
12-112A	Football Twins. A.S. Barnes & Co. 1953. Clothbound.

* * *

12-113	WARD CORNELL
12-113A	Fullback Fuller. 1953. Paperbound.

* * *

12-114	CLYDE GROSSCUP
12-114A	The Winning Spirit. A.S. Barnes & Co. 1953. Clothbound.

        For boys. By the father of pro quarterback Lee Grosscup.

Fiction

12-115   WILLIAM C. GAULT

12-115A   Mr. Fullback. E.P. Dutton & Co. 1953. Clothbound.

12-115B   Mr. Quarterback. E.P. Dutton & Co. 1955. Clothbound.

12-115C   Bruce Benedict, Halfback. E.P. Dutton & Co. 1957. Clothbound.

12-115D   Through the Line. E.P. Dutton & Co. 1961. Clothbound.

12-115E   Little Big Foot. E.P. Dutton & Co. 1963. Clothbound.

12-115F   Backfield Challenge. E.P. Dutton & Co. 1967. Clothbound.
           Racial prejudice in a football setting.

12-115G   Quarterback Gamble. E.P. Dutton & Co. 1970. Clothbound.

* * *

12-116   WILLIAM MACKELLAR

12-116A   Kickoff. Whittlesey House. 1955. Clothbound.

* * *

12-117   RAY MILLHOLLAND

12-117A   Lucky Shoes. Doubleday & Co. 1956. Clothbound.

* * *

12-118   GILBERT DOUGLAS

12-118A   Hard to Tackle. Thomas Y. Crowell Co. 1956. Clothbound. Dell Publishing Co. 1967, reissue. Paperbound.

* * *

12-119   HOWARD NEMEROV

12-119A   The Homecoming Game. Simon & Schuster. 1957. Clothbound.
           The story of the pressures applied to a college professor in an attempt to persuade him to give a passing grade to a football star.

12-120   ROBERT SCRIBNER

12-120A   Eggheads in the Endzone. Exposition Press. 1957. Clothbound.

Fiction

A satire concerning football-playing college professors.

* * *

12-121 HELEN D. FRANCIS

12-121A Double Reverse. Doubleday & Co. 1958. Clothbound.

12-121B Football Flash. Hastings House. 1961. Clothbound.

12-121C Big Swat. Follett Publishing Co. 1963. Clothbound. Signet. 1965, reissue. Paperbound.

* * *

12-122 WILLIAM R. COX

12-122A Gridiron Duel. Dodd, Mead & Co. 1959. Clothbound.

12-122B Third and Eight to Go. Dodd, Mead & Co. 1964. Clothbound.

12-122C The Valley Eleven. Dodd, Mead & Co. 1967. Clothbound.

12-122D Goal Ahead! Dodd, Mead & Co. 1967. Clothbound.

12-122E Third and Goal. Dodd, Mead & Co. 1971. Clothbound.

* * *

12-123 MATTHEW F. CHRISTOPHER

12-123A Touchdown for Tommy. Little, Brown & Co. 1959. Clothbound.

12-123B Wing-T Fullback. Franklin Watts. 1960. Clothbound.

12-123C Crackerjack Halfback. Little, Brown & Co. 1962. Clothbound.

12-123D The Counterfeit Tackle. Little, Brown & Co. 1965. Clothbound.

12-123E The Team That Couldn't Lose. Little, Brown & Co. 1967. Clothbound.

12-123F Catch That Pass. Little, Brown & Co. 1969. Clothbound.

12-123G Tough to Tackle. Little, Brown & Co. 1971. Clothbound.

Fiction

12-124	CHARLES VERRAL
12-124A	The Winning Quarterback. Thomas Y. Crowell Co. 1960. Clothbound.

* * *

12-125	MANLY WELLMAN
12-125A	Third String Center. I. Washburn. 1960. Clothbound.

* * *

12-126	ROBERT LECKIE (pseudonym Mark Porter)
12-126A	Keeper Play. Simon & Schuster. 1960. Clothbound. Tempo Books. 1963, reissue. Paperbound.

* * *

12-127	BEMAN LORD
12-127A	Quarterback's Aim. Henry Z. Walck. 1960. Paperbound. For young readers.
12-127B	Mystery Guest at Left End. Henry Z. Walck. 1965. Paperbound. For young readers.

* * *

12-128	SIDNEY OFFIT
12-128A	Cadet Quarterback. St. Martin's Press. 1961. Clothbound.

* * *

12-129	TEX MAULE
12-129A	Footsteps. David McKay Co. 1963. Clothbound.

* * *

12-130	LAWRENCE KEATING
12-130A	Runner Up. Westminster Press. 1961. Clothbound.
12-130B	Wrong-Way Neelen. Westminster Press. 1963. Clothbound.
12-130C	The Comeback Year. Westminster Press. 1966. Clothbound.

Fiction

12-131	DAVE CAMERER
12-131A	Nine Saturdays Make a Year. Doubleday & Co. 1962. Clothbound.
A novel about a college coach.

* * *

12-132	STEVE GELMAN
12-132A	Football Fury. Doubleday & Co. 1962. Clothbound.

* * *

12-133	JAMES SUMMERS
12-133A	Tiger Terwilliger. Westminster Press. 1963. Clothbound.
A humorous story of a female high school football coach.

* * *

12-134	NELSON HUTTO
12-134A	Breakaway Back. William Morrow & Co. 1963. Clothbound.

* * *

12-135	MIKE FREDERIC
12-135A	Freshman Quarterback. Nova Books. 1964. Paperbound.
12-135B	Frank Merriwell, Quarterback. Award Books. 1965. Paperbound.

* * *

12-136	BILL KNOTT (pseudonym Bill J. Carol)
12-136A	Scatback. Steck-Vaughn. 1964. Clothbound.
12-136B	Long Pass. Steck-Vaughn. 1966. Clothbound.
12-136C	Inside the Ten. Steck-Vaughn. 1967. Clothbound.
12-136D	Touchdown Duo. Steck-Vaughn. 1968. Clothbound.
12-136E	Crazylegs Merrill. Steck-Vaughn. 1969. Clothbound.
12-136F	Stop That Pass. Steck-Vaughn. 1970. Clothbound.

Fiction

12-136G	Linebacker Blitz.	Steck-Vaughn. 1971. Clothbound.
12-136H	Fullback Fury.	Steck-Vaughn. 1972. Clothbound.

* * *

12-137   PAUL DIETZEL AND EVERETT HOUGHTON

12-137A   Go, Shorty, Go. Bobbs, Merrill. 1965. Clothbound.
          An undersized boy's fight to make the school team. By a college coach.

* * *

12-138   LES ETTER

12-138A   Morning Glory Quarterback. Bobbs, Merrill. 1965. Clothbound.

12-138B   Big Down Gamble. Hastings House. 1968. Clothbound.

* * *

12-139   EDWIN MCDOWELL

12-139A   Three Cheers and a Tiger. Macmillan Co. 1966. Clothbound.
          A wry novel of college football.

* * *

12-140   ISADOR S. YOUNG

12-140A   Quarterback Carson. Follett Publishing Co. 1967. Clothbound.

* * *

12-141   STEPHEN MEADER

12-141A   Lonesome End. Harcourt, Brace & World. 1968. Clothbound.

* * *

12-142   CLEM PHILBROOK

12-142A   Ollie's Team and the Football Computer. Hastings House. 1968. Clothbound.

12-142B   Ollie's Team and the Two-Hundred Pound Problem. Hastings House. 1972. Clothbound.

Fiction

12-143	RICHARD DRDEK
12-143A	<u>The Game.</u> Doubleday & Co. 1968. Clothbound.

* * *

12-144	CHET GRANT
12-144A	<u>Fumblestumble Sandy.</u> Dujarie Press. 1969. Clothbound.
	The humorous story of a college halfback.

* * *

12-145	JIM MCKONE
12-145A	<u>Lone Star Fullback.</u> Vanguard Press. 1970. Clothbound.

* * *

12-146	DON DE LILLO
12-146A	<u>End Zone.</u> Houghton Mifflin Co. 1972. Clothbound.
	A "black humor" novel about college football.

* * *

12-147	J.A. DELL
12-147A	<u>Dan Workman's Big Game.</u> No date. Clothbound.

* * *

12-148	NOEL SAINSBURY (*pseudonym Charles Lawton)
12-148A	<u>Stirring Football Stories.</u> Cupples & Leon. No date. Clothbound.
	Republication of three novels in one edition: <u>Gridiron Grit.</u> 1934. *<u>Ros Hackney, Halfback.</u> 1937. *<u>The Winning Forward Pass.</u> 1940.

* * *

12-149	FRANK OWEN, Ed.
12-149A	<u>Teen-Age Football Stories.</u> Lantern Press. 1948. Clothbound. Grosset & Dunlap. Reissue. Clothbound.

* * *

12-150	LEO MARGULIES, Ed.
12-150A	<u>All-American Football Stories.</u> Cupples & Leon. 1948, 1949,

Fiction

reissue. Clothbound.

A fiction anthology.

* * *

12-151   CHARLES COOMBS

12-151A Young Readers Football Stories. Lantern Press. 1950. Clothbound. Grosset & Dunlap. Reissue. Clothbound.

Short stories.

* * *

12-152   JOSH FURMAN, Ed.

12-152A Teen-Age Gridiron Stories. Lantern Press. 1950. Clothbound.

A fiction anthology.

* * *

12-153   EDITORS OF BOYS' LIFE

12-153A Boys' Life Book of Football Stories. Random House. 1963. Clothbound.

An anthology from Boys' Life Magazine.

PULP MAGAZINES

Novels, novelettes, short stories, factual articles.

12-154   Football Stories. Fiction House. 1937-53. Paperbound.

Two issues in the fall.

12-155   All-American Football Magazine. Fiction House. 1939-51. Paperbound.

Two issues in the fall.

12-156   Football Action. Fiction House. 1939-53. Paperbound.

Two issues in the fall.

12-157   Thrilling Football. Standard Magazines. c 1940-52. Paperbound.

Fall and winter issues.

12-158   Popular Football. Standard Magazines. 1941-51. Paperbound.

Fiction

                Fall issue, winter issue.

12-159   Exciting Football. Better Publications, Inc. c 1941-51. Paperbound.

Professional Titles

12P-1   DONAL HAINES

12P-1A   Pro Quarterback. Farrar & Rinehart. 1940. Clothbound.

                *   *   *

12P-2   FRANK WALDMAN

12P-2A   Giant Quarterback. Houghton Mifflin Co. 1950. Clothbound.

12P-2B   Glory Boy. Ariel Books. 1953. Clothbound.

                *   *   *

12P-3   WILLIAM GAULT

12P-3A   Day of the Ram. Random House. 1956. Clothbound.
                A murder mystery.

                *   *   *

12P-4   TEX MAULE

12P-4A   The Rookie. David McKay Co. 1961. Clothbound.

12P-4B   The Quarterback. David McKay Co. 1962. Clothbound.

12P-4C   Championship Quarterback. David McKay Co. 1963. Clothbound.

12P-4D   The Linebacker. David McKay Co. 1965. Clothbound.

12P-4E   The Running Back. David McKay Co. 1966. Clothbound.

12P-4F   The Cornerback. David McKay Co. 1967. Clothbound.

12P-4G   The Receiver. David McKay Co. 1969. Clothbound.

                *   *   *

12P-5   C. PAUL JACKSON

12P-5A   Pro Football Rookie. Hastings House. 1962. Clothbound.

Fiction

12P-6	DICK FRIENDLICH
12P-6A	All-Pro Quarterback. Westminster Press. 1963. Clothbound.

* * *

12P-7	Y.A. TITTLE and HOWARD LISS
12P-7A	Pro Quarterback. Argonaut, Inc. 1963. Clothbound. Scholastic Book Services. 1964, reissue. Paperbound.
	Insights by all-time great quarterback.

* * *

12P-8	WILFRED MCCORMICK
12P-8A	The Pro Toughback. Duell, Sloan & Pearce. 1964. Clothbound.

* * *

12P-9	HASKEL FRANKEL
12P-9A	Pro Football Rookie. Doubleday & Co. 1964. Clothbound.

* * *

12P-10	ROBERT WELLS
12P-10A	Five-Yard Fuller. G.P. Putnam's Sons. 1964. Clothbound.
	A humorous novel of pro football.
12P-10B	Five-Yard Fuller and the Unlikely Knights. G.P. Putnam's Sons. 1967. Clothbound.
	Sequel to 12P-10A.

* * *

12P-11	DOUGLAS WALLOP
12P-11A	So This Is What Happened to Charlie Moe. W.W. Norton & Co. 1965. Clothbound. Avon Books. 1967, reissue. Paperbound.
	A humorous novel concerning a pro football hero, big-time TV and a sportswriter's love affair.

12P-12	CLYDE GROSSCUP
12P-12A	Pro Rookie. Grosset & Dunlap. 1965. Clothbound.

Fiction

	The story of rookie's attempt to win a spot on a pro team. The author is the father of Lee Grosscup, former pro quarterback, and has drawn on his son's experiences.
12P-12B	<u>Pro Passer.</u> Grosset & Dunlap. 1966. Clothbound. Sequel to 12P-12A.
12P-12C	<u>Pro Champion.</u> Grosset & Dunlap. 1966. Clothbound.
12P-12D	<u>Throw the Bomb.</u> Grosset & Dunlap. 1967. Clothbound.

* * *

12P-13	ROBERT DALEY
12P-13A	<u>Only a Game.</u> New American Library. 1967. Clothbound. Signet. 1968, reissue. Paperbound.
	The story of a star pro football player and his troubled off-field life.

* * *

12P-14	JACK LAFLIN
12P-14A	<u>Throw the Long Bomb.</u> Whitman Publishing Co. 1967. Clothbound.
	The story of a rookie pro quarterback.

* * *

12P-15	GARY CARTWRIGHT
12P-15A	<u>The 100-Yard War.</u> Doubleday & Co. 1968. Clothbound.
	A story about the intimate workings of a pro football team.

* * *

12P-16	WARREN TUFTS
12P-16A	<u>The Life and Hard Times of the Super Heroes.</u> Montgomery Ward. National Football League Properties. 1968. Booklet.
	A story in comic book form.
12P-17	JOE ARCHIBALD
12P-17A	<u>Pro Coach.</u> Macrae-Smith. 1969. Clothbound.

Fiction

12P-18   DAVID S. MILTON

12P-18A   The Quarterback. Dell Publishing Co. 1970. Paperbound.
> The on and off field problems of a star pro quarterback.

* * *

12P-19   JAMES WHITEHEAD

12P-19A   Joiner. Alfred A. Knopf, Inc. 1971. Clothbound.
> The story of an NFL lineman and his origins in the Deep South.

* * *

12P-20   DAN JENKINS

12P-20A   Semi-Tough. Atheneum. 1972. Clothbound.
> A humorous, earthy novel about pro football.

* * *

12P-21   FRANK DEFORD

12P-21A   Cut 'n Run. Viking Press. 1972. Clothbound.
> The humorous story of a group of fanatical Baltimore Colt fans.

* * *

12P-22   NATIONAL FOOTBALL LEAGUE PLAYERS ASSOCIATION

12P-22A   Players' Choice. Whitman Publishing Co. 1969. Clothbound.
> Seven fictional stories selected by pro players.

* * *

FOOTBALL UNDER THE NEW RULE

SHOWING HOW FORMER ROUGH PLAY HAS BEEN REPLACED BY HUMANE TACTICS AND ILLUSTRATING THE IMPOSSIBILITY OF ACCIDENT SINCE REFORMS HAVE BEEN INSTITUTED

13. Humor

13-1   Revised Football Rules. Burr McIntosh. 1895. Paperbound.

              Horse play and horse sense.

13-2   Evolution of the Pig-Skin. William Edwin Rudge. W.E. Rudge, Inc. 1925. Booklet.

              A satirical history of the game.

13-3   Hold 'em, Girls. Judson P. Phillips and Robert W. Wood, Jr. G.P. Putnam's Sons. 1936. Clothbound.

              The intelligent woman's guide to men and football. A humorous description and explanation of football, including drinking at games.

13-4   For Laughing Out Loud. Herman Masin. Scholastic Book Services. 1954. Paperbound.

              Humorous anecdotes.

13-5   Dear Coach. Horace Pertoot. William-Frederick Press. 1963. Paperbound.

              A plan to change the rules to allow the home team to win every game, with hilarious stories to keep the coach in a receptive mood. Written in the form of letters from a fan to the coach of his favorite team.

13-6   Football Wit and Humor. Gene Ward and Dick Hyman, eds. Grosset & Dunlap. 1970. Clothbound.

              Humorous anecdotes and recollections of college and pro football.

14. Drama, Verse, Ballads

14-1   Echoes of the Harvard-Yale Game of 1890. Charles H. Thurston. 1890. Booklet.

   Game lineups, an account of the post-game celebrating, the football dinner, poems, songs.

14-2   A Football Game. C.S. Turner. 1894. Paperbound.

   A one-act comedy.

14-3   A Collection of the Popular Dartmouth Football Cheers and Songs. C.G. Howes. 1902. Booklet.

   Prepared for the 1902 Brown game. Words to cheers and songs.

14-4   Stanford Football Songs. Associated Students of Leland Stanford University. 1907. Booklet.

   Words to songs and cheers.

14-5   The Football Game. Sara Wiley. Samuel French. 1904. Booklet.

   A one-act comedy.

14-6   Football: A Monologue. Frank Dumont. M. Witmark & Sons. 1905. Booklet.

   A humorous monologue for stage delivery.

14-7   Songs and Cheers. Coe & Young. 1905. Booklet.

   Words to Harvard and Yale football songs and cheers.

14-8   Official Yale-Princeton Songs and Cheers. C.G. Whaples & Co. 1907. Title page: The Yale-Princeton Song and Cheer Book. Booklet.

   Words to cheers and songs.

14-9   Yale-Harvard-Princeton Official Songs and Cheers. C.G. Whaples & Co. 1908. Title page: The Yale-Harvard-Princeton

Drama, Verse, Ballads

Songs and Cheers Book. Booklet.
Words to songs and cheers.

14-10 Football. I. Clous and R. Snow. 1908. Paperbound.
A drama.

14-11 The All America Eleven. M.N. Beebe. 1909. Booklet.
An entertainment for boys in one scene.

14-12 A Halfback's Interference. M.N. Beebe. W.H. Baker & Co. 1912. Booklet.
A one-act farce.

14-13 Football. W. Fitzsimmons and E. Metcalf. 1911. Paperbound.
A one-act comedy.

14-14 The Football Fiends. J. Burnett. 1912. Paperbound.
A one-act comedy.

14-15 A Football Romance. Anthony Wills. Dick & Fitzgerald. 1912. Paperbound.
A college comedy in four acts.

14-16 Poe's "Run" and Other Poems. McCready Sykes. Cannon Press Princeton. 1916. Clothbound.
Drawings by Booth Tarkington. Humorous verses and parodies.

14-17 Goal Lines. Frank D. Halsey and A.C.M. Azoy, Jr. Princeton University Press. 1922. Clothbound.
A collection of humorous Princeton football verse and campus chatter.

14-18 The Midget Substitute. Harold V. Lucas. Marcy Center Press. 1924. Booklet.
Poetry.

14-19 Intercollegiate Song Book. Thornton W. Allen. Thornton W. Allen Co. 1927. Clothbound.
Football songs of American colleges.

14-20 Play Ball. Dr. H.B. Hulbert. Northwestern College of Speech Arts, Inc. 1929. Booklet.
A one-act comedy of college football.

Drama, Verse, Ballads

14-21 <u>The Kick Off.</u> Olive Jenkins. Walter H. Baker. 1938. Booklet.

    A drama of college football.

14-22 <u>The All-American College Football Songs.</u> Melrose Music Corp. 1945. Paperbound.

    Text and music.

14-23 <u>Football Fever</u>. Curtis Bishop and H. Gregory. 1952. Booklet.

    A farce in three acts.

15. Pictorials

Professional Titles

15P-1   Field of Vision. Chris Schenkel. Columbia Broadcasting System. 1962. Paperbound.

             Published by CBS for promotional purposes. A photographic account of the National Football League games played on November 4, 1962. Rosters, statistics.

15P-2   The New York Giants. Don Rubin and Al DeRogatis. Duell, Sloan, and Pearce. 1964. Clothbound.

             A pictorial analysis of the team and the pro game as a whole.

15P-3   Charlie Charger Coloring Book. San Diego Chargers. 1966. Magazine.

15P-4   The Gladiators. Kimberly-Clark. National Football League Properties. 1966. Booklet.

             A color pictorial view of National Football League football.

15P-5   Official National Football League Autograph Book. Sports Underwriters, Inc. 1967. Booklet.

             Western Conference and Eastern Conference editions. Different covers for each team, with roster and schedule on inside front cover. Player photos, vital statistics, autographs.

15P-6   Official American Football League Autograph Book. Sports Underwriters, Inc. 1967. Booklet.

             Different covers for each team, with roster and schedule on inside front cover. Player photos, vital statistics, autographs.

15P-7   National Football League Action Stamp Album. 1972. Booklet.

             Player stamps.

Pictorials

15P-8   <u>NFL Action '72.</u>   National Football League Properties.   1972.
Paperbound.
           Player stamps.

16. Schedule and Record Booklets

16-1 <u>Football Calendar.</u> L.L. Longdon. 1921. Booklet.
        Records, schedules, reviews of all major colleges. Rule explanations.

16-2 <u>Braeburn University Red Book.</u> Holtz-Rochester, Inc. 1921-35. Booklet.
        Schedules, scores, All-American teams. Published as a pocket date and address book.

16-3 <u>Atchison's College Football Record.</u> G.A. Atchison. 1923. Booklet.
        1922 scores. 1923 schedules, with scores to November 1.

16-4 <u>Football in 1925.</u> "Football" 1925. Paperbound.
        Schedules, scores, photos.

16-5 <u>National Intercollegiate Football Schedule, Rules, Scorecard.</u> Official Football Schedule Publishing Agency. Stall & Dean. 1925-27. Booklet.
        Schedules with scores of previous year. Rule interpretations, photos of game action.

16-6 <u>The Football Fan's Dope Book.</u> B.A. Shively SS Co. 1928-42. Booklet.
        Schedules, scores, facts, and figures. Overprinted by various commercial firms for advertising purposes.

16-7 <u>Grantland Rice's Cities Service Football Guide.</u> Grantland Rice. Cities Service Oil Co. 1933-55. Booklet.
        Schedules, records, facts.

16-8 <u>National Football Schedules and Rules.</u> Stucker & Smith. 1934. Booklet.
        Arranged by state.

Schedule and Record Booklets

16-9   Heffelfinger's Football Facts. C.H. Pearson. 1935-53. Booklet.

         Later editions were overprinted by various commercial firms for advertising purposes. History, terms, playing hints, records, schedules, scores.

16-9A   Official Football Facts. C.H. Pearson. Booklet.

         Various editions of 16-9 bear this title.

16-10   Original Football Facts. C.H. Pearson. Pearson Productions, Inc. 1935-to date. Booklet.

         Records, schedules, data. Overprinted by various commercial firms for advertising purposes. College and pro coverage.

16-11   Gluek's Football Dopester. Rollie Johnson. Gluek Brewing Co. 1936. Booklet.

         Schedules, rosters, rules, records.

16-12   National Football Schedule. Bogardus and Bogardus. 1937. Booklet.

         Schedules, scores.

16-13   B.F. Goodrich Football Guide. H.E. (Suz) Sayger. Sayger Sports Syndicate. 1937-52. Title page: Football Fans Dope Book and Guide. Booklet.

         Schedules, scores.

16-14   Hood Football Guide. H.E. (Suz) Sayger. Sayger Sports Syndicate. 1946, 1947. Booklet.

         Schedules, scores, bowl games.

16-15   Etna Football Facts. 1937. Booklet.

16-16   New York Times Official Football Schedules. New York Times. 1937. Booklet.

         Schedules and other data.

16-17   Brown-Forman's Football Schedule. Brown-Forman Distillers. 1937-56, 1958-to date. Booklet.

         College and pro records, statistics, schedules.

16-18   Saturday Evening Post Football Schedule Book. Curtis Publishing Co. 1938. Booklet.

         Schedules, records, data.

16-19   Trevor's Football Handbook. George Trevor. Heffelfinger Publishing Co. 1938. Booklet.

Schedule and Record Booklets

16-20   **Atlantic Football Book.** Atlantic Refining Co. 1938, 1939. Booklet.

         Schedules, records, forecasts.

16-21   **Football Calendar.** A. Goes. 1939-41. Booklet.

         Records, other data. College and pro coverage. Overprinted.

16-22   **Hires Football Schedules.** Hires Root Beer. 1940, 1941. Booklet.

16-23   **Jones Foundry Football Schedule Booklet.** Jones Foundry. 1942-49. Booklet.

         Records, facts, data.

16-23A   **Jones Foundry Football Schedules and Statistics.** Jones Foundry. 1950-57. Booklet.

         Continuation of 16-23.

16-24   **Football Schedules and Record Book.** Athletic Publications. 1946-60. Booklet.

         College and pro coverage.

16-24A   **College Football Schedules and Record Book.** Athletic Publications. 1961. Booklet.

         Continuation of 16-24.

16-25   **1947 Football Schedule.** Frontier Oil Co. 1947. Booklet.

         College and pro coverage.

16-26   **Esso Football Handbook.** J.M. Sheehan and C.H. Pearson. Standard Oil; Humble Oil Co. 1947-61. Booklet.

         Scores, records, statistics, schedules, rules review. College and pro coverage.

16-26A   **National Football.** J.M. Sheehan and C.H. Pearson. Humble Oil Co. 1962. Booklet.

         Continuation of 16-26.

16-26B   **College and Pro Football.** J.M. Sheehan and C.H. Pearson. Humble Oil Co. 1963, 1964. Booklet.

         Continuation of 16-26A.

16-26C   **Football.** J.M. Sheehan and C.H. Pearson. Humble Oil Co. 1965-67. Booklet.

         Continuation of 16-26B.

Schedule and Record Booklets

16-27   Humble Oil Football Handbook. Humble Oil Co. 1949. Booklet.

16-28   Roble Football Roundup. 1948. Booklet.

16-29   Boston Post Football Facts. Boston Post. 1944. Booklet.
             Review, records, scores, data.

16-30   New York Journal American Football Facts. New York Journal American. 1948. Booklet.

16-31   PM Football Schedules. Woodrow Press. 1948, 1949. Booklet.
             Records, previews, data. College and pro coverage.

16-32   Facts on American Sports and Health. Health Publications. 1949. Booklet.
             Football edition. Schedules, facts covering college and pro teams. Health facts, illustrations.

16-33   Arch Ward's Football Facts. Arch Ward. 1949. Booklet.
             Schedules, scores.

16-34   Paul Brown's Sohio Football Handbook. Sohio Oil Co. 1949-62. Booklet.
             Spectating guides, playing instructions, schedules. College and pro coverage.

16-35   RCA Football TV Handbook. Radio Corporation of America. 1950- to date. Booklet.

16-36   Westinghouse Football Facts and Schedules. Charles Loftus, ed. Westinghouse Electric Corp. 1951. Booklet.

16-37   Herman Hickman Football Guide. 1951. Booklet.

16-38   Sinclair Football Guide. Sinclair Oil Co. 1951. Booklet.
             Scores, records. College and pro coverage.

16-39   Guckenheimer Football Schedules. American Distilling Co. 1952. Booklet.

16-40   Football Handbook and Schedules. National Research Bureau. 1953. Booklet.

16-41   Four Roses Football Schedules. Distillers Corp. 1953. Booklet.

16-42   Phillip Morris Football Schedule. Erwin D. Ettin, ed. Woodrow Press. 1951-53. Booklet.
             Forecasts, records, statistics. College and pro coverage.

Schedule and Record Booklets

16-42A   Phillip Morris Football Guide. Erwin D. Ettin, ed. Woodrow Press. 1954-56. Booklet.

          Continuation of 16-42.

16-42B   Marlboro Football Guide. Erwin D. Ettin, ed. Woodrow Press. 1957. Booklet.

          Continuation of 16-42A.

16-43   Sylvania TV Home Viewers' Official Football Guide. Sylvania Television. 1953-55. Booklet.

          College and pro rosters and records.

16-44   Football Handbook and Schedules. The Sporting News. 1954-66. Booklet.

          Reviews, previews, articles, photos. Schedules, statistics. College and pro coverage.

16-44A   The Sporting News Official NFL, AFL and College Schedules and Records. The Sporting News. 1967-to date. Booklet.

          Continuation of 16-44.

16-45   College Football Television Handbook. Gulf Oil Co. 1955. Booklet.

          Rosters, statistics.

16-46   Football Handbook and Schedules. International News Service-United Press International. 1955-to date. Booklet.

          College and pro coverage. Overprinted by various firms for advertising purposes.

16-47   Texaco Football Almanac. Texaco, Inc. 1958. Booklet.

16-48   Monti's Official Football Book. 1961, 1962. Booklet.

          Schedules, scores, forecasts.

16-49   Ford Football Televiewer. Ford Motor Co. 1962. Booklet.

          Rosters, photos, statistics. College and pro coverage.

16-50   Chrysler Football Almanac. Chrysler Motor Co. 1964. Booklet.

16-51   NCAA TV Game of the Week Football Almanac. Masthead Corp. 1964, 1965. Booklet.

          Rosters, schedules.

16-52   Chevrolet College Football Handbook. ABC TV Sports. American Broadcasting Co. and Rutledge Books. 1967. Booklet.

          Previews, rosters, schedules, player sketches. (See also 26-34)

Schedule and Record Booklets

Professional Titles

16P-1   Professional Football Highlights. Atlantic Refining Co. 1952. Booklet.

         Schedules, scores, reviews, previews.

16P-2   Professional Football. American Oil Co. 1954. Title page: Your Guide to Professional Football. Booklet.

         Team facts, records, schedules.

16P-3   Pro Football Handbook. Masthead Corp. 1957-60. 1962-to date. Booklet.

         Rosters, previews, reviews. Overprinted by various commercial firms for advertising purposes.

16P-3A   Pro Football Guide. Masthead Corp. 1961. Booklet.

         Continuation of 16P-3.

16P-4   National Football League Guide. Sports Illustrated. National Football League. 1960. Booklet.

         Rosters, schedules.

16P-5   National Football League Handbook. Zander Hollander and Norman Miller. Associated Features. 1963, 1964. Booklet.

         Rosters, reviews.

16P-6   NFL Football Flip-up Line-up. Masthead Corp. 1964. Booklet.

         Rosters, reviews, previews.

16P-7   NFL Record Book. Norelco. 1966. Paperbound.

         Records, statistics, schedules.

16P-8   The New American Football League. Masthead Corporation. 1960. Booklet.

         Overprinted by various firms for advertising purposes. History, schedules, rosters, television information.

16P-9   AFL TV Handbook. Mercury. Ford Motor Co. 1960-to date. Booklet.

         American Football League records and rosters.

16P-10   American Football League TV Roster Round-up. Institute of Life Insurance. Masthead Corporation. 1965. Booklet.

         Previews, records, schedules.

Schedule and Record Booklets

16P-11 American Football League. Chrysler Corp. 1968. Booklet.

        An advertising supplement containing schedules, photos, player sketches.

16P-12 TWA Official AFL TV Viewing Guide. Trans World Airlines. 1968. Booklet.

        Rosters, statistics, reviews, schedules covering American Football League teams.

16P-13 Pro Football Schedule and Record Book. Athletic Publications. 1961. Booklet.

        Rosters, schedules, records.

16P-14 First and Goal to Go. Columbia Broadcasting System. 1965. Booklet.

        A preview of the 1965 season. Team previews and schedules.

16P-15 Ballentine Beer Pro Football Television Manual. Zander Hollander. P. Ballentine & Sons. 1966. Booklet.

        Rosters, team previews, records, statistics, schedules.

16P-16 The Family Pro Football TV Handbook. Zander Hollander, ed. Associated Features. 1968. Booklet.

        Rosters, records.

17. Rating Systems

17-1 <u>Method of Ranking College Football Teams.</u> I.B. Thomas. Allen, Lane and Scott. 1922. Booklet.

    A point system, using won and lost records. Results for 1921.

17-2 <u>Azzi Ratem.</u> William F. Boand. 1930. Booklet.

    An explanation of a mathematical rating system. Ratings of leading teams.

17-2A <u>Azzi Ratem - Boand Football Ranking System.</u> William F. Boand. 1950. Booklet.

    Continuation of 17-2.

17-3 <u>National Football Champions.</u> William F. Boand. 1941. Booklet.

    Facts, ratings since 1924.

17-4 <u>An Examination of Football Scores.</u> William N. McFarland. Waverly Press. 1932. Paperbound.

    A rating system devised from game scores. Ratings of leading teams.

17-5 <u>Ten Thousand and One Scores.</u> Deke Houlgate. 1938. Paperbound.

    Team ratings based on scores of major games from 1928-37.

17-6 <u>Dickinson's Football Ratings.</u> Frank G. Dickinson. 1941. Booklet.

    An explanation of his rating system, with team ratings from 1924-40.

17-7 <u>National Football Champions.</u> Helms Athletic Foundation. 1942. Booklet.

    The record of each team picked by Helms as the

Rating Systems

national champion from 1883-1941. Sketches of great coaches.

17-8   <u>Junior College Football Rating Systems.</u> Clive Grafton. Statistics Bureau of the National Junior College Athletic Association. 1955. Booklet.

         The development of the junior college football rating systems and a comparison between the Williamson and Gridiron Index Systems.

18. Economic Matters

18-1   The Yale Bowl. Tuttle Co. 1914. Paperbound.

            The history and description of the stadium which was built in 1914. Color illustrations.

18-2   The Stadium. Myron Serby. American Institute of Steel Construction. 1930. Clothbound.

            The design of stadiums and their equipment for optimum football use.

18-3   What the 1925 Season Taught Us About Business Organization. Harold T. Marshall. American Management Association. 1926. Paperbound.

            A paper prepared by members of the Dartmouth football team, comparing football and business.

18-4   Night Football. Ralph A. Piper. 1941. Booklet.

            Status, lighting principles and standards.

18-5   The Effects of Television on College Football Attendance. National Opinion Research Center. 1952. Paperbound.

            Prepared for the National Collegiate Athletic Association. Two reports, covering 1949 and 1950.

18-6   Highlights of Pro Football. Grantland Rice. Prest-O-Lite Battery Co. 1952. Magazine.

            An advertising pictorial sponsored by various commercial firms.

Professional Titles

18P-1   Now It Can Be Told. Washington Redskins. 1945. Booklet.

            Reprints of correspondence dealing with the Redskins' part in the war effort.

Economic Matters

18P-2   The Professional Football Player. Paul Governali. Columbia University. 1951. Paperbound.

           A thesis written for a Doctor of Education degree. History of pro football, status of the player, legal aspects of the relationship between player and team. Conditions of employment, attitudes of the player toward the game and his environment. Conclusions drawn from response to questionnaires sent to players.

18P-3   The Story of Pro Football in Summary. Bert Bell. National Football League. 1957. Booklet.

           A defense of pro football sent to congressmen to aid the National Football League in its fight for exemption from antitrust laws. Entered in hearings conducted by the House Antitrust Sub-Committee.

18P-4   Organized Professional Team Sports. U.S. Congress. 1958, 1960. Paperbound.

           Hearings held before the Senate Judiciary Committee on Antitrust laws and the FTC Act as applicable to baseball and professional football.

18P-5   Telecasting of Professional Sports Contests. U.S. Congress. 1961. Paperbound.

           An examination of the economic aspects of major league television policies, including the National Football League.

18P-6   AFL vs. NFL. U.S. District Court. 1962. Booklet.

           A printed account of the court case (subsequently dismissed) and decision concerning the monopoly charges brought against the National Football League by the American Football League.

18P-7   AFL vs. NFL. U.S. Court of Appeals. 1963. Booklet.

           A printed account of the appeal (denied) from the U.S. District Court decision which dismissed monopoly charges brought by the American Football League against the National Football League.

18P-8   Professional Football League Merger. U.S. Congress. 1966. Paperbound.

           Hearings held before the House Anti-Trust Subcommittee to determine the legality of the merger between the National and American Football Leagues.

18P-9   NFLP. National Football League Properties, Inc. 1963. Booklet.

Economic Matters

                Guides to merchandising and promoting items produced under contract to National Football League Properties.

18P-10   <u>The Bert Bell NFL Player Benefit Plan</u>. National Football League. 1964. Booklet.

                The annual report on the player pension plan for the year ending March 31, 1964.

18P-11   <u>NFL Group Insurance Plan: The Bert Bell NFL Player Benefit Plan</u>. National Football League. 1966. Booklet.

                General information and lists of benefits offered under the group insurance plan.

19. Yearbooks

19-1 The Longhorn. University of Texas. 1914. Paperbound.
The story of the undefeated 1914 team. Game summaries, lineups, photos.

19-2 Football Report. United States Military Academy. 1916. Booklet.
A review of the 1915 season. Photos, play-by-play of the Navy game.

19-3 A Testimonial to the Players, Coaches, Management of Washington and Jefferson College, Football Season of 1921. Citizens of Washington, Pennsylvania. January 10, 1922. Booklet.
An account of the 1921 undefeated Rose Bowl team. Scores, roster, game accounts, player sketches. Reprints of newspaper articles, photos.

19-4 Southern Champions -- A Football Treasure. E.J. Howell and Karl Opryshek. 1922. Booklet.
An account of the post-season game played on January 2, 1922 between Texas A & M and Centre College for the mythical football championship of the South.

19-5 The Winning Team of Centre College. R. Ames Montgomery. 1923. Cover title: The Winning Team. Clothbound.
Talks delivered to the student body by the college president each Monday morning following the Saturday football game during the 1923 season. Football and the lessons of life. Foreword: background of Centre College and its football teams, and a defense of its athletic program.

19-6 Official Football Review. University of Notre Dame. 1924-to date. Magazine.
Scores, game accounts, player sketches, photos.

Yearbooks

19-6A   Notre Dame Scholastic Football Review. University of Notre Dame. Magazine.

           Later editions of 19-6 bear this title.

19-7   A Proud Tradition/Notre Dame. Daniel Moore, II. Mossberg & Co. 1967. Magazine.

           A photographic review of Notre Dame's 1964 and 1965 seasons. A critique of the university and the football program.

19-8   Illinois' Greatest Football Game. Charles L. Allen. 1925. Booklet.

           Reprints of the newspaper accounts of Illinois' 24-2 win over the University of Pennsylvania in 1925.

19-9   Georgia Tech's Golden Tornado Champions. Georgia Tech University. 1929. Magazine.

           Full-page sketch and photo of each player on the 1928 championship team. Review of season.

19-10   Golden Tornado, Georgia Tech, 1951. Hugh Folk and George D. Newton, Jr. 1952. Paperbound.

           Reprints of newspaper articles and game accounts covering the 1951 Georgia Tech conference and Orange Bowl champions.

19-11   The Georgia Tech Yellow Jackets. Robert B. Wallace, Jr. Sports Publications. 1966, 1967. Clothbound.

           A game-by-game review of the season. Results, statistics, photos.

19-12   A Football Classic. C.R. Gray. 1929. Clothbound.

           Privately printed. Reprints of newspaper accounts of the 1933 undefeated Princeton team. Roster, photos.

19-13   Going Back. A.G. Murray, Jr. 1934. Clothbound.

           Privately printed. Reprints of newspaper accounts of the 1933 undefeated Princeton team. Roster, photos.

19-14   Tiger Triumph. Peter Battin and Peter Gullick. 1951. Donald Edwards and George Gillespie, Jr. 1952. Paperbound.

           Game accounts of the undefeated 1950 and 1951 Princeton University teams. Reprints of newspaper and magazine articles and photos.

19-15   Jerry Dalrymple and His Tulane 1931 Green Wave National Champions. John Boyd. Franklin Printing Co. and Snider Publishing

Yearbooks

Agency. 1931. Clothbound.

Dalrymple was a two-time All-American end. Game accounts, statistics, outstanding plays. An account of Tulane's first football game.

19-16 The Minnesota Huddles. Stan Carlson. 1936-38. Magazine.

University of Minnesota football review. Articles, rosters, photos, scores.

19-17 Football Champions of 1938. Texas Christian University. 1938. Magazine.

Photos, game summaries, statistics of the undefeated 1938 team.

19-18 Following the Huskers. Bill Devreindt and Ken Ott. 1938-41. Booklet.

A game-by-game review of the University of Nebraska's previous season. Statistics, photos.

19-19 Hail the Champs! Indianapolis Star. 1945. Magazine.

Season review covering the University of Indiana's first Big 10 Football Championship. Game summaries, lineups, photos.

19-20 Michigan Football Review. S.F. Schneider. Franklin DeKleine Co. 1949. Magazine.

Game summaries of the 1947 and 1948 Michigan University seasons, in which the teams were undefeated. Photos.

19-21 The 500 Club. College of Pacific. 1949. Clothbound.

A game-by-game review of the 1949 season.

19-22 California Football Review. University of California. A.S.U.C. News Bureau. 1950-53. Booklet.

A game-by-game review of the previous season. Statistics, photos.

19-23 The Wow Boys. Cyclone Covey. Exposition Press. 1957. Clothbound.

A game-by-game account of Stanford University's 1940 undefeated Rose Bowl champion team.

19-24 Football at Texas A & M. Don Burt and Glendall Rand. 1957. Booklet.

A game-by-game review of the undefeated 1956 season.

Yearbooks

19-25   The Aggies Are Back. Alpha Delta Sigma. Texas A & M. 1968. Magazine.

                 A game-by-game review of Texas A & M's 1967 Southwest Conference championship season. Statistics, roster, photos.

19-26   Packard-Bell Presents UCLA Football. Packard Bell Corp. 1958. Booklet.

                 A preview of the team and the season. Photos.

19-27   Football Alabama Style. University of Alabama. 1961. Magazine.

                 A pictorial account of the 1961 national champion team. Review of each game.

19-28   College Football Digest Presents Alabama. Barry Copeland, ed. College Football Digest. 1969. Booklet.

                 Review, preview, roster, scores, records. Previews of leading teams.

19-29   Dartmouth's Undefeated Football Season. Ernie Roberts. University of Dartmouth. 1963, 1966. Paperbound.

                 Reviews of the undefeated teams of 1962 and 1965. Reprints of newspaper articles covering each game. Statistics, lineups, photos.

19-30   The Road to the Championship. Richard Kunkle. Waynesburg College Alumni Association. 1966. Booklet.

                 Game-by-game review of the 1966 NAIA championship season of Waynesburg (Pennsylvania) College.

19-31   College Football Digest Presents Georgia. Barry Copeland, ed. College Football Digest. 1969. Booklet.

                 Review, preview, roster, scores, records. Previews of leading teams.

19-32   Penn State's Finest Football Season. Dick Brown. Centre Daily Times. 1969. Booklet.

                 A photographic review of Penn State's undefeated 1968 season.

19-33   Penn State Football Season. Dick Brown. Centre Daily Times. 1970. Booklet.

                 A photographic review of Penn State's undefeated 1969 season.

19-34   The Unbeatable Rockets. Toledo Blade. 1971. Magazine.

Yearbooks

A review of the University of Toledo's 1969, 1970 and 1971 unbeaten seasons.

19-35 Collegiate Press Guides. c 1941-to date. Booklets. Paperbound. Magazines.

Issued by colleges prior to the opening of the season. Rosters, player sketches, all-time records and scores, history, review of the previous season, photos. Various titles.

Professional Titles

19P-1 Spartan Yearbook. Portsmouth Spartans. 1931. Paperbound.

Player sketches, review of the 1931 season, photos.

19P-2 The Baltimore Colts. American Visuals Corp. 1950. Booklet.

Player biographies in cartoon form.

19P-3 Baltimore Colts Picture Album. Baltimore Football, Inc. 1957-58. Magazine.

Action photos.

19P-3A Baltimore Colts Action Pictorial. Baltimore Football, Inc. 1959-61. Magazine.

Continuation of 19P-3.

19P-3B Baltimore Colts Tenth Anniversary Yearbook. Vince Bagli and Tom Gorman. 1962. Magazine.

Continuation of 19P-3A.

19P-4 Our '64 Colts. Tom Gorman. 1964. Magazine.

A review of each Baltimore Colts game during the 1964 season. Photos.

19P-5 Detroit Lions Photo Album. Ted Pitok. 1953, 1954. Magazine.

Player photos and sketches.

19P-6 San Francisco 49ers Yearbook. San Francisco 49ers. 1958-to date. Magazine.

Player sketches, records, statistics, other data, photos. The 1958 edition was the official press guide.

19P-7 Rams Yearbook. Los Angeles Ram Football Club. 1958-to date. Magazine.

Player sketches, records, statistics, other data. Photos.

Yearbooks

19P-8   Green Bay Packers Yearbook. Art Daley and Jack Yuenger. 1960-to date. Magazine.

          Player sketches, records, statistics, other data. Photos.

19P-9   Salute to the Packers. Fritz Van. Fritz Van Enterprises. 1962- to date.

          A review of the Green Bay Packers 1967 season. Articles, game summaries, statistics, player sketches, photos.

19P-10   Sports Focus Yearbook, Green Bay Packers. Jack Bundy, ed. Bundy & Associates. 1968-70. Magazine.

          Articles, statistics, photos.

19P-10A   Sports Focus Yearbook, Green Bay Packers, Wisconsin Badgers. Jack Bundy, ed. Bundy & Associates. 1971. Magazine.

          Continuation of 19P-10. Includes coverage of University of Wisconsin Football.

19P-11   Minnesota Vikings Official Cartoon Book. Minnesota Vikings. 1961. Magazine.

          Player sketches.

19P-12   Minnesota Vikings Fact Book. Ford Motor Co. 1965. Booklet.

          Records, statistics, roster.

19P-12A   Minnesota Vikings New Fact Book. Ford Motor Co. 1966. Booklet.

          Continuation of 19P-12.

19P-13   The Vikings. Minnesota Vikings. 1965. Magazine.

          A photographic review.

19P-14   New York Giants Yearbook. New York Giants. 1963-to date. Magazine.

          Player sketches, records, statistics, other data. Photos.

19P-15   The New York Giants. Complete Sports. 1964. Magazine.

          Articles, photos.

19P-16   Witness for the Defense. Dick Lynch and Jack Zanger. Parallax Publishing Co. 1966. Clothbound. Pocket Books. 1966, reissue. Paperbound.

          The story of the 1965 season as told by the star defen-

Yearbooks

sive halfback of the New York Giants. Insights into the game, behind-the-scene anecdotes.

19P-17　Seven Days to Sunday. Eliot Asinof. Simon & Schuster. 1968. Clothbound. Ace Books. 1970, reissue. Paperbound.

A week in the life of the New York Giants, leading up to a crucial game.

19P-18　Browns. Cleveland Browns. 1964. Paperbound.

A photographic review of the 1963 season.

19P-19　Atlanta Falcons. Atlanta Falcons Football Club. Sports Publications, Inc. 1966. Clothbound, 1967, 1968. Clothbound and Paperbound.

A game-by-game photographic review of the season. Statistics, roster.

19P-20　The Dallas Cowboys. Dave Campbell, ed. Southwest Sports Publications. 1967-to date. Magazine.

Player sketches, previews, roster, statistics, schedule.

19P-21　Next Year's Champions. Steve Perkins. World Publishing Co. 1969. Clothbound.

A daily diary of the Dallas Cowboys' 1968 season, as kept by a Dallas football reporter who has covered the team for six years. A frank, inside look at the Cowboys, who were picked to win the 1968 championship but failed to do so.

19P-22　The Dallas Cowboys: Winning the Big One. Steve Perkins. Grosset & Dunlap. 1972. Clothbound.

The story of the Dallas Cowboys' 1971 season, in which they won the championship.

19P-23　St. Louis Football Cardinals. St. Louis Cardinals. 1968. Magazine.

A game-by-game review of the 1967 season. Photos.

19P-24　New Orleans Saints. Dave Campbell, ed. Southwest Sports Publications. 1968-to date. Magazine.

Player reports, reviews, previews.

19P-25　NFL Library. Golden Press. 1964. Eight volumes. Booklet.

History, records, rosters, team analyses.

19P-25A　Baltimore Colts.

19P-25B　Chicago Bears.

Yearbooks

19P-25C	Cleveland Browns.
19P-25D	Detroit Lions.
19P-25E	Green Bay Packers.
19P-25F	New York Giants.
19P-25G	Eastern Conference.
19P-25H	Western Conference.

19P-26 American Football League Titans of New York. Jay Publishing Co. 1961. Magazine. Publishing Co. 1961. Magazine.

    Player sketches, statistics, roster, photos.

19P-27 The New York Jets. Complete Sports. 1964. Magazine.

    Articles, photos.

19P-28 New York Jets Official Yearbook. New York Jets. 1965-to date. Magazine.

    Player sketches, records, statistics, other data. Photos.

19P-29 The Violence Game. Bob Curran. Macmillan Co. 1966. Clothbound.

    An account of the 1965 New York Jets' season from the training camp through the 14-week schedule. A behind-the-scenes view of pro football.

19P-30 Countdown to Super Bowl. Dave Anderson. Random House. 1969. Clothbound. Signet. 1969, reissue. Paperbound.

    A chronicle of the New York Jets 1969 championship season.

19P-31 Boston Patriots Yearbook. Boston Patriots Football Club. 1964-67. Magazine.

    Player sketches, records, statistics, other data. Photos.

19P-32 Houston Oilers Action Album. Houston Oilers. 1966. Magazine.

    Action photos.

19P-33 Houston Oilers. Dave Campbell, ed. Southwest Sports Publications. 1968-to date. Magazine.

    Reviews and previews covering the Oilers and the other league teams.

Yearbooks

19P-34 Kansas City Chiefs Yearbook. Kansas City Chiefs. 1968-to date. Magazine.

> Game summaries, player sketches, team reviews, statistics, photos.

19P-35 Team Press Guides.

> Issued by teams before the season to provide information for newspaper, radio, and television reporters. Records, statistics, player sketches, rosters, historical facts, other data. Various titles.

National Football League:

19P-35A Atlanta Falcons. 1966-to date. Booklet.

19P-35B Baltimore Colts. 1950, 1953-to date. Booklet.

19P-35C Boston Redskins. 1936. Magazine.

19P-35D Boston Yanks. 1945-48. Booklet.

19P-35E Brooklyn Dodgers. 1943. Booklet.

19P-35F Chicago Bears. 1937-to date. Booklet.

19P-35G Chicago Cardinals. 1940-59. Booklet.

19P-35H Cleveland Browns. 1950-to date. Booklet.

19P-35I Dallas Cowboys. 1960-to date. Booklet.

19P-35J Dallas Texans. 1952. Booklet.

19P-35K Detroit Lions. 1940-44. Magazine. 1945-to date. Booklet.

> Two 1949 editions: Detroit Lions Facts and Team History. Official guide. Follow Those Detroit Lions.

19P-35L Green Bay Packers. 1930-46. Magazine. 1946-to date. Booklet.

> Two 1946 editions: Green Bay Packers Press Book. Magazine. Green Bay Packers Press and Radio Guide. Booklet. Separate roster booklets published, 1943-51: Green Bay Packer Personnel.

19P-35M Los Angeles Rams. 1946-to date. Booklet.

19P-35N Minnesota Vikings. 1961-to date. Booklet.

19P-35P New Orleans Saints. 1967-to date.

Yearbooks

19P-35Q	New York Bulldogs.	1949. Booklet.
19P-35R	New York Giants.	1925-44. Booklet. 1945. Magazine. 1946-to date. Booklet.
19P-35S	New York Yankees.	1950, 1951. Booklet.
19P-36T	Philadelphia Eagles.	1946-to date. Booklet.
19P-35U	Pittsburgh Steelers.	1946-to date. Booklet.
19P-35V	San Francisco 49ers.	1950-to date. Booklet. 1958. Magazine. 1959-to date. Booklet.
19P-35W	St. Louis Cardinals.	1960-to date. Booklet.
19P-35X	Washington Redskins.	1944-to date. Booklet. 1946 and 1947. Paperbound. 1948 and 1949. Booklet. See 4P-2.

All-American Football Conference: 1946 and 1947, Paperbound. 1948 and 1949.

19P-35Y	Baltimore Colts.	1947-49. Booklet.
19P-35Z	Brookleyn Dodgers.	1947-49. Booklet.
19P-35AA	Buffalo Bisons, Bills.	1946, 1948, 1949. Booklet.
19P-35BB	Chicago Rockets, Hornets.	1947-49. Booklet.
19P-35CC	Cleveland Browns.	1948-49. Booklet.
19P-35DD	Los Angeles Dons.	1947-49. Booklet.
19-35EE	New York Yankees.	1947-49. Booklet.
19-35FF	San Francisco 49ers.	1946-49. Booklet.

American Football League:

19P-35GG	Boston Patriots.	1962-to date. Booklet.
19P-35HH	Buffalo Bills.	1960-to date. Booklet.
19P-35II	Cincinnati Bengals.	1968-to date. Booklet.
19P-35JJ	Denver Broncos.	1961-to date. Booklet.
19P-35KK	Houston Oilers.	1961-to date. Booklet.

Yearbooks

19P-35LL	Kansas City Chiefs.	1963-to date. Booklet.
19P-35MM	Los Angeles Chargers.	1960. Booklet.
19P-35NN	Miami Dolphins.	1966-to date. Booklet.
19P-35PP	New York Jets.	1963-to date. Booklet.
19P-35QQ	Oakland Raiders.	1961, 1963-to date. Booklet.
19P-35RR	San Diego Chargers.	1961-to date. Booklet.

20. Boys and High School

High School—General

20-1	Spalding's Official Interscholastic Football Guide. A.G. Spalding & Brothers. 1925-31. Paperbound.	
20-1A	Pacific Coast or Western Edition. 1925-31.	
20-1B	Ohio Edition. 1925, 1931.	
20-1C	Pennsylvania and West Virginia Edition. 1925.	
20-1D	East Coast Edition. 1926-31.	
20-1E	Mid-Western Edition. 1926-31.	
20-1F	Southern Edition. 1926-31.	
20-1G	Southwestern Edition. 1930, 1931.	

    Records, rules, playing instructions, outstanding plays.

20-2   Official Interscholastic Football Rules. E.A. Thomas, Hugh L. Ray and H.V. Porter. National Federation of State High School Athletic Associations. 1930-41. Booklet.

    The 1940 and 1941 editions included six-man touch rules.

20-2A   Interscholastic Football Rules. E.A. Thomas, Hugh L. Ray and H.V. Porter. National Federation of State High School Athletic Associations. 1942. Booklet.

    Continuation of 20-2. Included six-man and touch rules.

20-2B   National Federation Football Rules. National Federation of State High School Athletic Association. 1943, 1944. Booklet.

    Continuation of 20-2.

Boys and High School

20-2C   Football Rules. E.A. Thomas, Hugh L. Ray and H.V. Porter. National Federation of State High School Athletic Associations. 1945-to date. Booklet.

                Continuation of 20-2. The 1945 edition included six-man and touch rules.

20-3   Football Rules through Play Situations. Hugh L. Ray. National Federation of State High School Athletic Associations. 1930. Booklet.

                For officials, coaches and players. A textbook for the study of the rules and game procedure.

20-3A   Football Play Situations. Hugh L. Ray. National Federation of State High School Athletic Associations. 1931, 1932. Booklet.

                Continuation of 20-3.

20-3B   Football Play Situations, Based on the Official Interscholastic Football Rules. Hugh L. Ray. National Federation of State High School Athletic Associations. 1933-47. Booklet.

                Continuation of 20-3.

20-3C   Football Case Book. Hugh L. Ray. National Federation of State High School Athletic Associations. 1948-to date.

                Continuation of 20-3.

20-4   Football Play Situations, Based on the NCAA Official Football Rules. Hugh L. Ray. National Federation of State High School Athletic Associations. 1933-35. Booklet.

20-5   Football Player Handbook. National Federation of State High School Athletic Associations. 1945-to date. Booklet.

                Elaborations of the rules, with explanations and interpretations.

20-6   National High School Football Annual. Universal Sports Press. 1948. Magazine.

                Records of leading teams in each state.

20-7   Football Magazine. Kurt Lenser. 1954. Magazine.

                Articles, reviews covering schoolboy football.

20-7A   Prep Football Magazine and Annual. Kurt Lenser. 1955, 1956. Magazine.

                Continuation of 20-7.

20-8   High School Football. Complete Sports Publications. 1963. Magazine.

Reviews, previews, articles, photos.

20-9 **Making College Count.** Ewald B. Nyquist and G. Hawes. National Football Foundation.

A guide to college for high school football players.

High School—Regional

20-10 **Kickoff.** W.A. Penney. Eastern Massachusetts Interscholastic Football Association. 1940. Magazine.

Schedules, rosters, forecasts, photos.

20-11 **That Old Rivalry.** Eustace L. Williams Morton & Co. 1940. Clothbound.

A year-by-year account of games between Manual and High School, Louisville, Kentucky, 1893-1900.

20-12 **Forty-Two Years of Hotchkiss Football.** Otto F. Monahan. Kennerly Press. 1941. Paperbound.

The story of Monahan's coaching career at the Connecticut prep school from 1896-1938. Greatest teams, players, games. Photos.

20-13 **A History of Football at Shortridge.** Thomas Koch. 1943. Paperbound.

The history of football at Shortridge High School, Indianapolis, Indiana.

20-14 **Massachusetts Official School Boy Football Annual.** Curt Noyes. 1947. Paperbound. Tom Lester. 1948. Paperbound.

Rules, regulations, schedules, records, other data.

20-15 **Chicago Prep Football Annual.** John Kuenster. 1948. Magazine.

Previews, schedules, records.

20-15A **Chicago and Area High School Football Annual Pictorial.** John Kuenster. 1949. Magazine.

Continuation of 20-15.

20-16 **57 Years of Phoenixville Football.** Wayne Jones, Jr. 1949. Clothbound.

The history of Phoenixville, Pennsylvania, high school and sandlot football. Yearly history, scores, photos.

Boys and High School

20-17   Down the Years with Cathedral Football. Matlock Printing Co. 1952. Paperbound.

        A history of football at Cathedral High School in Indianapolis, Indiana.

20-18   California Prep Football Guide. Lefty Stern and Dave Reznek. Tam Gibbs Company. 1953. Booklet.

20-19   California Prep Football. Calendar Sports Publications. 1966- to date. Magazine.

        Player sketches, team previews.

20-20   Bay and Pioneer Leagues Football Yearbook. Doug Stephen. 1960. Magazine.

        Coverage of high school football in Southern California.

20-21   No Gold Footballs. Warren N. Kellogg. Twayne Publishers. 1954. Clothbound.

        A study of the athletic program at Phillips Exeter Academy.

20-22   Down Memory Lane with Rayen and South. Victor Frolund. William-Frederick Press. 1961. Clothbound.

        A game-by-game account of the 50-year rivalry between two Youngstown, Ohio, high school teams.

20-23   Autumn's Mightiest Legions. Harold Ratliff. Texian Press. 1963. Clothbound.

        The history of Texas schoolboy football.

20-24   Gridfax. Clarence W. Funk. 1967. Clothbound.

        The 80-year history of scholastic football in south-central Pennsylvania.

20-25   Broward Football. Ken Small. Parker Printing. 1968, 1969. Magazine.

        Team previews, rosters, schedules, scores, statistics covering high school teams in Broward County, Florida.

20-26   A History of South Jersey Football. Douglas Frambes. Brooks-Irvine Memorial Football Club of South Jersey. 1969. Paperbound.

        A history of high school football in Southern New Jersey since 1919.

Boys and High School

20-27　　Team: A High School Odyssey. Richard Woodley. Holt, Rinehart & Winston. 1972. Clothbound.

　　　　An intimate insight into a Westchester County, New York, high school football team.

High School—Coaching

20-28　　Principles of Football. John Heisman. Sports Publishing Bureau. 1921, 1922. Paperbound.

　　　　Advice, fundamentals. Offensive and defensive strategy. Injuries, coaching. For high school and prep school players.

20-29　　A Manual of Football for High Schools. Charles Bachman. Kansas State College. 1923, 1926. Title page: A Manual of Football for High School Coaches. Clothbound.

　　　　General playing instructions, diagrams.

20-30　　High School Football Manual of Fundamentals. Clement Johnston. 1925. Paperbound.

　　　　Organization, drills, general fundamentals. Offense and defense, passing, signals, generalship, scouting.

20-31　　High School Football and How to Win Games. James W. Aiken. 1928. Clothbound.

　　　　Problems of the high school coach. How to deal with boys and their parents. Discipline, strategy, conditioning, scouting.

20-32　　Ball Carrying Made Easy. James W. Aiken. Standard Printing Co. 1935. Clothbound.

　　　　An insight into high school football for players, coaches and fans. Personal coaching experiences, playing instructions.

20-33　　Pre-College Football. Robert Barr. A. Stokes Co. 1939. Clothbound.

　　　　Equipment, coaching, conditioning. Playing in-instructions, the play of each position.

20-34　　Oklahoma Football Coaching School Manual. 1946. Paperbound.

　　　　Lectures by Otis Coffey, Fritz Crisler, Ed McKeever, others.

20-35　　Washington State High School Association Football Clinic. H. Bendele. Washington State High School Association. 1949-

55. Paperbound.

    Lectures by Wilkinson, Snavely, Frnka, Neely, other college coaches.

20-36   Football for All. Dr. Harold Parker. Saga Press. 1950. Paperbound.

    A complete manual for teachers and coaches of schoolboy football. Theory and fundamentals of Class Football. General instructions, drills, programs.

20-37   Wisconsin High School Coaches Summer Clinic. 1954. Paperbound.

    Lectures by Williamson, Daugherty, other coaches.

20-38   Winning High School Football. Charles Mather. Prentice-Hall. 1955. Clothbound.

    Organization, planning, strategy. Offense, defense, kicking. Player evaluations, mechanical aids, scouting, the player's notebook.

20-39   Abilene High School Football Organization. Charles H. Moser. 1959. Paperbound.

    Drills, quarterback practice, game organization and scouting as employed at Abilene High School, Abilene, Texas.

20-40   The Crying Towel. James M. Eason. Prestige Press. 1961. Clothbound.

    A discussion of football and coaching techniques by a successful high school coach. Recollections of games and incidents.

20-41   Football Coaches How to Do It Book. Lou Thom Howard. How to Do It Book Co. 1962. Paperbound.

    Instructions for high school coaches on various phases of the game.

20-42   Limited Material? Unlimited Results! John Austin. Inter-Collegiate Press. 1963. Clothbound.

    Football advice for young coaches. Plays, formations.

20-43   Drills for High School Football. Kermit B. Davis. Scott Publishing Co. 1964. Paperbound.

    Diagrams.

20-44   So You Want to Be a High School Football Coach. Johnny Mach. 1966. Paperbound.

Boys and High School

20-45 Football Forum. Bill Lucier, ed. Michigan Technology University. 1966, 1967. Paperbound.

   Articles by and for Michigan high school coaches. Plays, drills, diagrams.

20-46 How to Select and Develop Athletes for Winning High School Football. Stan Peters. Parker Publishing Co. 1967. Clothbound.

   Qualifications, organization, indoctrination, placement, conditioning, practice.

20-47 Ohio High School Football. Carl Benhase. Parker Publishing Co. 1967. Clothbound.

   Historical background, coaching programs, team organization. Practice, offense, defense, rebuilding.

20-48 Developing a Championship Football Program. Joe Talamo and Roy Lupinaccio. Parker Publishing Co. 1968. Clothbound.

   Team morale, organization, practice, signals, plays, passing, defense, drills, kicking.

20-49 Michigan-Style High School Football. Jay Stielstra. Parker Publishing Co. 1969. Clothbound.

   Building a program, offensive formatins, running, passing, defense, kicking, scouting.

20-50 Offensive and Defensive Football. Burt Smith. A.S. Barnes & Co. 1970. Clothbound.

   Offense, defense, scouting, developing a high school program.

20-51 Black Coach. Pat Jordan. Dodd, Mead & Co. 1971. Clothbound.

20-52 Football Fundamentals. Lawrence H. Battistini. No date. Booklet.

   Instructions for high school players.

High School—Offense

20-53 Successful Multiple Offense in High School Football. Robert E. Walker. Prentice-Hall. 1957. Clothbound.

   General discussion, personnel, basic formations. Organization, offense, defense, kicking, drills.

Boys and High School

20-54 Run and Shoot Football. Glenn (Tiger) Ellison. Parker Publishing Co. 1965. Clothbound.

    The high school offense of the future. Reasons for wide-open football, the "lonesome polecat" formation. Offensive plays and series, practicing, glossary.

20-55 Smorgasbord Offense for Winning High School Football. Joe Blount. Prentice-Hall. 1965. Clothbound.

    Blocking, line play, offensive plays, kicking.

20-56 Mesa's Power Attack. Roger Worsley. Parker Publishing Co. 1967. Clothbound.

    Football's winningest offense. The system employed by Mesa High School, Mesa, Arizona. Formations, personnel, line play. Rushing, passing, drills, off-season program.

20-57 Flip-Flop Offense in High School Football. Pete Dyer. Parker Publishing Co. 1967. Clothbound.

    Theory, advantages, personnel. Offense, defense, passing, quarterbacking.

20-58 Developing a Superior Football -- Control Attack. Vincent Dooley. Parker Publishing Co. 1969. Clothbound.

20-59 How to Coach Football's Running Trap Game. Jerry H. Laycock. Parker Publishing Co. 1972. Clothbound.

    Fundamentals, techniques, assignments, plays, drills.

High School—Plays

20-60 Sayger Illustrated Football Series. Sayger Sports Syndicate. Booklet. Purdue University. Noble Kizer. 1936. University of Minnesota. Bernie Bierman. 1936. University of Michigan. Harry Kipke. 1936. Ohio State University. Francis Schmidt. 1936. Los Angeles Rams. Bob Snyder. 1947. Booklet.

    Play diagrams and details by outstanding college and pro coaches for use by high school coaches.

20-61 Football Scout. Lew Elverson and C.D. Chesley. Schoolboy Sports. 1947. Paperbound.

    Diagrams and explanations of plays as used by various college and pro teams.

20-62   Football: Combatting the Changing Defenses. Harold H. Hoskins. 1953. Paperbound.
    Play diagrams for high school coaches.

20-63   99 Best High School Plays. David M. Nelson, ed. DuPont Co. 1966. Paperbound.
    Best plays submitted by high school coaches in a national contest as selected by a panel of college coaches.

20-64   Winning Play Sequences in Modern Football. Drew Tallman. Parker Publishing Co. 1971. Clothbound.
    Formations, series, variations.

High School—Formations

20-65   The Split-T in High School Football. Elvan George. Prentice-Hall. 1958. Clothbound.
    An analysis of the formation and an adaptation of new ideas.

20-66   The Complete Book of the I Formation. Roy Kramer. Parker Publishing Co. 1966. Clothbound.
    Features, numbering system, basic formation. Personnel, backfield and line play, passing, play series.

20-67   Wing-T Multiple Offense for High School Football. Harry Clarke. Prentice-Hall. 1962. Clothbound.
    Step-by-step outline. Passing and running.

20-68   The Pro-T Offense in High School Football. Harry Gamble. Prentice-Hall. 1962. Clothbound.
    Plays, assignments, drills.

20-69   Developing a Successful High School Pro Set Football Offense. Ed Henry. Parker Publishing Co. 1968. Clothbound.
    Fundamentals, techniques, running, passing, kicking, plays, drills, organization.

20-70   Winning Football with the Strategic Slot. Henry Harlow. Parker Publishing Co. 1969. Clothbound.
    Player requirements, fundamentals, position play, organization, formations, running, passing, kicking.

20-71   The New Doublewing Attack. Robert Tierney and Cliff Gray. Parker Publishing Co. 1971. Clothbound.

Boys and High School

	Advantages, blocking, plays, running, passing, line play.
20-72	Modern Belly T Football. A. Allen Black. Parker Publishing Co. 1972. Clothbound.
	Personnel, formations, techniques, plays, drills.

High School—Passing

20-73	How to Develop a Successful High School Passing Attack. Noel Reebenacker. Prentice-Hall. 1965. Clothbound.
	Selecting a passer, throwing positions, practice techniques. Passing offense, pass protection, the receiver. Game preparations, keeping records.
20-74	The Complete Football Passing Game. Don Read. Parker Publishing Co. 1970. Clothbound.
	Coaching the passer, coaching the receiver, formations.
20-75	Handbook for Coaching the Football Passing Attack. Homer Smith. Parker Publishing Co. 1970. Clothbound.
	Quarterbacking and receiving fundamentals, mechanics, strategies, practice, rules.

High School—Line Play

20-76	The Maze: A New Concept in Football Blocking. David Hurst. Parker Publishing Co. 1968. Clothbound.
	Foundation, attack, personnel, techniques.

High School—Defense

20-77	The Best of High School Defensive Football. David M. Nelson, ed. DuPont Co. 1967. Paperbound.
	Best defenses for specific plays, as submitted by high school coaches in a nationwide contest. Selected by a panel of college coaches.
20-78	Football's Master Defense Guide. Robert Troppmann. Parker Publishing Co. 1969. Paperbound.
	Formations, techniques, drills.
20-79	Directory of Football Defenses. Drew Tallman. Parker Publish-

ing Co. 1969. Clothbound.

Successful defenses and how to attack them.

20-80 The Radar Defense for Winning Football. Jules Yakapovich. Parker Publishing Co. 1970. Clothbound.

Development, naming and numbering individual moves, advantages, variations.

20-81 The Slanting Monster Defense in Football. Dale Foster. Parker Publishing Co. 1970. Clothbound.

Advantages, organization, line play, secondary play, drills, practice.

20-82 Winning High School Defensive Football. Leonard Jacobowitz. Parker Publishing Co. 1970. Clothbound.

Tackling, organization, pursuit, formations, strategy, personnel, scouting, training.

20-83 Developing a Flexible Defensive Secondary System. George Byers. Parker Publishing Co. 1971. Clothbound.

Organization, selection of personnel, alignments, coaching techniques.

20-84 Winning Football with the Blockbuster Defense. Paul S. Hatem. Parker Publishing Co. 1972. Clothbound.

Alignments, responsibilities, fundamentals, techniques, philosophy, organization.

High School—Kicking

20-85 How to Develop a Strong High School Kicking Game. Jim Leighty. Parker Publishing Co. 1967. Clothbound.

Selecting the kicker, development, correcting faults, conditioning. Protection, kicking off, punting.

High School—Officiating

20-86 Manual of Football Officiating Techniques. Pennsylvania Interscholastic Athletic Association. 1948. Booklet.

Boys

20-87 Football Plays for Boys. Ralph H. Barbour and LaMarr Sarra.

D. Appleton-Century. 1933, 1940, 1942. Clothbound.

Play diagrams from various formations.

20-88   Want to Be a Football Champion? B.W. (Bernie) Bierman. General Mills. 1945. Booklet.

Playing instructions for boys.

20-89   Terry and Bunky Play Football. Richard M. Fishel and Walter (Red) Smith. G.P. Putnam's Sons. 1945. Clothbound.

A fictionalized instructional for boys.

20-90   Football for the Beginner. George Staten. Educational Publishers. 1949. Clothbound.

General instructions, outline of the rules, spectating.

20-91   Midget Football Fundamentals. Reds Chapman. Pop Warner Conference. 1955. Booklet.

A handbook of Midget League Football. Generalship, training, playing instructions.

20-92   Football for Beginners. Thomas Walsh. 1951. Booklet.

Illustrated instructions for boys.

20-93   Football for Young Champions. Robert Antonacci and Jene Barr. Whittlesey House. 1958. Clothbound.

Development, general instructions.

20-94   Better Football for Boys. David Cooke. Dodd, Mead & Co. 1958. Clothbound.

General instructions. Formations, plays, terms.

20-95   The First Book of Football. Don Schiffer. Franklin Watts. 1958. Clothbound.

Instructions for boys.

20-96   How to Star in Football. Herman Masin. Scholastic Book Services. 1959. Paperbound. Four Winds Press. 1966. Clothbound.

Instructions for boys.

20-97   Football for Boys. Joe Kuharich and Marshall McClelland. Follett Publishing Co. 1960. Paperbound.

Offense, defense, the code of the gridiron.

20-98   Make the Team in Football. Clary Anderson. Grosset & Dunlap. 1961. Clothbound.

For schoolboys. Qualifications, fundamentals, quarterbacking. Line and backfield play, formations.

20-99   Punt, Pass and Kick. Ford Motor Co. 1961-to date. Booklet.

Illustrated promotional for the annual punt, pass and kick competition for boys sponsored by Ford. Playing tips.

20-100 The Young Sportsman's Guide to Football. Clary Anderson. Thomas Nelson & Sons. 1963. Clothbound.

General description, playing instructions.

20-100A Football. Clary Anderson. Thomas Nelson & Sons. 1966. Paperbound.

Reissue of 20-100.

20-101 Football for Boys. Tom Nugent. Ronald Press. 1962. Clothbound.

General instructions, fundamentals. By a college coach.

20-102 Football Skills. George H. Allen. Montgomery Ward. 1964, 1970, reissue. Booklet.

Illustrated playing instructions on running, passing, blocking, tackling, kicking, and training. By a pro head coach.

20-103 Frank Gifford's Football Guidebook. Frank Gifford. McGraw-Hill. 1965. Booklet.

Basic plays and techniques for boys playing Pop Warner League football.

20-104 Kick, Pass and Run. Leonard Kessler. Harper & Row. 1966. Clothbound.

A description of a game as played by a group of animals. Glossary.

20-105 Football Tips for Boys 18 and Under. Edsel B. Martz. 1971. Paperbound.

Offense, defense, strategy.

20-106 I Want to Be a Football Player. Eugene H. Baker. Childrens Press. 1972. Clothbound.

Playing instructions for young boys.

20-107 How to Play Better Football. C. Paul Jackson. Thomas Y. Crowell Co. 1972. Clothbound.

Boys and High School

Rules, equipment, basic techniques, glossary signals.

20-108   How to Play It Series. Don Smith. Stadia Sports Publishing. 1972. Booklet. Vol. 1. You Are the Quarterback. Vol. 2. You Are the Running Back. Pictorial Guides for young players. Play diagrams, photos of outstanding pro players.

21. Six-Man and Touch

21-1   Six-Man Football, a Handbook for Coaches and Players. Stephen Epler. University Publishing Co. 1935, 1936. Booklet.

      Evolution and purpose of the game. Rules, playing instructions, plays, review.

21-1A   Six-Man Football, the Official Handbook for Players, Coaches and Schoolmen. Stephen Epler. University Publishing Co. 1937, 1938. Booklet.

      Continuation of 21-1.

21-1B   The Official Six-Man Football Guide and Rulebook. Stephen Epler. University Publishing Co. 1939. Paperbound.

      Continuation of 21-1A.

21-2   Official Six-Man Football Guide and Rule Book. Stephen Epler. A.G. Spalding & Brothers. 1940. Paperbound.

      Development, rules, coaching. Outstanding teams, All-America selections.

21-2A   Spalding's Six-Man Official Guide and Rules Book. Stephen Epler. A.G. Spalding & Brothers. 1941. Paperbound.

      Continuation of 21-2.

21-2B   Six-Man Football Rules. H.V. Porter and Stephen Epler. National Federation of State High School Athletic Associations. 1942, 1944. Paperbound.

      Continuation of 21-2A. Including touch football rules.

21-2C   Official Six-Man Football Rules and Handbook. H.V. Porter and Stephen Epler. National Federation of State High School Athletic Associations. 1943, 1945-to date. Cover titles: Six Man Football Rules. 1943. Six-Man Football Rules and Handbook. 1945. Paperbound.

      Continuation of 21-2B.

21-3   Six-Man Football Manual. Alfred W. Larson. 1937-39. Paper-

Six-Man and Touch

bound.

> A description of the game. Fundamentals, playing instructions.

21-4 Practical Six-Man Football. Kurt Lenser. 1938, 1940. Clothbound.

> Organization, equipment, playing instructions, general discussion.

21-5 Six-Man Football, the Streamlined Game. Stephen Epler. Harper & Brothers. 1938. Clothbound.

> By the originator of the game. Principles for players, coaches and spectators. Growth and development of the game, philosophy, fundamentals, playing instructions.

21-6 Six-Man Football. J.D. Alexander. Edwards Brothers, Inc. 1938. Clothbound.

> Outline, fundamentals, instructions.

21-7 Deception in Six-Man Football. Herbert E. Phillips. Athletic Publishing Co. 1939. Clothbound.

> Rules, fundamentals, instructions.

21-8 How to Play Six-Man Football. Ralph Henry Barbour and LaMar Sarra. D. Appleton-Century. 1939. Clothbound.

> Instructions, drills, equipment, formations, plays.

21-9 Six-Man Football. Roy Duncan. A.S. Barnes & Co. 1940, 1954. Clothbound.

> General instructions.

21-10 Larson Simplified Scorebook for Six-Man Football. Alfred W. Larson. Walcott. 1937. Booklet. Ind. Publishing Co. 1937. Booklet.

21-11 National Survey of High School Six-Man Football Accidents. S. Voinoff. 1941. Booklet.

21-12 Six-Man Football Magazine. C.J. O'Connor, ed. 1946-58. Magazine.

> Two editions published in 1947. Photos, articles, records.

21-13 Spalding's Official Rules of Beeball. Clarence W. Beeman. A.G. Spalding & Brothers. 1929. Paperbound.

> A nine-man touch game for schoolyards.

Six-Man and Touch

21-14   Six-Man Two-Hand Touch Football Rules for Elementary Schools. Paul D. Kates. 1939. Paperbound.

         A description of the game, playing instructions.

21-15   Touch Football. John Grombach. A.S. Barnes & Co. 1942, 1958. Clothbound.

         Rules, playing instructions, plays.

21-16   Touch Football. Dean Stanbury and Frank DeSantis. Sterling Publishing Co. 1961. Clothbound.

         An explanation of the game. Fundamentals, tactics. Glossary, rules.

21-17   How To Succeed at Touch Football. Frederick Birmingham. Macmillan Co. 1962. Clothbound and Paperbound.

         A humorous commentary incorporating the current social and political scene.

21-18   The Violent World of Touch Football. James Wagenwoord. Doubleday & Co. 1968. Paperbound.

         A humorous recollection of the author's playing days.

21-19   Official Touch Football Play and Rule Book. National Football League Properties. Varsity House, Inc. 1969. Booklet.

         Offense, defense, plays, rules.

21-20   Flag Football. Royal Canadian Air Force. Queen's Printer. 1960. Paperbound.

         Playing, coaching, officiating.

22. Rule Books

22-1 The Book of Rules of the Game of Football. Charles W. Alcock. Peck & Snyder. 1871. Cover title: The Playing Rules of Football. Booklet.

    The first book of Rugby rules, as adopted and played by English Football Associations, expressly for the benefit of American colleges. Playing instructions, definitions of terms.

22-2 The Rugby Game. c 1875-1880. Booklet.

    Printed by different firms each year: Tuttle, Ford, others. Rules of the Rugby Union game.

22-3 Official Rule Books.

    The first of these was 2-1: 1876-82.
    Followed by 2-2: 1883-89.

22-3A Official Football Rules. A.G. Spalding & Brothers. 1908-12. Booklet.

    The official rules were published in the Spalding Football Guide beginning in 1885. They were also published separately from 1908-12, and from 1919-40 they were printed in the guide in a detachable booklet.

22-3B Official National Collegiate Athletic Association Football Rules. N.C.A.A. 1941-52. A.S. Barnes & Co. 1941-49. N.C.A.A. 1950-51. Booklet.

    Rules and interpretations for coaches and officials.

22-3C Official National Collegiate Athletic Association Football Handbook. N.C.A.A. 1952-to date. Booklet.

    Continuation of 22-3B.

22-4 The Rules of Football, As Played by the American College Teams. Edward Plummer. New York Sportsman Print. 1879. Booklet.

    With an account of the 1879 Harvard-Princeton game.

Rule Books

22-5   <u>Rules of American Football.</u> Henry Chadwick. A.G. Spalding & Brothers. 1879. Paperbound.

           The first Spalding football publication.

22-6   <u>Rugby Football Rules.</u> A.G. Spalding & Brothers. 1880. Paperbound.

22-7   <u>The Revised and Latest Rules of Football.</u> Peck & Snyder. 1879. Paperbound.

           Rugby Union and Association rules. Definitions of terms.

22-8   <u>American Intercollegiate Football Rules and Constitution.</u> Peck & Snyder. 1890. Booklet.

           Rules and constitution of the American Intercollegiate Association.

22-9   <u>Football Rules.</u> Walter Camp. Wright & Ditson. 1880. Booklet.

           With hints for practice.

22-10   <u>Referee's Book on Football Rules.</u> Walter Camp. Wright & Ditson. 1883. Booklet.

           Rule interpretations, duties of the referee. Incorporated into the official rule book, 1884-89.

22-11   <u>Football Rules and Referee's Book.</u> J.R. Judd. Wright & Ditson. 1888. Booklet.

           A copy of the 1888 edition of 2-2.

22-12   <u>Rules of the Rugby Game of Football.</u> Lester Dole & Co. 1882. Booklet.

           1881 American Intercollegiate Association rules with amendments for the 1882 season.

22-13   <u>Spalding's Code of Football Rules for 1909.</u> Charles W. Short, Jr. A.G. Spalding & Brothers. 1909. Paperbound.

           Groupings of rules under general headings.

22-13A   <u>Digest of Football Rules for 1910.</u> Charles W. Short, Jr. A.G. Spalding & Brothers. 1910. Paperbound.

           Continuation of 22-13.

22-13B   <u>Digest of Football Rules for 1911.</u> Charles W. Short, Jr. A.G. Spalding & Brothers. 1911. Paperbound.

           Continuation of 22-13A.

22-14   <u>Football Rules.</u> Albert M. Barron. A.J. Reach & Co. 1926,

1926, revised. Booklet.

>A complete interpretation of the 1926 official rules.

22-15 The American Football Quizzer. William J. Sheeley. Bruce Publishing Co. 1926, 1927. Paperbound. Central Publishing Co. 1928, 1929. Paperbound.

>Questions and answers on the rules, with approved rulings and decisions. The football code with illustrative cases. For players, coaches and officials.

22-15A The Football Quizzer. William J. Sheeley. A.S. Barnes & Co. 1930-31. Paperbound.

>Continuation of 22-15.

22-16 Changes in the Football Rules, 1928. F.A. Lambert. Ohio Association of Football Officials. 1928. Paperbound.

22-17 How to Study the Football Rules. Eastern Association for Selection of Football Officials. 1929. Booklet.

>A digest of rules.

22-18 Football Problems. Samuel S. Scott. Campbell Co. 1932. Clothbound.

>Two hundred questions and answers based on the 1932 official NCAA rules.

22-19 A Study of the Football Rules, 1932. F.A. Lambert. Bexley Publishing Co. 1932. Paperbound.

>Rule interpretations.

22-20 Illustrated Football Rules Book. H.E. (Suz) Sayger. Sayger Sports Syndicate. c 1934. Booklet.

>Rule changes, knotty problems.

22-21 Official Rules of Football and Soccer Ball. Thomas E. Wilson & Co. 1939. Booklet.

>Rules with special notes and examples.

22-22 A Chronology of Changes in Collegiate Football Rules. Lawrence J. Green. State University of Iowa. University Microfilms. 1955. Paperbound.

>Rules changes from 1873-1954. College thesis.

22-23 Official National Collegiate Athletic Association Football Rules: Interpretations. David Nelson, ed. N.C.A.A. 1962-to date. Booklet.

>Rule interpretations and elaborations.

Rule Books

22-23A   Official Read-Easy Football Rules. Bert McGrane, ed. National Collegiate Athletic Association. 1969-to date. Booklet.

        Continuation of 22-23

22-24   Official Football Statisticians' Manual. National Collegiate Athletic Association. 1955-to date. Booklet.

        Basic interpretations. Official rules covering football statistics.

22-25   Football Rules in Pictures. Don Schiffer and Lud Duroska. Grosset & Dunlap. 1964, 1969. Magazine.

        Offense and defense, fouls, signals, definitions.

22-26   Collegiate Football Rules. John Waldorf and Cliff Harper, eds. Collegiate Commissioners Association. 1966-to date. Booklet.

        For coaches, players, and officials. Illustrated.

22-27   Booing Is a "No No". Sheldon Wilson. Craft-Tex. 1970. Clothbound.

        Rule explanations and interpretations.

Professional Titles

22P-1   National Football League Revised Rules. National Football Leagues. 1933, 1934. Booklet.

        The first official pro publication. Intercollegiate rules with amendments.

22P-2   Official Football Rules of the National Football League. 1939-44. A.G. Spalding & Brothers. 1939-40. A.S. Barnes & Co. 1941. National Football League. 1942-44. Hugh L. Ray. 1941-44. Paperbound.

        Intercollegiate rules with amendments. The rules were incorporated in the Official National Football League Guide from 1935-38.

22P-3   Official Rules for Professional Football. National Football League. 1945-to date. Hugh L. Ray. 1945-52. C. Rebele. 1953-55. S.M. Wilson. 1956-62. Joe Kuharich. 1963-65. Mark Duncan. 1966-to date. Paperbound.

        Separate codifications for pro football.

22P-4   The National Football League Digest of Rules. National Football League. 1966-to date. Paperbound.

        For players and the press. Rule summaries and explanations.

23. Officiating

23-1 <u>Eastern Association of Intercollegiate Football Officials, By-Laws.</u> Eastern Association of Intercollegiate Football Officials. 1923-to date. Booklet.

23-2 <u>Eastern Association of Intercollegiate Football Officials, Annual Report.</u> Eastern Association of Intercollegiate Football Officials. 1926-to date. Booklet.

23-3 <u>Manual of Football Officiating.</u> A.R. Hutchens. Southern Football Officials Association. 1935. Booklet.

> General principals, reminders. Principal duties and responsibilities of each official. Code of ethics, signals.

23-4 <u>Manual of Football Officiating.</u> A.R. Hutchens. Eastern Intercollegiate Football Association. 1938. Booklet.

> Similar to 23-3.

23-5 <u>Manual of Football Officiating.</u> A.R. Hutchens and Asa Bushnell. Eastern Intercollegiate Football Association. Harbas Co. 1939. Booklet.

> Combined features of 23-3 and 23-4.

23-6 <u>Football Officiating Procedures.</u> Eastern Intercollegiate Football Association. 1959-to date. Booklet.

23-7 <u>New Jersey Football Officials Association Official Handbook.</u> New Jersey Football Officials Association. 1931, 1932. Booklet.

> Playing rules, the relationship between the official and the game. Reminders, equipment, rules for referees, linemen and umpires.

23-8 <u>Manual of Football Officiating.</u> Western Conference. 1949. Booklet.

23-9 <u>Football Officiating and Interpretation of the Rules.</u> F.A. Lambert. R.G. Adams & Co. 1926. Clothbound.

Officiating

Qualifications, attitudes, mechanics, equipment. Photos of game action illustrating various formations and situations.

23-10   How to Officiate Football. F.A. Lambert. Bexley Publishing Co. 1931, 1932. Booklet.

23-11   Questions and Answers on the Football Rules. Earl C. Krieger. Lawhead Press. 1931, 1934-50. Paperbound.

         Rule interpretations, officiating procedures, hints for field captains and players. Play diagrams, correcting past errors.

23-11A   Two Hundred Practical Questions and Answers on the 1932 Football Rules. Earl C. Krieger. Lawhead Press. 1932. Paperbound.

         Continuation of 23-11..

23-11B   Two Hundred and Fifty Practical Questions and Answers on the Football Rules. Earl C. Krieger. Lawhead Press. 1933. Paperbound.

         Continuation of 23-11A.

23-12   Football Officiating. Earl C. Krieger. Lawhead Press. 1935, 1937, 1939, 1941, 1943, 1946-49. Paperbound.

         General discussion and advice for each phase and situation.

23-13   The Technique of Football Officiating. 1940. Booklet.

         Instructions by leading officials.

23-14   Manual of Football Officiating. National Association of Football Commissioners. 1945, 1948. Booklet.

         General principles, important reminders, assignments, and duties. Explanations of various game situations.

23-15   Sammy Blows His Whistle. George E. Kelly. Progress Press. 1947. Clothbound.

         The biography of Samuel A. Weiss, judge and football official.

23-16   Fanfare on a Tin Whistle. J. Burghalter. 1958. Clothbound.

         Reminiscences of a famous Western Conference official. Reprint of a 1958 newspaper series of five articles entitled "Inside Football."

Officiating

Professional Titles

23P-1   <u>Official's Manual</u>. National Football League. 1944-to date. Booklet.

   General comments on officiating, instructions, rule interpretations.

24. Post-Season Games

24-1   Bowl Game Press Guides. c. 1939-to date. Booklets. Paperbound. Magazines.

             Issued by bowl committees and by participating colleges. Season review, rosters, records, photos.

24-2   Georgia's Wallace Butts: "Bowlmaster." Ed Thilenius. 1951. Booklet.

             Reviews, statistics of the seven bowl games played by Butts' University of Georgia teams. Photos, other data.

24-3   Bowl-Manac. James Edson. Johnson Printing Co. 1956. Paperbound.

             Scores, lineups, and summaries of every Rose, Sugar, Orange, Cotton and Gator Bowl game.

24-4   Big Bowl Football. Fred Russell and George Leonard. Ronald Press. 1963. Clothbound.

             Lineups, photos, statistics, accounts of all Rose, Orange, Sugar, Cotton, and Gator Bowl games.

24-5   Bowl Game Thrills. Joseph Bell. Julian Messner, Inc. 1963. Clothbound.

             Twelve outstanding games since 1922. Lineups, statistics, season records of participating teams.

24-6   College Division Regional Football Championship Handbook. National Collegiate Athletic Association. 1965. Booklet.

             Policies and procedures governing the administration and conduct of post-season bowls for the college division championships.

24-7   Bowl Record Guide. Ray Franks Publications. 1969. Booklet.

             All-time scores of major and minor bowl games.

24-8   Cambridge to Pasadena and Return. Taylor Press. 1920. Booklet.

Post-Season Games

> A day-by-day account of Harvard's west coast trip to play Oregon in the 1920 Rose Bowl, with a report of the game.

24-9   A Rose Bowl Tour. Curley Grieve. Los Angeles Examiner. 1940. Paperbound.

> A preview of the 1941 game. Photos, statistics, rosters.

24-10   The Rose Bowl Trip. University of Nebraska. 1941. Paperbound.

> Team roster, photos, itinerary of the trip to Pasadena for the 1941 Rose Bowl game.

24-11   Tournament of Roses Football Game Record. Helms Athletic Foundation. 1943. Paperbound.

> Game summaries, records.

24-12   The Rose Bowl. Maxwell Stiles. Sportsmaster Publications. 1946. Paperbound.

> Game accounts, lineups, statistics, play-by-play charts. Season scores of participating teams.

24-13   Rose Bowl Cartoon History. Souvenir Publication Press. 1947, 1948. John Cross and Jerry Corcoran. 1947. John Olds. 1948. Booklet.

> Scores, records, reviews, cartoons.

24-14   The Rose Bowl Game. Rube Samuelson. Doubleday & Co. 1951. Clothbound.

> Narrative account of each game. Lineups, statistics, season's records.

24-15   The Rose Bowl Game. Rube Samuelson. Packard Motor Car Co. 1951. Booklet.

> Records, review.

24-16   Does the Big Ten Always Win? Fred Russell. Packard Motor Car Co. 1954. Booklet.

> A review of the Rose Bowl games involving the Big Ten and Pacific Coast Conferences.

24-17   The Tournament of Roses. Joe Henderson and Maxwell Stiles. Brooke House. 1971. Clothbound.

> A yearly review of the festival and parade held in conjunction with the Rose Bowl game, and accounts of the games.

Post-Season Games

24-18   The Story of the Orange Bowl. Orange Bowl Committee. 1940. Booklet.

> A promotional booklet publicizing the Orange Bowl Festival and Game. A brief review of the games since 1933.

24-19   The Orange Bowl Story. Robert Daly. Orange Bowl Committee. 1958. Clothbound.

> An account of each game. Statistics, records, photos.

24-20   The New Orleans Sugar Bowl Football Classic. Fred Digby. New Orleans Mid-Winter Sports Association. 1946-to date. Booklet.

> Title later changed to: The Sugar Bowl. Origin, history, all-time records. Game accounts, lineups, photos.

24-21   The Navy in High Cotton. Naval Reserve Public Relations Co. 1958. Paperbound.

> An account of the 1958 Naval Academy-Texas University Cotton Bowl Game. Reprints of newspaper articles.

24-22   The Cotton Bowl. Lee Cruse. Debka Publications. 1963, 1964. Cover title: About the Cotton Bowl. Paperbound.

> Scores, statistics, lineups, and accounts of each game. Team and player records, photos.

24-23   Football's Finest Hour. Maxwell Stiles. Nashunal Publishing Co. 1950. Clothbound.

> The story of the Shrine East-West game. Background account and lineups of each game, team photos. Records, all-time teams, the Shrine Hall of Fame.

24-24   A Rebel in Sports. Champ Pickens. A.S. Barnes & Co. 1956. Clothbound.

> The autobiography of the founder of the Blue-Gray game. Rosters and scores of all games since 1939.

Professional Titles

24P-1   National Football League World Championship Game. National Football League. 1962-65. Booklet.

> Press guide. Rosters, statistics, records, season reviews, other data.

Post-Season Games

24P-1A *National Football League Championship Game.* National Football League. 1966–to date. Booklet.

    Continuation of 24P-1.

24P-2 *National Football League Playoff Bowl.* National Football League. 1963–to date. Booklet.

    Press guide. Rosters, statistics, records, season reviews, other data.

24P-3 *American Football League Championship Game.* American Football League. 1966–to date. Booklet.

    Press guide. Rosters, statistics, records, season reviews, other data.

24P-4 *Super Bowl Press Guides.* National Football League. 1967 to date. American Football League. 1967-69. Booklet.

    Various titles, rosters, statistics, records, season reviews, other data.

24P-5 *Pro Bowl Press Book.* Los Angeles Metropolitan Newspapers. 1951–to date. Newspaper.

    Player records and statistics.

24P-6 *Wheaties Pro Bowl Football Player Stamp Album and Fact Book.* General Mills. 1965. Booklet.

    National Football League and Pro Bowl history and records. Color stamps.

24P-7 *Here's Why It Was the Best Football Game Ever.* Tex Maule. Helicon Press. 1959. Booklet.

    An account of the 1958 Baltimore-New York pro championship game.

24P-8 *Playoff.* Howard Liss. Delacorte Press. 1966. Clothbound. Dell Publishing Co. 1969, reissue. Paperbound.

    Descriptions of the ten greatest National Football League championship games. Game statistics, photos.

24P-9 *Championship.* Jerry Izenberg. Four Winds Press. 1966, 1968, 1970. Clothbound. Scholastic Book Services. 1966, reissue. 1968, reissue, 1971. Paperbound.

    An account of each National Football League championship game since 1933. Game statistics, records, photos.

24P-10 *Super Bowl.* National Football League Properties. 1970. Booklet.

Post-Season Games

      A review of the first four games. Statistics, photos.

24P-11   Cord Sportfacts Super Bowl Special Report. Cord Communications. 1971. Magazine.

      Team previews, super bowl review, photos.

24P-12   Super Bowl! John Devaney. Random House. 1971. Punt, Pass and Kick Library. Clothbound.

      Descriptions of the first five games.

24P-13   Super Bowl. Martin Ralbovsky. Hawthorn Books. 1971. Clothbound. 1972. Paperbound.

      Rosters, statistics, news dispatches, photos covering each game.

24P-14   The Fifth Anniversary of the Super Bowl. Don Smith and Art Poretz. Stadia Sports Publishing. 1971. Booklet.

      Statistics and review of each game.

24P-15   Super Bowl. Don Smith. Stadia Sports Publishing. 1972. Paperbound.

      Expanded edition of 24P-14.

24P-16   Super Bowl: Pro Football's Greatest Games and Stars. Steve Gelman. Scholastic Book Services. 1972. Paperbound.

      Descriptions of the first six games.

25. Conference and Sectional

Sectional

25-1 <u>Constitution of the Pennsylvania Intercollegiate Football Association.</u> Pennsylvania Intercollegiate Football Association. 1891. Booklet.

> Member schools: Bucknell, Dickinson, Franklin and Marshall, Haverford, Penn State, Swarthmore.

25-2 <u>Indiana Football.</u> Andrew Stott. Carlon and Hollenbeck Printers. 1896. Clothbound.

> History and development of football at the University of Indiana and Purdue University. 1895 player sketches, scores and reviews of Purdue, Indiana, Wabash, De Pauw, Butler, and Notre Dame. Explanation of the game, the play of each position. Club and high school coverage.

25-3 <u>Fans Handbook.</u> H.E. Vandiver and L.R. McCoy. Coaches Directory Association. 1932. Paperbound.

> Coverage of Indiana college and high school football. Schedules, reviews, directories. Records, photos.

25-4 <u>Watertown Athletic Association.</u> Harry Goodwin. Hungerford-Holbrook Co. 1900. Booklet.

> A yearly chronicle of an amateur team organized in Watertown, New York, in 1892 to play against area high school and college teams. Game lineups, photos.

25-5 <u>Virginia College Football Directory.</u> R.D. Wright. 1934. Magazine.

> Rosters, reviews, scores, schedules of all Virginia college teams.

25-6 <u>Football in Virginia.</u> J. Malcolm Pace, III, ed. Sports Media, Inc. 1971. Magazine.

Conference and Sectional

High school and college team previews, photos.

25-7   Fifty-Seven Years on Pittsburgh Gridirons. Ray Byrne. 1947. Booklet.

         Records of the University of Pittsburgh, Carnegie Tech. Duquesne University and the Pittsburgh Steelers.

25-8   Panhandle Pigskin Preview. Robert Franks. Pigskin Publications. 1953. Paperbound.

         Coverage of college and high school football in the Texas Panhandle. Records, schedules, forecasts.

25-9   Texas Football. Dave Campbell. Southwest Sports Publications. 1960-to date. Magazine.

         Previews of all Texas high school and college teams, as well as those in the Southwest Conference and professional leagues. Photos, records.

25-10   East Texas Football. 1968, 1969. Magazine.

         High school and college coverage.

25-11   Arkansas Football. Dave Campbell, ed. Southwest Sports Publications. 1963-to date. Magazine.

         Reviews and previews of Arkansas University, Southwest and Arkansas Intercollegiate Conferences and high school teams. Photos.

25-12   College Football in Iowa. Robert Rutland. State Historical Society of Iowa. 1953. Paperbound. The Palimpsest: Vol. 34, no. 9.

         Early history and development of football in Iowa. Iowa college rivalries.

25-13   The Iowa Conference Story. J.E. Turnbull. 1961. Paperbound.

         Coverage of all sports. Great coaches, star players, yearly standings.

25-14   Ohio Collegiate Football. Pepper Wilson. 1953. Booklet.

         Individual and team records for all Ohio college teams.

25-15   Buckeye Football. Pat Riley. Buckeye Football, Inc. 1967. Magazine.

         Reviews and previews of all Ohio college and high school teams. Photos.

25-16   All-South Carolina Football Annual. B. Hammett and H. Jacobs. Jacobs Press. 1954, 1955. Magazine.

Conference and Sectional

Coverage of high-school and college teams.

25-17 **Official All-North Carolina Football Annual.** Curtis Cates. Charles Cates and Perrin Anderson. 1956. Magazine.

    College and high school forecasts and schedules.

25-18 **Hail, West Virginians.** Kent Kessler. Park Press. 1959. Paperbound.

    Yearly narrative summaries of football at all West Virginia colleges. Scores, coaches, famous events, letterman, undefeated teams, leading scorers, West Virginians in pro football. Basketball also covered.

25-19 **Southern California Football.** Euclid Sports. 1958. Magazine.

    Coverage of college, junior college, high school and pro football.

25-20 **Southern California Grid Index.** Will Kern. 1959. Magazine.

    Records and data on high school and college football.

25-21 **California Quarterback.** Richard W. Juline. Llewellyn Publications. 1960. Paperbound.

    Scores, records, schedules, facts on all California college and pro teams.

25-22 **Football in Illinois.** Illinois State Historical Society. November 1961. Booklet. **Illinois History.** Vol. 15, no. 2.

    Articles on the history of college and pro football in Illinois. Photos.

25-23 **Alabama Football.** S-W Publishers. 1965. Magazine.

    College and high school team reviews and previews.

25-24 **The Blue Book: Who's Who in Michigan Football.** John Heston. 1966. Paperbound.

    All-time ratings of Michigan high school and college players and teams.

25-25 **Michigan Football.** Sportspress. 1968-to date. Magazine.

    Rosters, schedules, scores covering high school, college, and pro football. Feature articles.

25-26 **Football Schedules.** The Milwaukee Journal. 1966. Booklet.

    Wisconsin high school, college and pro schedules.

25-27 **Pelican State Pigskin Preview.** Dudley Downing, ed. Wil-do Enterprises. 1966. Magazine.

Conference and Sectional

A review of high school, college, and pro football in Louisiana.

25-28 Minnesota Football. Gerald Hoffman, ed. Sports Publications, Inc. 1967. Magazine.

Articles on a variety of topics covering high school, college and pro football in Minnesota.

25-29 Football Oklahoma. Oklahoma Sports Publishers. 1967. Magazine.

College and high school team previews and rosters.

25-30 Miami Football. Ken Small. Parker Printing. 1967-69. Magazine.

Team previews, rosters, scores, schedules, statistics covering the University of Miami, Miami Dolphins, and high schools in Dade County, Florida.

25-31 History of Southern Football, 1890-1928. Fuzzy Woodruff. Walter W. Brown. 1928. Clothbound.

Three volumes: Vol. 1. 1890-1915. Vol. 2. 1915-1923. Vol. 3. 1923-1928. A year-by-year narrative. Lineups and accounts of important games.

25-32 All-South Football Annual. B. Hammett. Jacobs Press. 1953, 1954. Magazine.

A review of the Atlantic Coast, Southern and North Carolina State Conferences. Coverage of North Carolina high school teams.

25-33 The Impact of Southern Football. Zipp Newman. Moros-Bell. 1969. Clothbound.

A review and history of football in the South. Great coaches and teams, bowl games, historical sketches of football at various colleges.

25-34 Football '71. William B. Tanner. Hike Publications. 1971. Magazine.

College and pro team previews, with emphasis on Southern teams.

25-35 Western Football Roundup. Tidewater Oil. 1947. Booklet.

Team reviews, forecasts.

Conference and Sectional

Conference

25-36 **Complete Football Records of the Western Conference.** Thaddeus A. Kucharski. 1924. Cover title: **Big Ten Football Records.** Booklet.

   Yearly scores for each team.

25-37 **The Big Nine.** Howard Roberts. G.P. Putnam's Sons. 1948. Clothbound.

   A narrative history of the Western Conference. Yearly standings since 1896.

25-38 **Big Ten Football Digest.** Marathon Oil Co. 1965. Booklet.

   Records, reviews covering Western Conference teams.

25-39 **The Big Ten.** Kenneth L. Wilson and Jerry Brondfield. Prentice-Hall. 1967. Clothbound.

   A yearly summary of games in all sports. Player sketches, photos, records, chronology.

25-40 **Pacific Coast Intercollegiate Football.** Pacific Gravure Co. 1927. Magazine.

   Team reviews, rosters, photos.

25-41 **Who's Who in Football on the Pacific Coast.** Harold P. Muller, Francis Tappaan and George Wilson. Brown, Davis & Co. 1931. Booklet.

   Compiled by former All-Americans. Rosters, player sketches, scores.

25-42 **Pacific Coast Conference Football Record.** Helms Athletic Foundation. Pacific Coast Intercollegiate Athletic Conference. 1939. Booklet.

   Yearly standings, team records, coaching records. Player records, history of the conference.

25-43 **Pacific Coast Conference Football Record Book.** Helms Athletic Foundation. 1959. Paperbound.

   A detailed compilation of team, player, and coaching records from 1916-59. Scores, All-America teams, coaches.

25-44 **Pacific Eight Football News Facts.** Walter T. Ride, Jr. 1967. Magazine.

   Player and team records. Rosters, photos.

Conference and Sectional

25-45   Touchdown. E.W. Peek & Co. 1940. Booklet.

         Schedules, records, facts covering the Southwest Conference.

25-46   Southwest Football Dope Book. Zeke Handler. 1946-49. Booklet.

         Schedules, records, facts covering the Southwest Conference.

25-47   The Touchdown of 1947. Jim Abel. Wallace Engraving Co. 1948. Cover title: Touchdown 1947. Clothbound.

         Complete account of football in the Southwest Conference in 1947. Reprints of newspaper articles, photos.

25-48   Sizzling Southwest Football for 60 Years. J.W. Williams. 1956. Paperbound.

         Outstanding games, yearly summaries, scores, great teams, photos.

25-49   The Power and the Glory. Harold Ratliff. Texas Tech Press. 1957. Clothbound.

         The history of football in the Southwest Conference. A narrative year-by-year account.

25-50   Football Texas Style. Kern Tips. Doubleday & Co. 1964. Clothbound.

         An informal pictorial history of football in the Southwest Conference.

25-51   Football: The Greatest Moments in the Southwest Conference. Will Grimsley. Little, Brown & Co. 1968. Clothbound.

         Accounts of outstanding games. Photos.

25-52   Southwest Conference Football. Ralph Wall and Ray Herndon. Football History, Inc. 1968-to date. Clothbound.

         Game resumes covering the previous season. Statistics, scores, photos.

25-53   The Big Eight. Hank Keitz, ed. Football Enterprises, Inc. 1972. Magazine.

         Coverage of football in the Big Eight Conference. Team reviews and previews, player sketches, photos. Two supplements.

25-53A   Inside the Big Eight.

25-53B   The Big Eight Supplement.

Conference and Sectional

25-54   Peek's Football Fact Book. E.W. Peek & Co. 1942. Booklet.
Schedules, records, facts covering the Southwestern Conference.

Major Conference Official Record Books

Scores, rosters, records, all-time data, other facts. Published by the individual conferences.

25-55   *Official Western Conference Records Book of Big Nine Sports. 1946, 1948, 1949. Title page: The Western Conference Records Book. Paperbound.

25-55A   *Big Ten Records Books. 1950-to date. Title page: The Western Conference Records Book. 1950-61. Paperbound.

25-56   Big Ten Football Rosters Manual. 1949-50. Booklet.

25-57   Pacific Coast Conference Football. 1947-50. Booklet.

25-57A   Pacific Coast Conference Football Press Book. 1951-59. Booklet.

25-57B   *Big Five AAWU Fall Sports Information. 1960, 1961. Booklet.

25-57C   *AAWU Fall Sports Information. 1962, 1963. Booklet.

25-57D   *Athletic Association of Western Universities Fall Sports Information. 1964-66. Booklet.

25-57E   *Pacific Eight Fall Sports Information. 1967-to date. Booklet.

25-58   *Pacific Coast Conference Records Book. 1949-59. Paperbound.

25-59   Southeastern Conference Press and Radio Dope Book. 1948. Paperbound.

25-59A   Southeastern Conference Football Data. 1949-to date. Paperbound.

25-60   Southeastern Conference Football Statistics. 1959-to date. Booklet.

25-61   Missouri Valley Intercollegiate Athletic Association Big Seven Football Roster Manual. 1949-56. Booklet.

25-61A   Missouri Valley Intercollegiate Athletic Association Big Eight Football Roster Manual. 1957-61. Booklet.

* Other Sports Covered.

Conference and Sectional

25-61B	Big Eight Conference Football Record Book. 1962-65. Paperbound.	

                    Only ten printed in 1963.

25-61C   Big Eight Conference Football Year Book. 1966-to date. Paperbound.

25-62   The Official Southwest Athletic Conference Football Roster Book. 1950. Booklet.

25-62A   The Official Southwest Athletic Conference Football Roster-Records Book. 1951-61. Paperbound.

25-62B   The Official Southwest Athletic Conference Football Information Book. 1962. Paperbound.

25-62C   Southwest Conference Football Guide. 1963-to date. Paperbound.

25-63   *Southern Conference Fall Brochure. 1952-63. Cover title: Southern Conference Fall Sports Press Data. Booklet.

25-63A   *Southern Conference Fall Press Data. 1964-to date. Paperbound.

25-64   Eastern Intercollegiate Football Association Press and Radio Guide. 1952. Paperbound.

25-64A   Eastern Intercollegiate Football Association Press, Radio and TV Guide. 1953-55. Paperbound.

25-64B   Eastern College Athletic Conference Press, Radio and TV Football Guide. 1956-to date. Paperbound.

25-65   Atlantic Coast Conference Football Yearbook. 1954-to date. Paperbound.

                    Title page varies.

25-66   Ivy League Press, Radio and TV Football Guide. 1954-55. Booklet.

25-66A   Ivy League Football. 1956-to date. Paperbound.

25-67   *Missouri Valley Conference Handbook. 1956. Paperbound.

25-67A   *Missouri Valley Conference All-Sports Handbook. 1957-64. Paperbound.

25-67B   *Missouri Valley Conference Records Book. 1965-to date. Paperbound.

25-68   Border Conference Football Press Book. 1958-62. Booklet.

Conference and Sectional

25-69 *Skyline Football. Mountain States Athletic Conference. 1958-62. Paperbound.

25-70 *Western Athletic Conference Yearbook. 1963-to date. Paperbound.

25-71 Mid-American Conference Football. 1963-to date. Paperbound.

Professional Titles

25P-1 Pacific Coast Football League Constitution and By-Laws. Pacific Coast Football League. 1946. Booklet.

> Minor League.

25P-2 American Football League Roster Guide. Chemstrand Corp. Sports Illustrated. 1966. Booklet.

> Team rosters.

25P-3 Continental Football League Press, Radio and TV Guide. Continental Football League. 1966-69. Booklet.

> Minor league. Records, statistics, schedules, history, rules, scores.

25P-4 Atlantic Coast Football League Directory and Schedule. Atlantic Coast Football League. 1966-to date. Booklet.

> Minor league history, rules, statistics, records, rosters, schedules, scores.

26. Dictionaries and Spectators' Guides

26-1   Simple Explanations of the Great Game of Football with Diagrams for, Spectators. Amos Alonzo Stagg and Henry Williams. Case, Lockwood and Brainard Co. 1893. Clothbound.

         The "Explanations" were reprinted from A Scientific and Practical Treatise on American Football for Schools and Colleges: play diagrams, discussion of team play.

26-2   Football for Player and Spectator. Fielding H. Yost. University Publishing Co. 1905. Clothbound.

         Origin and development, prestige and popularity of the game, benefits to players. The spectator's viewpoint, football as played in different parts of the country. The play of each position, development of the team, signals, team play. Training, diagrams, generalship, rules. Yost's philosophy.

26-3   Football for the Spectator. Walter Camp. R.G. Badger. 1911. Clothbound.

         The general plan of play. Penalties, duties of officials.

26-4   Football for Public and Player. Herbert Reed. Frederick A. Stokes. 1913. Clothbound.

         Football and warfare, captain-coach relationships, building a team. Offensive and defensive systems, training, team play. Zones of play, coaching, ethics. How to watch a game, famous stars.

26-5   Football Made Plain to the Spectator. P.P. Douglas and Elmer Burrell. 1917. Booklet.

         Positions, officials, fundamentals of the game.

26-6   Football and How to Watch It. Percy Haughton. Marshall Jones Co. 1922. Clothbound. Little, Brown & Co. 1924, reissue. Clothbound.

         Offense, defense, preseason preparation.

Dictionaries and Spectators' Guides

26-7   How to Watch and Understand Football. Percy Haughton. Marshall Jones Co. 1922. Booklet.

Chapter 1 of 26-6, issued as a promotional publication.

26-8   How to Enjoy Football. John Wilce and L.W. St. John. Ohio State University Athletic Board. 1923. Booklet.

Fundamentals, the kickoff, offense, and defense. The kicking game, generalship, touchbacks, and safeties. Officials and penalties, terms.

26-9   The ABC's of Football. Vic H. Householder and C.L. Michael. 1927. Booklet.

Explanations for the fan. Playing positions, officiating, terms. Details of game action.

26-10   Football for the Spectator. H.S. Crocker Co. 1928. Booklet.

An explanation of the game. Plays, formations, glossary.

26-11   Football for the Fan. Howard H. Jones and Alfred F. Wesson. Times-Mirror Press. 1929. Clothbound.

A general discussion of the game. The line, the backfield, offense, defense, anticipating the play. Questions and answers, including answers to questions asked by movie stars.

26-12   Understand Football. Grantland Rice and John Heisman. Mac-Hill Publishing Co. 1929. Paperbound. Isaac Goldman Co. 1932, reissue. Paperbound. General Foods. 1932, reissue. Paperbound.

Offense, defense, generalship. Watching a game, plays and play situations. Glossary, penalties, outstanding records.

26-13   How to Watch a Football Game. M.P. Jeffrey and M.E. Reker. Richfield Oil Co. 1931. Booklet.

Explanations, schedules, glossary, all-time records.

26-14   How to Watch Football. Sol Metzger. Fawcett Publishing Co. 1931. Magazine.

Definitions, penalties, explanations of various phases of the game. Schedules, rules, scoring.

26-15   Lou Little's Football. Lou Little and Arthur Sampson. Leominster Printing. 1934. Clothbound.

Dictionaries and Spectators' Guides

Terms, fundamentals, team strategy, scouting, spectating.

26-16   <u>Football for Fans.</u> Arthur Sampson. Boston Herald. 1952. Booklet.

       Explanations of various phases of the game.

26-17   <u>Football for Fans.</u> William G. Kline. Educational Athletic Foundation. 1934. Booklet.

       What to watch for, play diagrams, how the game is played.

26-18   <u>How to Watch Football.</u> Lou Little and Robert Harron. Whittlesey House. 1935. Clothbound.

       Before the game, offense, defense, generalship. Fundamentals, kicking, passing, scouting. Officials, coaching, evolution of the rules. Pro football, game photos.

26-19   <u>How to Watch a Football Game.</u> Mal Stevens and Harry Shorten. Leisure League of America. 1937. Clothbound and Paperbound.

       The warmup, kickoff, and opening scrimmage. Watching the individual player. Passing, dropkicking, razzle-dazzle, glossary.

26-20   <u>Ernie Nevers' Spectator's Football Guide.</u> Ernie Nevers. 1943. Booklet.

       Records, photos, reviews, bowls. Coverage in intercollegiate, pro and service football.

26-21   <u>Do You Know Your Football?</u> Dr. L.H. Baker. A.S. Barnes & Co. 1946. Clothbound.

       Questions and answers on football history, All-Americans, bowl games, coaches, players, rules, and techniques.

26-22   <u>Everybody's Football.</u> Maurice Dubofsky and Francis Stann. American Publishing Co. 1947. Paperbound.

       Explanations and diagrams of formations, systems, plays. Glossary.

26-23   <u>Tom Harmon's Gridiron Guide.</u> Tom Harmon. 1950. Paperbound.

       Rules, formations, plays, explanation of the game.

26-24   <u>How to Get More Fun Out of Watching Football.</u> Doak Walker. Haggar Slacks. 1950. Booklet.

       Explanations of rules, terms, penalties.

Dictionaries and Spectators' Guides

26-25   Football for Fun. Ben Hodge. Football Hobbies. 1950, 1955, 1960, 1969. Booklet.

         History, the field and equipment, procedure of the game, team organization, scoring.

26-26   Football for the Fan. Irwin Rickel. 1951. Booklet.

         How to enjoy a game.

26-27   How to Watch and Enjoy a Football Game. Leo Fisher. Packard Motor Car Co. 1952. Booklet.

26-28   How to Watch Football. Phillips Petroleum Co. 1952. Booklet.

         By 11 famous coaches. Offense, running, kicking, blocking, records.

26-29   How to Watch Football. Oldsmobile. 1953. Booklet.

         By 13 famous coaches. Similar to 26-28.

26-30   Modern Football for the Spectator. Charles Caldwell. J.B. Lippincott, Inc. 1953. Clothbound.

         Development, discussion of football as a spectator sport. Formations, personnel, referee's signals. How to watch and what to watch for. Strategy, quarterbacking, analysis of game accounts and statistics.

26-31   The American Game of Football. Helms Athletic Foundation. 1954. Booklet.

         A reprint of the October 1887 Century Magazine article, the first magazine article on football. A general description of the game with illustrations.

26-32   TV College Football Program. National Collegiate Athletic Association. 1956-65. Booklet.

         Rosters, facts covering nationally televised games.

26-33   Football Viewer's Guide. Royco Athletic Publications. 1966. Booklet.

         Data on televised National Collegiate Athletic Association games. Rosters, photos, statistics, lineups.

26-34   Chevrolet College Football Handbook. ABC TV Sports. American Broadcasting Co. and Rutledge Books, Inc. 1967. Booklet.

         Sectional roundups, All-America players, rosters of teams appearing on the National Collegiate Athletic Association TV game of the week. (See also 16-52)

26-35   Football: How to Understand and Enjoy the Game. John Austin.

Dictionaries and Spectators' Guides

T.S. Denison & Co. 1966. Paperbound.

    Offense, defense, running, passing. Penalties, game action, glossary.

26-36   How to Watch Football Like an Expert. Leo Fischer. Chicago American. 1967. Paperbound.

    What coaches and spotters look for. Offensive and defensive formations, options, passing and blocking patterns, reading plays. Statistics, records, schedules.

26-37   Football for Feminine Fans. Amy (Mrs. Len) Watters. The Printer Wick. 1933. Clothbound.

    By a coach's wife. A general explanation of the field, teams, game, offenses, fouls, and penalties. Terms.

26-38   Women's Guide to Football Watching. Sports Illustrated. 1962. Booklet.

    Explanations, glossary.

26-39   Ladies' Guide to Football. Pat Kiely. 1966. Booklet.

    Illustrated explanations. Facts.

26-40   Instant Football for Females. Marion Lamb. Vantage Press. 1968. Clothbound.

    A generalized, humorous explanation. Recipes, glossary.

26-41   Football Lingo. Howard Bonham. Diversified Publishing Co. 1962, 1963. Booklet.

    An explanation of modern football in the form of a glossary. Coaches' viewpoints, clarifications of rules, strategy. Diagrams, photos.

26-42   Football Handbook. Everett L. Storey. West Magazine. 1966. Clothbound.

    Historical background, top coaches and players, various formations. Detailed glossary.

26-43   Football Lingo. Zander Hollander and Paul Zimmerman. W.W. Norton & Co. 1967. Clothbound.

    A detailed glossary of football terms.

26-44   Football Talk for Beginners. Howard Liss. Julian Messner, Inc. 1970. Clothbound.

    A dictionary of terms, explanation of plays, function

Dictionaries and Spectators' Guides

of players.

Professional Titles

26P-1 Football: How to Play and Watch It. Lee Grosscup. Sterling Publishing Co. 1963. Clothbound.

    Film strips of game action with captions and commentary by a former pro quarterback.

26P-2 How to Watch and Enjoy Pro Football. Minnesota Vikings. 1963. Booklet.

    Player duties, glossary, formations, scouting reports.

26P-3 Pro Football Tele-Spotter. Snibbe Sports Publications. 1964. Paperbound.

    Rosters, depth charts.

26P-4 How to Be a TV Quarterback. Alex Kroll. McGraw-Hill. 1964. Paperbound.

    Schedules, rosters, records. Play diagrams, signals, photos. By a pro lineman.

26P-5 How to Watch Football on Television. Chris Schenkel. Viking Press. 1964. Clothbound. Paperback Library. 1967, reissue. Paperbound.

    The evolution of the pro game. Offensive and defensive strategy, officials, glossary. How games are broadcast. By a television sports announcer.

26P-6 Pro Football for the Fan. Kyle Rote and Ray Siegener. Doubleday & Co. 1964, 1965. Clothbound.

    History, player requirements, player sketches. Offensive and defensive formations, officials, glossary, records. How to watch a game. By a pro halfback.

26P-7 The Big Play. Harold Rosenthal. Random House. 1965. Punt, Pass and Kick Library. Clothbound.

    Exciting and dramatic plays from nineteen important National Football League games. Photos, index.

26P-8 The Strategy of Pro Football. Fred Morrison and Howard Liss. MKIM Productions Ltd. c 1965. Paperbound.

    A television viewers' guide to National Football League football for Canadians.

26P-9 The Language of Pro Football. Kyle Rote and Jack Winter.

Dictionaries and Spectators' Guides

Random House. 1966. Clothbound.

>Play diagrams and explanations. Terms, strategy, glossary. Index.

26P-10 How to Watch Pro Football on TV. Y.A. Tittle. Benjamin Co. Inc. 1966, 1967. Paperbound. Essandess. 1967, reissue. Paperbound.

>Formations, plays, offensive and defensive fundamentals, strategy, glossary, schedules.

26P-11 Televiewing Guide. Masthead Corp. 1966. Booklet.

>A spectator's guide to watching National Football League football. Overprinted by various commercial firms for advertising purposes.

26P-12 How to Be an Armchair Quarterback. Bart Starr. North American Philips Co. 1966. Paperbound.

>National Football League rosters, depth charts, schedules. Records, statistics.

26P-13 A Family Guide to Football. NFL Properties, Inc. 1967. Booklet.

>Explanations of various phases of the game.

26P-14 This Is NFL Football. National Football League Properties, Inc. 1967, 1968. Booklet.

>An advertising newspaper supplement containing articles and photos.

26P-15 How to See Football. Roman Gabriel. National Football League Properties. 1968. Booklet.

>Diagrammed plays to match specific situations.

26P-16 The Football Playbook. Sam DeLuca. Jonathan David Publishers. 1972. Clothbound.

>An explanation of the pro game for fans. Position play, formations, game plans, glossary.

26P-17 Bluffer's Guide to Football. Joe Singer. Crown Publishers. 1972. Paperbound.

>A general explanation of the pro game with humorous comments.

26P-18 Your Guide to Monday Night Football. The Savings and Loan Foundation, Inc. 1972. Paperbound.

>Previews for each game in the television series.

Dictionaries and Spectators' Guides

26P-19   Football Fundamentals for Feminine Fans. Perian Conerly. 1963. Joe Pollack. 1970. The Sporting News. Paperbound.

                Rules, signals, terminology. The 1963 edition is by the wife of a former pro quarterback.

26P-20   A Wife's Guide to Pro Football. Elaine Tarkenton and Michael Rich. Viking Press. 1969. Clothbound.

                An explanation of the game by the wife of quarterback Fran Tarkenton, with notes by Tarkenton.

26P-21   This Is Pro Football. George Sullivan. Dodd, Mead & Co. 1970. Clothbound.

                An explanation for the TV "Football Widow." Interviews with players and coaches, diagrams, photos.

26P-22   The Football Dictionary. Ron Rice and Chuck Moore. Ron Rice. 1968. Paperbound.

                A glossary accompanied by humorous illustrations.

26P-23   The Language of Pro Football. National Football League Properties. 1968. Booklet.

                A glossary.

26P-24   The ABC's of NFL Football: A Primer. National Football League Properties. 1972. Booklet.

                An illustrated glossary.

27. Anecdotes and Recollections

27-1   Football Days. William H. Edwards. Moffat, Yard & Co. 1916. Clothbound.

> Recollections of a Princeton player of the 1890's. Observations on various phases of the game. Anecdotes about coaches and players.

27-2   Football Fables. Stan W. Carlson. Olympic Press. 1939, 1949. Clothbound.

> A collection of humorous verse, incidents, anecdotes.

27-3   Personal Reminiscences of a Yale Football Player of the Early 'Eighties. Henry B. Twombly. Yale University Press. 1940. Paperbound.

> An account of early football by the Yale University quarterback of 1881-83. Descriptions of important games, recollections about Walter Camp.

27-4   Bill Stern's Favorite Football Stories. Bill Stern. Blue Ribbon Books. 1948. Clothbound. Pocket Books. 1948, reissue. Paperbound.

> Unusual and memorable incidents and games.

27-5   Dementia Pigskin. Francis Wallace. Rinehart & Co. 1951. Clothbound.

> Humorous recollections of the game, on and off the field.

27-6   The Herman Hickman Reader. Herman Hickman. Simon & Schuster. 1953. Clothbound.

> Anecdotes and recollections by a famous player, coach and raconteur.

27-7   My Favorite Football Stories. Harold (Red) Grange. A.S. Barnes & Co. 1955. Clothbound. Dell Publishing Co. 1955, reissue. Paperbound.

> Anecdotes and stories of the immortals.

Anecdotes and Recollections

27-8   Strange but True Football Stories. Zander Hollander. Random House. 1967. Punt, Pass and Kick Library. Clothbound.

    Thirteen unusual stories of college and pro football.

27-9   Football's Unforgettables. Mac Davis. Bantam Books. 1971. Paperbound.

    Strange happenings, outstanding achievements, amusing incidents.

Professional Titles

27P-1   The Professionals Look at Pro Football. Kimberly-Clark. 1967. Booklet.

    Observations on and impressions of the game by various players.

27P-2   Young Sports Photographer with the Green Bay Packers. John Biever and George Vecsey. W.W. Norton & Co. 1969. Clothbound.

    The story of a teen-age photographer, the son of the Green Bay Packers' official photographer. Recollections, anecdotes concerning the team and players.

27P-3   Pro Football's Rag Days. Bob Curran. Prentice-Hall. 1969. Clothbound.

    Interviews with 15 early stars.

27P-4   The Game That Was. Myron Cope. World Publishing Co. 1970. Clothbound.

    The early days of pro football as described by the players themselves.

27P-5   From Out of the Huddle. Mike Rathet, ed. Rutledge Books and The Benjamin Co. 1970. Paperbound.

    Amusing anecdotes of pro football.

28. Conditioning and Injuries

28-1 Archery, Cricket and Football. Andrew Peck & Co. 1868. Booklet.

    Peck and Snyder's Series of Out Door Sports. Training instructions.

28-2 Football Casualties. Romulus Foster. 1894. Booklet.

    A reprint of an article in the April 1, 1894, issue of the American Medico-Surgical Bulletin.

28-3 Treatment of Football Injuries. Harry Stewart, M.D. November 15, 1921. Booklet.

    A reprint from an article in the Medical Record. Diagnosis and treatment.

28-4 Football Conditioning. Holger C. Langmack. A.S. Barnes & Co. 1926. Clothbound.

    An illustrated handbook of drills for coaches, students, and players.

28-5 Training, Conditioning and the Care of Injuries. W.E. Meanwell and Knute Rockne. 1931. Clothbound.

    Training and conditioning, the coach's viewpoint, Rockne's ten fundamentals. The team physician's viewpoint, off-season training, game preparation, diet.

28-6 Survey of Football Fatalities. American Football Coaches Association and Football Rules Committee of the National Collegiate Athletic Association. 1931-to date. Paperbound.

    A summary of various types of injuries with discussion and recommendations. Tables, case studies.

28-7 Football Fatalities of 1931. University of Michigan. 1932. Booklet.

    An investigation into the causes of deaths ascribed to football.

Conditioning and Injuries

28-8   The Control of Football Injuries. Marvin Stevens, M.D. and Winthrop Phelps, M.D. A.S. Barnes & Co. 1933. Clothbound.

> A definitive study. Training, terms, therapy. Types of injuries, statistics.

28-9   Football Injuries Survey for the 1952 Season. G. Kenneth Hawk. National Athletic Trainers Association. 1954. Paperbound.

> Injuries classified by month, week, position, and game situation. Types of injuries, tables.

28-10   Football in February. Lous Chiesi. Packard Motor Car Co. 1957. Booklet.

> Winter preparations for the coming season.

28-11   Weight Training for Football. Elvan George and Ralph E. Evans. Prentice-Hall. 1959. Clothbound.

> Conditioning exercises. Photos.

28-12   Functional Isometric Contraction for Football. Bob Hoffman, Martin Broussard, Alvin Roy and Dr. Francis Drury. Bob Hoffman Foundation. 1962. Magazine.

> Training and exercises illustrated with photos.

28-13   Psychological Changes During Periods of Football Training and Detraining. Willard M. Hammer. University of Oregon. 1963. Paperbound.

> Doctoral thesis.

28-14   Bud Wilkinson's Guide to Modern Physical Fitness. Charles (Bud) Wilkinson. Viking Press. 1967. Clothbound.

> By an outstanding former college football coach and chairman of President's Council on Physical Fitness.

28-15   Conditioning for Football. Robert R. Spackman, Jr. Charles C. Thomas. 1968. Clothbound.

> Pre-season, during-season and off-season drills and exercises.

28-16   Explosive Muscular Power for Championship Football. John Jesse. Athletic Press. 1968. Paperbound.

> Exercises, training.

28-17   Conditioning for Football. Ernest Biggs, Sr. William C. Brown. 1968. Paperbound.

> Training routines for developing football skills.

28-18   Prevention of Football Injuries. O. Charles Olson. Lea &

Conditioning and Injuries

Febiger. 1971. Clothbound.

How to protect the health of the student athlete.

Professional Titles

28P-1   National Football League Guide to Physical Fitness. Richard Pickens, ed. Random House. 1965. Paperbound.

    Exercises, weight training, conditioning. Comments by coaches, doctors and trainers of NFL teams.

28P-2   Weeb Ewbank's Pro Football Way to Physical Fitness. Weeb Ewbank and Lud Duroska. Grosset & Dunlap. 1967. Paperbound.

    Exercises illustrated with photographs.

28P-3   Off-Season Football Training. Paul Wiggin, Floyd Peters and Dr. Harvey E. Williams. World Publishing Co. 1967. Clothbound.

    By National Football League players. Programs to develop power, agility and speed. General principles, nutrition, the total program.

28P-4   Medicine and the Green Bay Packers. James W. Nellen, M.D. Upjohn Co. 1968. Paperbound.

    A description of the diagnostic and therapeutic methods employed by the Green Bay Packers team physician.

29. Controversies

29-1 <u>Football Facts and Figures.</u> Walter Camp. Harper & Brothers. 1894. Paperbound.

> A defense against criticism of football. Statistics to show the scholastic achievement and physical development of college players. Letters from captains and players. Statistics on football injuries.

29-2 <u>Opinions of Educators on the Value and Total Influence of Intercollegiate and Interscholastic American Football as Played in 1903-09.</u> Calvin M. Woodward. 1910. Paperbound.

> A criticism citing opinions of educators at Harvard, Kansas, Columbia, Michigan, Stanford, and Illinois. A discussion of the "serious injury inflicted on the character and work of the student body by the magnitude of the interest in football, and the corruption by gate receipts, professional coaches and the desire to win."

29-3 <u>Football and Warfare.</u> George Gundelfinger. The New Fraternity. 1917. Booklet.

> An argument for the abolition of football and competitive collegiate athletics.

29-4 <u>The 18th Amendment and Football.</u> George Gundelfinger. The New Fraternity. 1923. Booklet.

> An argument against alcohol and football.

29-5 <u>Why the Bulldog Is Losing His Grip.</u> George Gundelfinger. The New Fraternity. 1923. Booklet.

> A critical history of Yale football from 1913-23 with arguments for abolishing the game.

29-6 <u>Has the Bulldog Regained His Grip?</u> George Gundelfinger. The New Fraternity. 1924. Booklet.

> A supplement to 29-5 covering the 1924 season.

Controversies

29-7   The Decay of Bulldogism. George Gundelfinger. The New Fraternity. 1930. Clothbound.

             Includes 29-5 and 29-6, plus new material advocating the abolition of college football, with emphasis on Yale University.

29-8   College Football. E.K. Hall. New York Sun. 1925. Booklet.

             A reprint of an address by Hall, Chairman of the Football Rules Committee, at the 1925 All-America Dinner, detailing what he believed to be the faults of college football, and his suggestions for remedying them.

29-9   King Football, the Vulgarization of the American College. Reed Harris. Vanguard Press. 1932. Clothbound.

             By a former varsity player. A criticism of football policies and overemphasis of football at large universities.

29-10   What Price Football. Barry Wood. Houghton Mifflin Co. 1932. Clothbound.

             A player's defense of the game. The organization of football, its complexities and its hold on the public. Importance of the football problem, description of game day, practice during the week. Injuries, coaches, scouts, the quarterback. The benefits to schools resulting from football revenues. Overemphasis and ballyhoo resulting from the press coverage.

29-11   College Football, Asset or Liability? Celestin J. Steiner, S.J. University of Detroit. 1951. Booklet.

             An answer to critics of football by the president of the University of Detroit. A blueprint for the preservation of college football.

29-12   The Truth about Big-Time Football. Richard I. Miller. William Sloane Associates. 1953. Clothbound.

             Football as a big business. A criticism of bowl games, television, spring practice, sportswriter and broadcasters. The position of the college president, history of football, the future of intercollegiate football. Cartoons.

29-13   The Libel Case of Wally Butts vs. the Saturday Evening Post. Fred Russell. Nashville Banner. 1963. Paperbound.

             Reprints of Russell's articles in the Nashville Banner.

29-14   The Fifth Down: Democracy and the Football Revolution. Neil Amdur. Coward McCann. 1971. Clothbound. Dell Publishing

Co. 1972, reissue. Paperbound.

> An expose of college football based on the principles and problems of coach George Davis, with an examination of recruiting, payoffs to players, alumni pressure, authoritarian coaches, exploitation of players.

29-15 Meat on the Hoof. Gary Shaw. St. Martin's Press. 1972. Clothbound.

> A criticism of college football at the University of Texas, by a former player.

Professional Titles

29P-1 Exclusive - Paul Brown. Hal Lebovitz, ed. RA-KA, Inc. 1963. Paperbound.

> Articles by Cleveland sportswriters concerning the firing of Coach Paul Brown by the Cleveland Browns. Compiled and published because of a Cleveland newspaper strike in effect at that time.

29P-2 Pro Football Broadside. Elinor Kaine. Collier-Macmillan. 1969. Clothbound.

> A critical inside look at pro football by a woman sports writer.

29P-3 And Every Day You Take Another Bite. Larry Merchant. Doubleday & Co. 1971. Clothbound. Dell. 1972, reissue. Paperbound.

> A comprehensive discussion and criticism of various aspects of pro football, on and off the field.

29P-4 They Call It a Game. Bernie Parrish. Dial Press. 1971. Clothbound. Signet. 1972, reissue. Paperbound.

> An indictment of the management of pro football. By a former player.

30. Administrative Works

30-1 <u>American Football Coaches Association: Proceedings of Annual Meeting.</u> American Football Coaches Association. 1924-to date. Booklet.

    Committee reports, rule changes, speeches.

30-2 <u>American Football Coaches Association: Digest.</u> American Football Coaches Association. 1948-to date. Booklet.

    History of the Association, constitution, roster, data.

30-3 <u>The Press and the Football Coach.</u> Football Writers Association of America and the American Football Coaches Association. 1961. Booklet.

    Guides for establishing harmonious press relations.

30-4 <u>College Football and Television.</u> National Collegiate Athletic Association. 1951. Booklet.

    An explanation of the planned program for televising games.

Professional Titles

30P-1 <u>Annual Meeting, National Football League.</u> National Football League. 1942-to date. Booklet.

    Minutes of the meeting.

30P-2 <u>National Football League Constitution and By-Laws.</u> National Football League. 1935-to date. Paperbound.

    Annotated.

30P-3 <u>American Football League Constitution and By-Laws.</u> American Football League. 1960-to date. Booklet.

    Annotated.

30P-4 <u>Guide for Visiting National Football League Publicity Directors.</u>

Administrative Works

National Football League. 1961. Booklet.
Data on reporters and announcers in each league city.

Promotional Books

Issued by the various teams to prospective players to provide background information. Dates are approximate.

30P-5 Life with the Dallas Cowboys in the National Football League. Dallas Cowboys. 1961-67.

30P-6 Your Future with the New York Jets. New York Jets. 1963.

30P-7 Life with the San Francisco 49ers. San Francisco 49ers. 1965.

31. All-Time and All-American

31-1 <u>All-Time Football Teams of Nineteen Eastern Colleges.</u> George Trevor. New York Sun. 1930. Booklet.

> A reprint of articles appearing in the New York Sun in 1927. Western Conference also covered.

31-2 <u>Football in War and Peace.</u> Clark Shaughnessy. Jacobs Press. 1943. Magazine.

> The 12 greatest games, backfields, and plays. The 11 greatest players. Lineups, diagrams, photos.

31-3 <u>Collier's Original All-America.</u> Collier's Magazine. Crowell-Collier. 1948. Booklet.

> Background and origin of the All-American selection system. Yearly All-American teams.

31-4 <u>An Inquiry into the Matter of Priority in the Selection and Publication of All-American Football Teams for the Years 1889-96.</u> Clarence G. McDavitt. 1950. Booklet.

> An attempt to resolve the question of whether Walter Camp or Casper Whitney originated the idea of the All-American team. Presents evidence pointing to Whitney as the originator. Also covers teams from 1897-99.

31-5 <u>A Talk at the National Football Foundation and Hall of Fame Dinner.</u> Chester J. LaRoche. National Football Foundation. 1956. Booklet.

> The policies and plans of the National Football Foundation.

31-6 <u>Announcing the 68th All-American Football Team.</u> American Football Coaches Association. All-America Board of Coaches. General Mills. 1957. Booklet.

> Continuation of Walter Camp's Grantland Rice's All-American teams. Lists of teams since 1889. Photos.

All-Time and All-American

31-7 Footballetter. Football Hall of Fame. 1959-to date.

   A monthly pamphlet containing articles, schedule of events, Hall of Fame selections.

Professional Titles

31P-1 National Professional Football Hall of Fame. Gervis Brady. 1960. Magazine.

   Background and planning of the Pro Football Hall of Fame in Canton, Ohio.

31P-2 National Pro Football Hall of Fame Dedication. Dick McCann, ed. National Football Museum. 1963. Magazine.

   Issued for the dedication of the Pro Football Hall of Fame on September 7 and 8, 1963. Development and description of the Hall, historical sketch of pro football, biographical sketches of the inductees.

31P-3 Pro Football's Hall of Fame. Arthur Daley. Quadrangle Books. 1963. Clothbound. Grosset & Dunlap. 1968, reissue, 1971, reissue. Clothbound. Tempo Books. 1969, reissue. Paperbound.

   Sketches of players elected to the Pro Football Hall of Fame.

31P-4 Pro Football's All-Time Greats. George Sullivan. G.P. Putnam's Sons. 1968. Clothbound.

   Sketches of the players and executives who have been inducted into the Pro Football Hall of Fame.

31P-5 Hall of Fame Yearbook. National Football League Properties. Standard Packaging Corp. 1970. Magazine.

   Calendar, schedules, player sketches.

31P-6 Football. John Mosedale. World Publishing Co. 1972. Clothbound.

   Sketches of players in the pro Football Hall of Fame.

32. Scouting

32-1 <u>How to Scout Football</u>. George H. Allen. School Aid Co. 1953. Clothbound.

    History and development, qualifications, theories. Techniques, scouting, reports, and forms. Sections on high school and pro scouting.

32-2 <u>Handbook of Football Scouting and Film Analysis</u>. Edward L. Teague, Jr. and Emmett Cheek. William C. Brown. 1955. Paperbound.

32-3 <u>Basic Football Scouting</u>. Charles J. Spalten. Royal Publishing Co. 1958. Paperbound.

    A guide for the player, scout, coach, and fan. Illustrations.

32-4 <u>A Football Scouting Workbook</u>. Joseph S. Dienhart and Homer Allen. Tri-State Offset Co. 1960. Paperbound.

    A practical guide for college and high school scouts.

32-5 <u>Football Scouting Methods</u>. Steve Belichick. Ronald Press. 1962. Clothbound.

    By the Naval Academy chief scout. Preparation, analysis, recognizing offenses and defenses, forms and terminology. Final report, post-game analysis.

Professional Titles

32P-1 <u>Football Scouting</u>. Robert MacKenzie. Prentice-Hall. 1955. Clothbound.

    By a Cleveland Browns scout. Qualifications, phases of game scouting, talent scouting.

33. Miscellaneous

33-1   **Parlour Football.** Ezra H. Snow. McLoughlin Brothers, Inc. 1891. Paperbound.
    Rules for playing an indoor table game.

33-2   **Football Poker.** Madison Book Co. 1904. Booklet.
    Combining all the interest and excitement of the two great American games.

33-3   **Universal Football and Handball.** Thomas W. Graham. 1908. Booklet.
    Rules and diagrams for a new game.

33-4   **National Football.** Harry Bromley. W.E. Rudge, Inc. 1912. Booklet.
    A new, clean, open, active, safe, and sane American game for boys and girls. A modification of rugby and soccer.

33-5   **A Complete Bibliography of Football.** John DaGrosa. American Football Institute. 1935. Paperbound.
    Listing of books, fiction titles, and periodicals contained in the Library of Congress.

33-6   **Gridiron Pageantry.** Charles B. Righter. C. Fisher, Inc. 1941. Paperbound.
    The story of the football marching band. Organization, development, preparation of routines.

33-7   **Six Football Programs.** Savage and Painter. Gamble Hinged Music Co. 1943. Paperbound.
    Six complete halftime shows with band drills. Illustrations.

33-8   **Gridiron Cookery.** Frances Daugherty and Aileen Brothers. David McKay Co. 1961. Clothbound.

Miscellaneous

Favorite recipes of 250 coaches' wives.

Professional Titles

33P-1 <u>Gridiron Gourmet.</u> American Football League Women's Association. National Business Forms. 1966. Clothbound.

Favorite recipes of AFL stars.

General Index

A

A. A. Stagg, Grand Old Man of Football 59

AAWU Fall Sports Information 233

ABC'S of Football, The 238

Abilene High School Football Organization 200

About the Cotton Bowl 223

Aggies Are Back, The 186

Alabama Football 229

Alabama's Crimson Tide 44

Alan Ameche 64

Alexander of Georgia Tech 62

All-America Eleven, The 164

All-American 138

All-American College Football Songs, The 165

All-American Football Coaching Course, The 97

All-American Football Dope Book 18

All-American Football Magazine 155

All-American Football Stories 154

All-Conference Tackle 143

All-South Carolina Football Annual 228

All-South Football Annual 230

All-Star Sports Football 25

All-Star Sports Special 28

All-Time Football Teams of Nineteen Eastern Colleges 257

All-Time History of the Battling Buckeyes 49

American Football (Camp) 1

American Football (Daly) 88

American Football Coaches Association: Digest 255

American Football Coaches Association: Lectures Delivered at the Football Clinics 92

American Football Coaches Association: Proceedings of Annual Meeting 255

American Football Coaches Association: Summer Manual 92

General Index

American Football for Women 87

American Football, Its History and Development 35

American Football League, The 4

American Football Quizzer, The 215

American Football Statistical Bureau 18

American Game of Football, The 240

American Intercollegiate Association Rule Book 7

American Intercollegiate Football Rules, The 7

American Intercollegiate Football Rules and Constitution 214

American Medico-Surgical Bulletin 247

Amos Alonzo Stagg 59

Analysis of "T" Formation with Man-in-Motion 99

Andy at Yale 130

Andy Kerr, a Man Who Served 66

Annapolis, Ahoy 141

Announcing the 68th All-American Football Team 257

Arch Ward's Football Facts 172

Archery, Cricket and Football 247

Arkansas Football 228

Army-Navy Football Story, The 42

Army-Navy Game, The 42

Army vs. Navy 42

Army vs. Notre Dame 42

Around the End 122

At Good Old Siwash 127

Atchison's College Football Record 169

Athletic Association of Western Universities Fall Sports Information 233

Athletic Leadership 86

Athletic Record of the University of Michigan 53

Athletic World, The 115

Athletics and Football 15

Athletics at Dartmouth 52

Athletics at Lafayette College 52

Athletics at Princeton 52

Athletics at Wesleyan 53

Athletics in the University of North Carolina 52

Atlantic Coast Conference Football Yearbook 234

Atlantic Football Book 171

Atlas Football Handbook 19

Autobiography of Knute K. Rockne, The 60

Autumn Madness 134

Autumn Mightiest Legions 198

Azzi Ratem 177

Azzi Ratem - Boand Football Ranking System 177

General Index

B

Baby Elton, Quarterback   124

Backfield Ace   147

Backfield Blues   140

Backfield Buckaroo   140

Backfield Challenge   149

Backfield Comet   129

Backfield Feud, The   137

Backfield Play   129

Backfield Twins   142

Backup Quarterback   148

Ball Carrying Made Easy   199

Barclay Back   124

Barry Goes to College   131

Barry Locke, Halfback   123

Baseball and Football   15

Basic Football Scouting   259

Bay and Pioneer Leagues Football Yearbook   198

Beadles's Dime Book of Cricket and Football   1

Before Rockne at Notre Dame   47

Behind the Line   122

Bell Haven Eleven, The   130

Ben Martin's Flexible T Offense   101

Ben Stone at Oakdale   128

Ben Strong Football   28

Bert Wilson on the Gridiron   129

Bertie Comes Through   141

Best of Football from the Coaching Clinic   95

Best of High School Defensive Football, The   204

Better Football for Boys   206

B.F. Goodrich Football Guide   170

Big Bowl Football   221

Big Down Gamble   153

Big Eight, The   232

Big Eight Conference Football Record Book   234

Big Eight Conference Football Year Book   234

Big Eight Supplement, The   232

Big Five AAWU Fall Sports Information   233

Big Football Man   136

Big Game (Beach & Moore)   42

Big Game, The (Russell)   51

Big Game (Wallace)   134

Big Nine, The   231

Big Strike at Siwash, The   127

Big Swat   150

Big Ten, The   231

Big Ten Football Digest   231

Big Ten Football Records   231

General Index

Big Ten Football Rosters Manual 233

Big Ten Records Book 233

Bigger Game, The 146

Bill Stern's Favorite Football Stories 245

Black Champions of the Gridiron 68

Black Coach 201

Black Knights of West Point, The 41

Blaine of the Backfield 136

Block That Kick (Archibald) 142

Block That Kick! (Sherman) 133

Blocking Back (Bowen) 145

Blocking Back (Chute) 138

Blue Book: Who's Who in Michigan Football, The 229

Bob Mathias, Champion of Champions 63

Bob Neyland, 37 Years a Volunteer 65

Bob Suffridge, Football Beyond Coaching 65

Bobby Dodd on Football 92

Boltwood of Yale 122

Booing is a "No No" 216

Book of Football, The 2

Book of Rules of the Game of Football, The 213

Border Conference Football Press Book 234

Borleske, Never Far from Hope 66

Boston Post Football Facts 172

Bowl Game Press Guides 221

Bowl Game Thrills 221

Bowl-Manac 221

Bowl Record Guide 221

Boys of St. Timothy's 125

Boys' Life Book of Football Stories 155

Boys' Life Magazine 155

Braeburn University Red Book 169

Breakaway Back (Harkins) 142

Breakaway Back (Hutto) 152

Brick Barton and His Winning Eleven 138

Brief History of Football at the University of Delaware, A 49

Brief History of Intercollegiate Football at the US Military Academy, A 41

Broward Football 198

Brown-Forman's Football Schedule 170

Bruce Benedict, Halfback 149

Buckeye Football 228

Bucking the Line 129

Bud Baker, T Quarterback 143

Bud Plays Junior High Football 143

Bud Wilkinson's Guide to Modern Physical Fitness 248

General Index

Buddy and His Old Pro 138

Building a Championship Football Team 93

Bulldogs with a Bite 45

Bunny Plays the Game 128

Buttonhooks to Bombs! 68

Buzzy Plays Midget League Football 143

C

Cadet Quarterback 151

Cadets at Kings Point 145

California Football History 42

California Football Review 185

California Prep Football 198

California Prep Football Guide 198

California Quarterback 229

Calling Life's Signals 66

Cambridge to Pasadena and Return 221

Candidate for the Line 124

Captain Dan Richards 127

Captain Jack Lorimer 125

Captain Johnny Ford 138

Captain of the Eleven (Knipe) 128

Captain of the Eleven (Sherman) 133

Captain of the Schoolteam 126

Captive Coach, The 146

Career Coach 137

Carl Hall of Tait 127

Carolina-Clemson Game, The 50

Catch That Pass 150

Cavalcade 50

Center Rush Rowland 123

Championship Football (Bible) 91

Championship Football (Crisler) 86

Championship Football by Twelve Great Coaches 94

Championship Football Drills 94

Change Signals! 122

Changes in the Football Rules, 1928 215

Chevrolet College Football Handbook 173, 240

Chicago and Area High School Football Annual Pictorial 197

Chicago Prep Football Annual 197

Choo Choo: The Charlie Justice Story 64

Chris Plays Small Fry Football 143

Chris Schenkel's Sportscene: Football 117

Chronology of Changes in Collegiate Football Rules, A 215

Chrysler Football Almanac 173

Coach, The 125

Coach Tom Cahill 66

General Index

Coach Tommy of the Crimson Tide 64

Coaching (Rockne) 89

Coaching, Book V 91

Coaching on Explosive Passing Offense 99

Coaching Football (Dietzel) 95

Coaching Football (Zuppke and Olander) 89

Coaching Football and the Split-T Formation 100

Coaching Linebackers and the Perimeter Defense 104

Coaching of Football Line Play, The 104

Coaching the Offensive and Defensive Line Game 104

Coaching the Quarterback 98

Coaching the T Formation 100

Coaching, the Way of the Winner 89

Coaching Today's Athlete: A Football Textbook 95

Collection of the Popular Dartmouth Football Cheers and Songs, A 163

College and Pro Football (Hewfred Publishing Co.) 28

College and Pro Football (Sheehan and Pearson) 171

College and Pro Football Guide 20

College Division Regional Football Championship Handbook 221

College Football (Complete Sports Publications) 27

College Football (Hall) 252

College Football (Walsh) 17

College Football All-Time Galaxy 20

College Football All-Time Record Book 20

College Football and Television 255

College Football, Asset or Liability? 252

College Football Digest Presents Alabama 186

College Football Digest Presents Georgia 186

College Football Illustrated 26

College Football in Iowa 228

College Football Schedules and Record Book 171

College Football Television Handbook 173

Collegiate Football Rules 216

Collegiate Football Summary 19

Collegiate Press Guides 187

Collier's Original All-America 257

Columbus Discovers Football 49

Comeback Year, The 151

Complete Bibliography of Football, A 261

Complete Book of Backfield Play, The 96

General Index

Complete Book of the I Formation, The 203

Complete Book of Winning Football Drills 92

Complete Football 26

Complete Football Passing Game, The 204

Complete Football Records of the Western Conference 231

Complete Guide to the Split-Pro Defense 106

Complete Kicking Game, The 104

Complete Sports 28

Complete Sports College Football 27

Concessionary Rules from 1873-1874 35

Conditioning for Football (Biggs) 248

Conditioning for Football (Spackman, Thomas) 248

Conley's Football Guide 9

Constitution of the Pennsylvania Intercollegiate Football Association 227

Contributions Sixteen Millimeter Cinematographic Techniques Make to Coaching Football, The 93

Control of Football Injuries, The 248

Cornell University, a History 52

Cotton Bowl, The 223

Counterfeit Tackle, The 150

Course in Football for Players and Coaches, A 88

Course in Football Tactics for 1911, A 88

Crackerjack Halfback 150

Crashing Through! 133

Crazy Legs McBain 142

Crazylegs Merrill 152

Crimson Road, The 138

Crimson Tide: A Story of Alabama Football, The 44

Crimson Sweater, The 122

Crucial Games and the Plays That Won Them 97

Crying Towel, The 200

D

Dan Workman's Big Game 154

Danforth Plays the Game 122

Danny the Freshman 127

Darrell Royal Talks Football 94

Dartmouth Athletics 52

Dartmouth's Undefeated Football Season 186

Dave Porter's Return to School 125

David Cheers the Team 139

Dear Coach 161

Decay of Bulldogism, The 252

Deception in Six-Man Football 210

Defense, Book IV 91

General Index

Defense Spartan Style   105

Defense: The Winning Difference in Football   106

Defensive Football (Leahy)   105

Defensive Football (Oshins)   3

Defensive Fundamentals, Book II   91

Dell Sports   26

Dell Sports Magazine: Stanley Woodward's Football   26

Dell Sports: Stanley Woodward's Football   26

Dementia Pigskin   245

Developing a Championship Football Program   201

Developing a Flexible Defensive Secondary System   205

Developing a Successful High School Pro Set Football Offense   203

Developing a Superior Football--Control Attack   202

Development of Intercollegiate Football   35

Diary of a Line Smasher, The   135

Dick Arnold of Raritan College   131

Dick Hamilton's Football Team   128

Dick Merriwell's Power   122

Dick Merriwell's Way   122

Dick of the Bruins   146

Dickinson's Football Ratings   177

Digest of Football Rules for 1910   214

Digest of Football Rules for 1911   214

Directory of Football Defenses   204

Ditto Practice Lessons in Football   85

Doak Walker, Three-Time all American   62

Do You Know Your Football?   239

Dr. Henry L. Williams   62

Does the Big Ten Always Win?   222

Double Reverse   150

Down Memory Lane with Rayen and South   198

Down the Years with Cathedral Football   198

Drills for High School Football   200

Dub, Halfback   143

E

East Texas Football   228

Eastern Association of Intercollegiate Football Officials, Annual Report   217

Eastern Association of Intercollegiate Football Officials, By-Laws   217

Eastern College Athletic Conference Press, Radio and TV Football Guide   234

Eastern Intercollegiate Football Association Press and Radio Guide   234

General Index

Eastern Intercollegiate Football Association Press and Radio Guide 234

Echoes of the Harvard-Yale Football Game of 1890 163

Eckersall of Chicago 64

Effect of Variations in Hand and Foot Spacing on Movement Time and on Force of Charge 103

Effects of Television on College Football Attendance, The 179

Eggheads in the Endzone 149

18th Amendment and Football, The 251

Encyclopedia of Football Drills 92

End Zone (Delilo) 154

End Zone, The (Scholz) 140

Eric and Dud's Football Bargain 144

Ernie Nevers, Football Hero 66

Ernie Nevers' Spectator's Football Guide 239

Esso Football Handbook 171

Etna Football Facts 170

Everybody's Football 239

Evolution of Formations from 1880-1910 35

Evolution of the Pig-Skin 161

Examination of Football Scores, An 177

Exciting Football 156

Explosive Muscular Power for Championship Football 248

Explosive Short-T, The 101

F

Fabulous Redmen, The 48

Facts on American Sports and Health 172

Fair Play! 129

Falcons to the Fight 142

Famous Feats of Football 113

Famous Football Players 67

Famous Names in Football 3

Fanfare on a Tin Whistle 218

Fans Handbook 227

Field Goal 141

Fielding Yost's Legacy to the University of Michigan 62

Fielding H. Yost, Football Immortal 62

5th Down, The 116

Fifth Down: Democracy and the Football Revolution, The 252

Fifty Football Plays by Fifty Great Coaches Coaches 97

57 Years of Phoenixville Football 197

Fifty-seven Years on Pittsburgh Gridirons 228

Fifty Years of Colgate Football 44

Fifty Years of Football 44

Fifty Years of Football at Syracuse University 43

Fifty Years of Vanderbilt Football 43

General Index

Fifty Years on the Quad   52

Fight 'em, Big Three   133

Fight Like a Falcon   143

Fight, Team, Fight   142

Fighting Blood   129

Fighting Captain, and Other Stories, The   129

Fighting Chance   140

Fighting Coach (Archibald)   142

Fighting Coach (Scholz)   139

Fighting Guard   124

Fighting Halfback   145

Fighting Quarterback   140

Fighting Scrub, The   123

Fighting Tigers, The   43

Fireside Book of Football, The   113

First and Ten (Daugherty and Wilson)   94

First and Ten (McCormick)   146

First Book of Football, The   206

First Common Set of Rules from 1873-1874   35

First Down, Kentucky!   128

500 Club, The   185

Five-Man Line Defense, The   103

Five Yards to Glory   146

Five Yards to Go   129

Flag Football   211

Flip-Flop Offense in High School Football   202

Fluor Football Forecast   116

Fly-T Football   101

Flying Tackle   145

Follow the Ball   123

Following the Ball   124

Following the Huskers   185

Football (Anderson)   207

Football (Camp and DeLand)   2

Football (Clous and Snow)   164

Football (Fitzsimmons and Metcalf)   164

Football (Johanson)   83

Football (Killinger)   91

Football (Leahy)   86

Football (Miers)   36

Football (Office of the Chief of Naval Operations)   85

Football (Otto)   86

Football (Sheehan and Pearson)   171

Football (Wilce)   89

Football: A Monologue   163

Football, a Popular Handbook of the Game   15

Football Action   155

Football Alabama Style   186

General Index

Football Alibis and Postmortems 116

Football and How to Watch It 237

Football and Love 121

Football and Warfare 251

Football at Minnesota 42

Football at Ohio State 93

Football at Rutgers 51

Football at Texas 48

Football at Texas A & M 185

Football at the University of Richmond 46

Football, Blocking and Tackling 85

Football Book 88

Football Boys 139

Football Boys of Lakeport, The 126

Football Calendar, The (Camp) 87

Football Calendar (Goes) 171

Football Calendar (Longdon) 169

Football Cartoons and Features 2

Football Case Book 196

Football Casualties 247

Football Champions of 1938 185

Football Classic, A (Gray) 184

Football Classic, A (Wonder Publications) 60

Football Coach 138

Football Coaches How to Do It Book 200

Football Coaching 95

Football Coach's Complete Handbook, The 94

Football Coach's Guide to Secondary Defense 105

Football Coach's Guide to Successful Pass Defense 106

Football: Combatting the Changing Defenses 203

Football Conditioning 247

Football, CU-Style 51

Football Data for Associated Sportcasters and Commentators 19

Football Days 245

Football Defense 84

Football Digest (Schroeder) 115

Football Digest (Simons) 113

Football Digest (Writers' Digest Publishing Co.) 25

Football End Play 104

Football Fables 245

Football: Facts and Figures (Baker) 19

Football Facts and Figures (Camp) 251

Football: Facts and Figures Supplement 19

Football Facts and Fun 3

Football Fan's Dope Book, The 169

Football Fan's Dope Book and Guide 170

Football Fatalities of 1931 247

273

General Index

Football Fever (Bishop)   140

Football Fever (Bishop and Gregory)   165

Football Fiends, The   164

Football Figures Weekly   116

Football Flash   150

Football for All   200

Football for Beginners   206

Football for Boys (Kuharich and McClelland)   206

Football for Boys (Nugent)   207

Football for Coaches and Players   88

Football for Fans (Kline)   239

Football for Fans (Sampson)   239

Football for Feminine Fans   241

Football for Fun   240

Football for Player and Spectator   237

Football for Public and Player   237

Football for the Beginner   206

Football for the Fan (Jones and Wesson)   238

Football for the Fan (Rickel)   240

Football for the Spectator (Camp)   237

Football for the Spectator (H. S. Crocker Co.)   238

Football for the Young Champions   206

Football Forecast (Fawcett Publishing Co.)   27

Football Forecast (Roberts)   25

Football Form   116

Football Form and Digest   115

Football Forum   201

Football from 1800-1868   35

Football from the Ground Up   3

Football Fundamentals (Bateman and Governali)   93

Football Fundamentals (Battistini)   201

Football Fundamentals (Faulkenberry)   90

Football Fury   152

Football Game, A   163

Football Game, The   163

Football Grandma   125

Football Gravy Train   147

Football Handbook   241

Football Handbook and Schedules (International News Service - United Press International)   173

Football Handbook and Schedules (National Research Bureau)   172

Football Handbook and Schedules (The Sporting News)   173

Football, How to Coach a Team   87

Football, How to Play the Game   84

General Index

Football, How to Understand and Enjoy the Game 240

Football Immortals 67

Football in February 248

Football in Illinois 229

Football in 1925 169

Football in the Gay Nineties 46

Football in the Rough 146

Football in Virginia 227

Football in War and Peace 257

Football Injuries Survey for the 1952 Season 248

Footballetter 258

Football Line Play for Players and Coaches 103

Football Lingo (Bonham) 241

Football Lingo (Hollander and Zimmerman) 241

Football Made Plain to the Spectator 237

Football Madness 125

Football Magazine 196

Football News, The 115

Football Newsletter 116

Football Notes (Rockne) 90

Football Notes (Yost, Little and Wieman) 89

Football Offense (Griffith and Clark) 84

Football Offense (Smith) 96

Football Offense in Revolution 96

Football Officiating 218

Football Officiating and Interpretation of the Rules 217

Football Officiating Procedures 217

Football Oklahoma 230

Football Play Situations 196

Football Play Situations, Based on the NCAA Official Rules 196

Football Play Situations, Based on the Official Interscholastic Football Rules 196

Football Player Handbook 196

Football Plays for Boys 205

Football Poker 261

Football Prevues 26

Football; Principles and Play 94

Football Problems 215

Football, Punting and Passing 85

Football Quizzer, The 215

Football Rebels, The 140

Football Record and Rule Book 9

Football Records of American Teams 17

Football Report 183

Football Review, The (Boyd) 18

Football Review, The (Northern Collegiate Sports) 116

General Index

Football Review (Writers' Digest Publishing Co.)   25

Football Review Scrapbook   18

Football Review Scrapbook Supplement   18

Football Romance, A   164

Football Roundup   27

Football Rudiments   84

Football Rules (Barron)   214

Football Rules (Camp)   214

Football Rules (National Federation of State High School Athletic Associations)   196

Football Rules, American Intercollegiate Association   7

Football Rules and How They Are Applied   3

Football Rules and Referee's Book (Camp)   7

Football Rules and Referee's Book (Judd)   214

Football Rules as Recommended by the Rules Committee   8

Football Rules as Recommended to the University Athletic Club by the Rules Committee   8

Football Rules from 1880   35

Football Rules from 1876-1878   35

Football Rules in Pictures   216

Football Rules of the Game   1

Football Rules through Play Situations   196

Football Schedules and Record Book   171

Football Schedules   229

Football Scorebook   18

Football Scout   202

Football Scouting Methods   259

Football Scouting Workbook, A   259

Football, Secrets of the Split-T Formation   100

Football '71   230

Football Skills   207

Football Skills Test Manual   87

Football Stars   26

Football Stories   155

Football, Straight Line Philosophy   103

Football Talk for Beginners   241

Football Techniques   90

Football Technique and Tactics   89

Football Techniques Illustrated   86

Football Texas Style   232

Football, The American Intercollegiate Game   35

Football: The Greatest Moments in the Southwest Conference   232

Football, the Rugby Game   15

Football, the Rugby Union Game   15

General Index

Football, The T Formation   85

Football Thesaurus   19

Football Thrills   67

Football Through the Years   36

Football Tips for Boys 18 and Under   207

Football, Today and Tomorrow   2

Football Trees   144

Football Twins   148

Football Viewers' Guide   240

Football Wit and Humor   161

Football Without a Coach   87

Football World, The   115

Football Y Men   67

Football Yearbook   27

Football Yearbook Kickoff   27

Football's Finest Hour   223

Football's Greatest Coaches   68

Football's Greatest Games   36

Football's Iron Men Teams   51

Football's Master Defense Guide   204

Football's Medicine Men   68

Football's Multiple Spread T Offense   102

Football's Unforgettable Games   36

Football's Unforgettables   246

Footsteps   151

For Laughing Out Loud   161

For the Good of the Team   123

For the Honor of the School   122

Ford Football Televiewer   173

Fortunes of the Team   123

Forty Years of Football   62

Forty-Two Years of Hotchkiss Football   197

Forty-Two Years on the Tiger Gridiron   43

Forward Pass   122

Forward Pass and its Defense, The   99

Forward Pass in Football, The   98

Forward Passing (Griffith and Clark)   84

Forward Passing (Kerr)   99

Forward Passing (Thomas E. Wilson & Co.)   84

Four Decades of Yale-Princeton Football   48

Four Horsemen of Notre Dame, The   67

Four Roses Football Schedules   172

Four Winners, The   131

Fourth Down (Barbour)   123

Fourth Down (Bowen)   145

Fourth Down, The (Quirk)   124

Fourth Down Pass   143

277

General Index

Fourth Down Showdown   144

Frank Allen, Captain of the Team   132

Frank Armstrong at College   128

Frank Armstrong, Drop Kicker   128

Frank Gifford's Football Guidebook   207

Frank Leahy and the Fighting Irish   62

Frank Merriwell as Coach   122

Frank Merriwell at Yale   121

Frank Merriwell, Quarterback   152

Frank Merriwell's Champions   122

Frank Merriwell's Return to Yale   122

Fred Fenton in the Line   129

Freddy Plays Football   145

Freshman, The   128

Freshman Quarterback (Bee)   144

Freshman Quarterback (Frederic)   152

Friends and Rivals   125

From T to T at UT   47

Front Man   134

Fullback, The   130

Fullback Afloat, A   125

Fullback Fever   140

Fullback for Sale   139

Fullback Foster   123

Fullback from Nowhere   147

Fullback Fuller   148

Fullback Fury (Archibald)   142

Fullback Fury (Knott)   153

Fullback in the Large Fry League   143

Fumbled Pass, The   124

Fumblestumble Sandy   154

Functional Football   91

Functional Isometric Contraction for Football   248

Fundamental Football   93

Fundamental Line Drills for Line Skills in the T Formation   103

Fundamentals of an Original System of Offensive Play in Football, The   96

Fundamentals of Football Training   84

Fundamentals of the T Formation   101

Fundamentals, Tackling, Blocking, Etc.   84

G

Game, The   154

Game of Football, The (Chadwick)   8

Game of Football, The (Newcombe)   36

Game of the Century   48

Game Plan College Football   28

General Index

Games of California and Stanford, The 52

Gangway for Navy 41

Gary Grayson's Hill St. Eleven 132

Gary Grayson Football Rivals 132

Gary Grayson at Lennox High 132

Gary Grayson at Stanley Prep 132

Gary Grayson Showing His Speed 132

Gary Grayson's Winning Kick 132

Gary Grayson Hitting the Line 132

Gary Grayson's Winning Touchdown 133

Gary Grayson's Double Signals 133

Gary Grayson's Forward Pass 133

General Ship 88

Georgetown Hoyas, The 44

Georgia Tech Yellow Jackets, The 184

Georgia Tech's Golden Tornado Champions 184

Georgia's Wallace Butts: "Bowlmaster" 221

Gerrit Smith Miller 59

Ghosts of Herty Field, The 45

Giant Quarterback 156

Gipp of Notre Dame 63

Gladiators, The 53

Glance at Amherst Athletics, A 53

Glory of Notre Dame, The 47

Glory Runners, The 68

Gluek's Football Dopester 170

Go, Big Red 44

Go, Gators 50

Go, Navy, Go 142

Go, Shorty, Go 153

Go, Team, Go 138

Goal Ahead! 150

Goal Line Stand 147

Goal Lines 164

Goal to Go (Barbour) 124

Goal to Go (Bishop) 140

Goal to Go (Scholz) 139

Goal to Go! (Sherman) 133

Goals, the Life of Knute Rockne 60

Going Back 184

Golden Hurricane, The 49

Golden Tornado, Georgia Tech, 1951 184

Graduate Coach, A 126

Grantland Rice's Cities Service Football Guide 169

Gray Line and Gold 139

Great Moments in Stanford Sports 52

Grid Star 136

General Index

Grid Wars Rage through Seventy-Fifth Year   36

Gridfax   198

Gridiron   117

Gridiron Challenge   139

Gridiron Cookery   261

Gridiron Courage   145

Gridiron Crusader   147

Gridiron Duel   150

Gridiron Gambler   141

Gridiron Glory (Bishop)   141

Gridiron Glory (Heyliger)   129

Gridiron Grenadiers   41

Gridiron Grit   136

Gridiron Pageantry   261

Gridiron Stranger   148

Gridiron Weekly   116

Grizzly Gridiron, The   50

Guckenheimer Football Schedules   172

Gulf Football Manual   17

H

H Book of Harvard Athletics, The   52

Hackberry Jones, Split End   141

Halfback!   144

Halfback, The   122

Halfback on His Own   140

Halfback's Interference, A   164

Half-Time Hero   140

Hail The Champs!   185

Hail, West Virginians   229

Hall of Fame Flankerback   143

Hammersmith: His Harvard Days   121

Handbook for Coaching the Football Passing Attack   204

Handbook of Football Scouting and Film Analysis   259

Handy Football Library, A   2

Handy Illustrated Guide to Football, A   2

Hard Nosed Halfback   142

Hard to Tackle   149

Harding of St. Timothy's   125

Harvard Teams   52

Has the Bulldog Regained His Grip?   251

Haughton Instructional Series   87

Haunted Halfback   143

Head Coach, The   128

Headwork Wins Football Games   97

Heffelfinger's Football Facts   170

Hell for Leather   48

Herb Kent, West Point Cadet   137

Herb Kent, West Point Fullback   137

General Index

Here Come the Texas Longhorns   48

Herman Hickman Football Guide   172

Herman Hickman Reader, The   245

Hero, The   144

Hero at Halfback   140

High School Captain of the Team, The   127

High School Football   196

High School Football and How to Win Games   199

High School Football Manual of Fundamentals   199

High School Freshman, The   127

High School Left End, The   127

Highlights of Pro Football   179

Hints to Coaches   84

Hip-Pocket Football   85

Hires Football Schedules   171

Historical Sketch of the Oneida Football Club of Boston, 1862-1865   43

History and Strategy of the Forward Pass   99

History of American Football   36

History of Athletics at Maryville College   53

History of Athletics at Pennsylvania, A   52

History of Athletics at the University of Pennsylvania, The   52

History of Football at Dickinson College, The   51

History of Football at Harvard, The   44

History of Football at Shortridge, A   197

History of Football at the University of Delaware   49

History of Football from the Beginnings to 1871   15

History of Minnesota Football   42

History of South Jersey Football, A   198

History of Southern Football, 1890-1928   230

History of Springfield College Football, The   43

History of Yale Athletics, A   51

Hitting the Line   123

Hold 'em, Girls   161

Hold 'em, Navy!   132

Hold 'em Wyndham   123

Hold That Line! (Archibald)   142

Hold That Line! (Sherman)   133

Homecoming Game, The   149

Hood Football Guide   170

Horace Higby and the Field Goal Formula   148

Horace Higby and the Gentle Fullback   148

How Champions Play Football   86

General Index

How I Play My Position 85

How to Be a Successful Coach 93

How to Coach a Football Team 7

How to Coach and Play Football 89

How to Coach Football's Forty-four Stack Defense 106

How to Coach Football's Running Trap Game 202

How to Coach Winning Football 93

How to Develop a Strong High School Kicking Game 205

How to Develop a Successful High School Passing Attack 204

How to Enjoy Football 238

How to Get More Fun Out of Watching Football 239

How to Meet the Five-Man Line Shifting and Changing Defenses 103

How to Officiate Football 218

How to Organize and Conduct Football Practice 94

How to Play Better Football 207

How to Play Football (Bierman) 85

How to Play Football (Caldwell) 86

How to Play Football (Camp) 83

How to Play Football (Eckersall) 85

How to Play Football (Rawlings Manufacturing Co.) 87

How to Play Football (Waldorf) 92

How to Play Football (Wilkinson) 85, 86

How to Play It Series 208

How to Play Plain and Fancy Football 85

How to Play Quarterback and Other Football Positions 84

How to Play Six-Man Football 210

How to Play Winning Football 86

How to Scout Football 259

How to Select and Develop Athletes for Winning High School Football 201

How to Star in Football (Crisler) 86

How to Star in Football (Masin) 206

How to Study the Football Rules 215

How to Succeed at Touch Football 211

How to Train the Quarterback 98

How to Watch a Football Game (Jeffrey and Reker) 238

How to Watch a Football Game (Stevens and Shorten) 239

How to Watch and Enjoy a Football Game 240

How to Watch and Understand Football 238

How to Watch Football (Little and Harron) 239

General Index

How to Watch Football (Metzger) 238

How to Watch Football (Oldsmobile) 240

How to Watch Football (Phillips Petroleum Co.) 240

How to Watch Football Like an Expert 241

Huddle! 134

Hughes' Collegiate Football Guide 9

Humble Oil Football Handbook 172

Hunt Holds the Center 123

"Hurry Up" Yost in Story and Song 62

I

I Play to Win 67

I Want to Be a Football Player 207

Illinois History 229

Illinois' Greatest Football Game 184

Illustrated Football Annual 25

Illustrated Football Rules Book 215

Illustrated Football Techniques 87

Illustrated Guide to Championship Football 95

Impact of Southern Football, The 230

Imposter, The 121

In the Line 124

Indiana Football 227

Ingersoll's Football Tactics 83

Inquiry into the Matter of Priority in the Selection and Publication of All-American Football Teams for the Years 1889-96, An 257

Inside Dope on Football Coaching 88

Inside Football (Allen and Weiskopf) 93

Inside Football (Cavanaugh) 88

Inside Football (A.G. Spalding & Brothers) 86

Inside Football (Sport Magazine) 27

Inside Tackle 142

Inside The Big Eight 232

Inside the Ten 152

Instant Football for Females 241

Intercollegiate and Professional Football 9

Intercollegiate Football 17

Intercollegiate Football Annual 17

Intercollegiate Football Pictorial, The 25

Intercollegiate Football Review 9

Intercollegiate Football Summary 18

Intercollegiate Song Book 164

Interference, and Other Football Stories 133

Interscholastic Football Rules 195

General Index

Iowa Conference Story, The   228

Iron Duke   138

It Was a Different Game   66

It's a Pass!   133

It's Always Too Soon to Quit   66

I've Seen 'em All   45

Ivy League Football   234

Ivy League Press, Radio and TV Football Guide   234

J

Jack Hall at Yale   127

Jack Lorimer, Freshman   125

Jack Lorimer's Champions   125

Jack Lorimer's Holidays   125

Jack Lorimer's Substitute   125

Jack Winters' Gridiron Chums   130

Jackson of Hillsdale High   131

Jake Gaither: Winning Coach   66

Jericho   105

Jerry Dalrymple and His Tulane 1931 Green Wave National Champions   184

Jim Thorpe   63

Jim Thorpe, All-Around Athlete   63

Jim Thorpe, Indian Athlete   148

Jim Thorpe Story, The   63

Jimmy Makes the Varsity   133

Jo Dunn, All-American   140

Jock Sutherland, Architect of Men   64

Joe Bellino   65

Joe Boland, Notre Dame Man   65

Joe McGuire, Freshman   135

Joe Paterno: Football My Way   67

Johnny King, Quarterback   139

Jones Foundry Football Schedule Booklet   171

Jones Foundry Football Schedules and Statistics   171

Junior College Football Rating Systems   178

Junior in the Line, A   126

Junior Quarterback   148

K

Keeper Play   151

Kent of Malvern   126

Kick Formation   123

Kick, Pass and Run   207

Kicking the American Football   104

Kickoff! (Baldwin)   135

Kickoff (Fenner)   113

Kickoff! (Fitzgerald)   113

Kick Off, The (Jenkins)   165

Kickoff (Penny)   197

General Index

Kickoff (MacKellar)   149

King Football, the Vulgarization of the American College   252

King of Coaches   61

Kings of American Football   49

Kingsford, Quarter   122

Knute Kenneth Rockne   60

Knute Rockne   61

Knute Rockne, Football Wizard of Notre Dame   61

Knute Rockne, Man Builder   60

Knute Rockne: Notre Dame's Football Great   61

Knute Rockne on Football   90

Knute Rockne, Young Athlete   147

Knute Rockne's Career   60

L

Ladies' Guide to Football   241

Lardy the Great   135

Larson Simplified Scorebook for Six-Man Football   210

Last Play, The   123

Last Quarter, The   124

Last White Line, The   145

Lateral Pass Technique and Strategy, The   99

Laws of Football, The   15

Leading a Bulldog's Life   45

Learning How: Football   87

Left End Edwards   122

Left End Luisetti   148

Left End Scott   147

Left Guard Gilbert   123

Left Half Harmon   123

Left Tackle Thayer   122

Legend of Hobey Baker, The   66

Letters from Brother Bill, Varsity Sub, to Tad, Captain of the Beechville High School Eleven   84

Libel Case of Wally Butts vs. the Saturday Evening Post, The   252

Life and Hard Times of the Super Heroes, The   158

Life of Knute Rockne, The   60

Limited Material? Unlimited Results!   200

Line Coaching   103

Line Man's Bible, The   103

Line Smasher   147

Linebacker Blitz   153

Little Big Foot   149

Lone Star Fullback   154

Lonesome End (Bishop)   141

Lonesome End (Meader)   153

Long Pass, The (Archibald)   142

General Index

Long Pass, The (Barbour)   123

Long Pass (Knott)   152

Longhorn, The   183

Lost Art of Kicking, The   104

Lost Eleven, The   140

Lou Little's Football   238

Lucky Shoes   149

M

M Book of Athletics, Mississippi A & M College, The   53

M Book of Athletics, Mississippi State College, The   53

Make the Team in Football   206

Making College Count   197

Making the Eleven at St. Michael's   132

Making the Freshman Team   126

Man in Motion   146

Manual for Functional Football   90

Manual of Football for High School Coaches, A   199

Manual of Football for High Schools, A   199

Manual of Football Officiating (Eastern Intercollegiate Football Association, 1938)   217

Manual of Football Officiating (Eastern Intercollegiate Football Association, 1939)   217

Manual of Football Officiating (National Association of Football Commissioners)   218

Manual of Football Officiating (Southern Football Officials Association)   217

Manual of Football Officiating (Western Conference)   217

Manual of Football Officiating Techniques   205

Manual of Punting, A   88

Many a Saturday Afternoon   65

Marlboro Football Guide   173

Marshall Newell, a Memorial   59

Massachusetts Official School Boy Football Annual   197

Maze: A New Concept in Football Blocking, The   204

Meat on the Hoof   253

Memorable Moments in Michigan Sports   53

Mesa's Power Attack   202

Method of Ranking College Football Teams   177

Miami Football   230

Michigan All-Time Athletic Record Book   53

Michigan Football   229

Michigan Football Review   185

Michigan on the Gridiron, 1904   41

Michigan State Multiple Offense   96

Michigan-Style High School Football   201

General Index

Michigan's All-Time Athletic Record 53

Michigan's Kicking Game 104

Mid-American Conference Football 235

Midget Football Fundamentals 206

Midget Substitute, The 164

Million Dollar Fumble, The 145

Minnesota Football 230

Minnesota Football History 42

Minnesota Huddles, The 185

Missouri Power Football 94

Missouri Valley Conference All-Sports Handbook 234

Missouri Valley Conference Handbook 234

Missouri Valley Conference Records Book 234

Missouri Valley Intercollegiate Athletic Association Big Eight Football Roster Manual 233

Missouri Valley Intercollegiate Athletic Association Big Seven Football Roster Manual 233

Mobil Pigskin Prophet 115

Mobil Touchdown Tips 115

Modern Belly T Football 204

Modern Defensive Football 105

Modern Football 91

Modern Football for Players and Coaches 88

Modern Football for the Spectator 240

Modern Football, How to Play the Game 83

Modern Notre Dame Formation, The 102

Modern Short Punt: A Winning Formation, The 102

Modern Single Wing Football 102

Modern T Formation with Man-In-Motion 99

Modern Winged-T Play Book, The 101

Monti's Official Football Book 173

Morning Glory Quarterback 153

Mountaineer Football 51

Mr. Football: Amos Alonzo Stagg 60

Mr. Fullback 149

Mr. Quarterback 149

Mud and Glory 134

Murder on the Ten-Yard Line 134

My Favorite Football Stories 245

My Greatest Day in Football 113

My Little Brother's Coming Tomorrow 67

Mystery Guest at Left End 151

N

Nation-Wide Football 116

National Champions 51

General Index

National Federation Football Rules   195

National Football (Bromley)   261

National Football (Sheehan and Pearson)   171

National Football Champions (Boand)   177

National Football Champions (Helms Athletic Foundation)   177

National Football Schedule   170

National Football Schedules and Rules   169

National High School Football Annual   196

National Intercollegiate Football Schedule, Rules, Scorecard   169

National Survey of High School Six-Man Football Accidents   210

Navy Blue and Gold   137

Navy in High Cotton, The   223

NCAA TV Game of the Week Football Almanac   173

Ned Beals, Freshman   131

Ned Beals Works His Way   131

New Boy, The   125

New Doublewing Attack, The   203

New Jersey Football Officials Association Official Handbook   217

New 1948 Plays: Football   98

New Orleans Sugar Bowl Football Classic, The   223

New York Journal American Football Facts   172

New York Times Official Football Schedules   170

Nicky's Football Team   139

Night Football   179

Nine Saturdays Make a Year   152

1959 Football Story, The   3

1947 Football Schedule   171

99 Best High School Plays   203

No Gold Footballs   198

No Ifs, No Ands, a Lot of Butts   65

No-Talent Letterman   143

Norman Sper's Football Almanac   18

Notre Dame Football   46

Notre Dame Football, The T Formation   100

Notre Dame, from Rockne to Parseghian   47

Notre Dame Scholastic Football Review   184

Notre Dame Story, The   46

Number 44, and Other Football Stories   133

O

Of Tigers and Touchdowns   48

Off Side   129

Offense, Book III   91

Offensive and Defensive Football   201

General Index

Offensive and Defensive Line Play 103

Offensive Football (Olivar) 96

Offensive Football (Oshins) 3

Offensive Fundamentals, Book I 90

Official All-North Carolina Football Annual 229

Official Collegiate Football Record Book 9

Official Football and Soccer Rules 2

Official Football Facts 170

Official Football Review 183

Official Football Rules 213

Official Football Rules and Guide 2

Official Football Statisticians' Manual 216

Official Intercollegiate Football Rules 2

Official Intercollegiate Football Schedules and Rules 2

Official Intercollegiate Football Statistical Summary 18

Official Interscholastic Football Rules 195

Official National Collegiate Athletic Association Football Guide 9

Official National Collegiate Athletic Association Football Handbook 213

Official National Collegiate Athletic Association Football Rules: Interpretations 215

Official Read-Easy Football Rules 216

Official Rule Books 213

Official Rules of Football and Soccer Ball 215

Official Six-Man Football Guide and Rulebook, The 209

Official Six-Man Football Guide and Rule Book 209

Official Six-Man Football Rules and Handbook 209

Official Southwest Athletic Conference Football Information Book, The 234

Organizational Keys and Checklists for Successful Football Coaching 95

Original Football Facts 170

Out of Bounds 136

Over the Line 133

P

Pacific Coast Conference Football 233

Pacific Coast Conference Football Press Book 233

Pacific Coast Conference Football Record 231

Pacific Coast Conference Football Record Book 231

Pacific Coast Conference Records Book 233

Pacific Coast Intercollegiate Football 231

General Index

Pacific Eight Fall Sports Information 233

Pacific Eight Football News Facts 231

Packard-Bell Presents UCLA Football 186

Panhandle Pigskin Preview 228

Parlour Football 261

Parseghian and Notre Dame Football 95

Pass and a Prayer, A 144

Pass Defense Drills 106

Pass Receiver 144

Passing and Kicking, 109

Passing and Kicking Game, The 99

Passing Game, The (Pelfrey and Owens) 99

Passing Game in Football, The 99

Paul Brown's Sohio Football Handbook 172

Peek's Football Factbook 233

Pelican State Pigskin Preview 229

Penn State Football Season 186

Penn State's Finest Football Season 186

Perfect Football Coach, The 68

Personal Reminiscences of a Yale Football Player of the Early 'Eighties 245

Phantom Backfield 144

Phantom Blitz 142

Phillip Kent 126

Phillip Kent in the Lower School 126

Phillip Kent in the Upper School 126

Phillip Morris Football Guide 173

Phillip Morris Football Schedule 172

Pic Quarterly Football Pictorial 25

Pigskin 134

Pigskin Parade at Trinity 50

Pigskin Tactics 91

Pigskin Soldier 133

Pigskin Warriors 139

Pink Pants 136

Play Ball 164

Play Football Safely 86

Play of the Backs 87

Play of the Quarterback 88

Play That Won, The 123

Players' Football Manual and Notebook 84

Playing Rules of Football, The 213

PM Football Schedules 172

Poe's Football 1

Poe's Run and Other Poems 164

Popular Football 155

Popular Sports Kickoff 27

Possibilities in Coaching Football 91

Power and the Glory, The 232

Power Back 142

Power T Football 102

Practical Football 90

Practical Football and How to Teach It 90

Practical Six-Man Football 210

Pre-College Football 199

Pre-Game Football 94

Prep Football Magazine and Annual 196

Press and the Football Coach, The 255

Prevention of Football Injuries 248

Primer of College Football, A 83

Principles of Football 199

Pro and College Football 28

Pro-T Offense in High School Football, The 203

Professor Fodorski 146

Progressive and Fundamental Football 91

Proud Tradition/Notre Dame, A 184

Psychological Changes During Periods of Football Training and Detraining 248

Punt Formation 142

Punt, Pass and Kick 207

Purple Tide, The 145

Q

Quaker Oats Instructional Series 86

Quarterback, The 116

Quarterback, All-American 145

Quarterback and Son 142

Quarterback Bates 123

Quarterback Carson 153

Quarterback Gamble 149

Quarterback Generalship and Strategy 98

Quarterback Hothead 129

Quarterback Reckless 129

Quarterback Strategy 98

Quarterback's Aim 151

Quarterback's Pluck, A 126

Questions and Answers on the Football Rules 218

Quick Kick 146

R

Rackety Rax 135

Radar Defense for Winning Football, The 205

Rainy Day Coach, The 90

Rainy Day Coach Supplement, The 90

General Index

Rambling Halfback   146

Rawlings Official Football Guide   9

Ray Graves' Guide to Modern Football Defense   105

Ray Graves' Guide to Modern Football Offense   96

Razzle Dazzle   134

RCA Football TV Handbook   172

Real Magaine's Football Yearbook Kickoff   27

Rebel Coach   67

Rebel Halfback   141

Rebel in Sports, A   223

Red-Dog Center   142

Red Dynamite   137

Red Grange, Football's Greatest Halfback   63

Red Grange Story, The   63

Red-Headed Halfback, The   131

Red Morton, Waterboy   135

Referee's Book on Football Rules   214

Resolution Adopted by the Intercollegiate Football Rules Committee on the Death of Walter Camp, A   59

Revised and Latest Rules of Football, The   214

Revised Football Rules   161

Revolutionary Football   92

Rex Kingdon at Walcott Hall   130

Right End Emerson   123

Right End Option, The   146

Right Guard Grant   123

Right Half Rollins   123

Right Tackle Todd   123

Rivals for the Team   123

Road to the Championship, The   186

Road to the Top, The   44

Roble Football Roundup   172

Rock Taylor, Football Coach   147

Rockne   61

Rockne, Idol of American Football   61

Rockne of Notre Dame (Lovelace)   61

Rockne of Notre Dame (Rockne Memorial Association, Inc.)   61

Rockne's Football Problems   89

Rockspur Eleven, The   122

Rocky Malone   148

Ronald Encyclopedia of Football   19

Rookie Coach   135

Rookie Quarterback   140

Ros Hackney, Halfback   136

Rose Bowl (Meincke)   137

Rose Bowl, The (Stiles)   222

General Index

Rose Bowl All-American 143

Rose Bowl Cartoon History 222

Rose Bowl Game, The (Doubleday & Co.) 222

Rose Bowl Game, The (Packard Motor Car Co.) 222

Rose Bowl Linebacker 143

Rose Bowl Pro 144

Rose Bowl Tour, A 222

Rose Bowl Trip, The 222

Rough Stuff 146

Route of the Boilermakers, The 48

Rugby Football 15

Rugby Football Rules (American Intercollegiate Association) 7

Rugby Football Rules (Spalding) 214

Rugby Game, The 213

Rules of American Football 214

Rules of Football, as Played by the American College Teams, The 213

Rules of the Rugby Game of Football 214

Run and Shoot Football 202

Runner Up 151

Rushton Boys at Rally Hall, The 130

S

Saga of American Football, The 36

Salesman from the Sidelines 61

Salute to Notre Dame, A 47

Sammy Blows His Whistle 218

Saturday Evening Post Football Schedule Book 170

Saturday Heroes 140

Saturday's America 3

Sayger Illustrated Football Series 202

Scarlet of Avalon, The 131

Scatback 152

School That Didn't Care, The 124

Scientific and Practical Treatise on American Football for Schools and Colleges, A 1

Scoring Play, The 124

Scoring Power with the Winged T Offense 101

Scrambler, The 142

Scrambling Quarterback 148

Second H Book of Harvard Athletics, The 52

Second String Hero 148

Secret Play, The 122

Secrets of Kicking the Football 105

Selected Football Plays from Nine Standard Formations 97

Senior Quarterback 126

Seven in Front 146

Seventy-Five Years with the Fighting Hawkeyes 46

General Index

Seventy-Seven Grange of Illinois 63

70,000 Witnesses 134

She Produces All-Americans 42

Shorty Carries the Ball 143

Sideline Pass 141

Sideline Quarterback 141

Sideline Victory 143

Simple Explanations of the Great Game of Football 237

Simplified Multiple Defense 105

Simplified Single Wing Football 102

Sinclair Football Guide 172

Six Decades of Yale-Princeton Football 48

Six Football Programs 261

Six-Man Football (Alexander) 210

Six-Man Football (Duncan) 210

Six-Man Football, a Handbook for Coaches and Players 209

Six-Man Football Magazine 210

Six-Man Football Manual 209

Six-Man Football Rules 209

Six-Man Football Rules and Handbook 209

Six-Man Football, the Official Handbook for Players, Coaches and Schoolmen 209

Six-Man Football, the Streamlined Game 210

Six-Man Two-Hand Touch Football Rules for Elementary Schools 211

Sixty-Six Years on the California Gridiron 43

Sizzling Southwest Football for 60 Years 232

Skyline Football 235

Slanting Monster Defense in Football, The 205

Slater of Iowa 64

Slot T Football 101

Small College Preview 2

Smorgasbord Offense for Winning High School Football 202

So You Want to Be a High School Football Coach 200

Soaring Eagles 49

Son of the Coach 142

Songs and Cheers 163

Sophomore Halfback 126

Southeastern Conference Football Data 233

Southeastern Conference Football Statistics 233

Southeastern Conference Press and Radio Dope Book 233

Southern California Football 229

Southern California Grid Index 229

Southern Champions--A Football Treasure 183

General Index

Southern Conference Fall Brochure 234

Southern Conference Fall Press Data 234

Southern Conference Fall Sports Press Data 234

Southwest Conference Football 232

Southwest Conference Football Guide 234

Southwest Football Dope Book 232

Spalding Football Guide 7

Spalding's Code of Football Rules for 1909 214

Spalding's Inter-Collegiate Association Football Rules 7

Spalding's Official Football Guide 8

Spalding's Official Interscholastic Football Guide 195

Spalding's Official Rules of Beeball 210

Spalding's Six-Man Official Guide and Rules Book 209

Spartan Saga 53

Spice's Football 143

Spirit of Menlo, The 131

Split-Line T Offense 100

Split-T in High School Football, The 203

Sporting News Official NFL, AFL and College Schedules and Records, The 173

Sports Forecast Football 27

Sports History of the University of the South, A 53

Sports Illustrated Football: Offense 97

Sports Quarterly Presents Football Roundup 27

Sports Review Football 26

Sportscasters Bulletin 117

Spotlighting the Husker Greats of Yesterday and Today 44

Spread Formation Football 102

Springfield College Football Team Defense 106

Springfield College Football Team Offense 96

Springfield Football 43

Stadium 134

Stadium, The 179

Stan Kent, Freshman Fullback 129

Stan Kent, Varsity Man 129

Stanford Football Songs 163

Stanley Woodward's Football 26

Star Kicker 143

Stirring Football Stories 154

Stop that Pass 152

Story of a Football Season, The 84

Story of Football, The 36

Story of Football at the University of Texas, The 47

Story of Football in Text and Pictures, The 36

General Index

Story of the Orange Bowl, The   223

Straight Ahead!   129

Strange but True Football Stories   246

Stranger in the Backfield   146

Street and Smith Football Yearbook   25

Street and Smith's Football Pictorial Yearbook   25

Street and Smith's Football Yearbook   25

Study of Linemen Stances and Body Alignments and Their Relationship to Starting Speed in Football, A   103

Study of the Football Rules, 1932, A   215

Substitute, The   126

Substitute Jimmy   123

Substitute Quarterback, The   124

Successful Multiple Offense in High School Football   201

Sugar Bowl, The   223

Summary of Nation-Wide 1937 Football Statistics   18

Supplement to AMERICAN FOOTBALL   35

Supplement to INTERCOLLEGIATE FOOTBALL   17

Survey of Football Fatalities   247

Swing-End Offense   102

Sylvania TV Home Viewers' Official Football Guide   173

T

T Formation from A to Z, The   100

T Quarterback   139

Tackle Play   88

Tackle, Quarterback and Other Stories   124

Tail of the Terrible Tiger, The   139

Tale of the Wildcats, The   53

Talk at the National Football Foundation and Hall of Fame Dinner, A   257

Target Pass   124

Team: A High School Odyssey   199

Team That Couln't Lose, The   150

Teamwork   140

Technique of Football Officiating, The   218

Techniques of Football Coaching   95

Teen-Age Football Stories   154

Teen-Age Gridiron Stories   155

Ten Seconds to Play!   144

Ten Thousand and One Scores   177

Ten Top Trojan Football Thrillers   46

Ten Years Athletics at Harvard   52

Tennessee, Football's Greatest Dynasty   47

General Index

Tennessee's Dazzling Decade 47

Terry and Bunky Play Football 206

Terry Brennan of Notre Dame 64

Testimonial to the Players, Coaches, Management of Washington and Jefferson College, A 183

Texaco Football Almanac 173

Texas Football 228

That Football Game 121

That Old Rivalry 197

That's My Boy 134

Third and Eight to Go 150

Third and Goal 150

Third String Center 151

Thirteen Years of Winning Oklahoma Football 45

Thirty Selected Trick Football Plays 84

This Game of Football 92

This Is Harry Gilmer 62

This Was Football 64

Thorpe 63

Thorpe of Carlisle 63

Three Cheers and a Tiger 153

Three Yards and a Cloud of Dust 49

Three Years of Football at Dartmouth 41

Thrilling Football 155

Through the Line 149

Tiger Terwilliger 152

Tiger Triumph 184

Tim, the Football Nut 143

Tod Hale on the Scrubb 124

Tom Fairfield in Camp 129

Tom Fairfield's Pluck and Luck 129

Tom Harmon and the Great Gridiron Plot 141

Tom Harmon's Book of Sports Information and Football Almanac 19

Tom Harmon's Gridiron Guide 239

Tom Mosely, Midget Leaguer 144

Tommy Carries the Ball 139

Tommy Tiptop and His Football Eleven 128

Too Late to Quit 146

Top Lineman 129

Touch Football (Grombach) 211

Touch Football (Stanbury and DeSantis) 211

Touchdown (E. W. Peek & Co.) 232

Touchdown (Powell) 141

Touchdown (Sherman) 133

Touchdown! (Stagg and Stout) 59

Touchdown and After 130

General Index

Touchdown Duo   152

Touchdown for Doc, A   139

Touchdown for the Enemy   146

Touchdown for Tommy   150

Touchdown Glory   142

Touchdown Kid   145

Touchdown Maker   147

Touchdown 1947   232

Touchdown of 1947, The   232

Touchdown Pass   144

Touchdown Plays   86

Touchdown to Victory   136

Touchdown Trouble   137

Touchdown Twins   142

Touchdowns   130

Tough to Tackle   150

Tournament of Roses, The   222

Tournament of Roses Football Game Record   222

Traditional Rules from 1868-1870   35

Training, Conditioning and the Care of Injuries   247

Treasury of Notre Dame Football, A   47

Treatment of Football Injuries   247

TREVOR'S FOOTBALL Handbook   170

Triple Threat   136

Triple Threat Trouble   144

True Football Yearbook   26

True's Football Yearbook   27

Truth about Big-Time Football, The   252

TV College Football Program   240

Twenty Football Plays for 1912   97

Twenty Modern Football Plays   97

Twenty-Five Years of Football at Washington and Jefferson College   42

Two Hundred and Fifty Practical Questions and Answers on the Football Rules   218

Two Hundred Practical Questions and Answers on the 1932 Football Rules   218

Two Quarterbacks, The   138

U

Umbrella Defenses   105

Unbalanced Line Open End T Offense, The   101

Unbeatable Rockets, The   186

Uncensored Truth about Rockne's Strange Death, The   60

Under the Goal Posts   136

Understand Football   238

Universal Football and Handball   261

University Football   1

University Football through the Years   46

General Index

University of Arkansas Football Clinic 95

University of California Football Records 42

University of Southern California Athletics 53

Unofficial Prefect 125

Unreconstructed Amateur, The 60

U.S. Rubber Co. Instructional Series 85

V

Valley Eleven, The 150

Varsity Athletic Record Book, University of Maine 53

Varsity Football Play Set, The 97

Varsity Jim 134

Victory Pass 147

Villanova University Football 50

Violent World of Touch Football, The 211

Virginia College Football Directory 227

Volunteers, The 47

W

Walter Camp 59

Walter Camp's Book of Football 2

Want to Be a Football Champion? 206

War Eagle 49

Washington State High School Association Football Clinic 199

Watch That Pass! 124

Watertown Athletic Association 227

Way the Ball Bounces, The 65

Waynesburg College Football Records, 50

Wearers of the "T", The 50

Weekly Football Guide 117

Weekly Gridiron Record 116

Wehman's Book on Football 1

Weight Training for Football 248

Western Athletic Conference Yearbook 235

Western Conference Records Book, The 233

Western Football Roundup 230

West Point Wingback 142

West Pointers on the Gridiron 137

Westinghouse Football Facts and Schedules 172

What Price Football 252

What the 1925 Season Taught Us About Business Organization 179

What's Right Now with Harvard Football 45

What's the Matter with Harvard Football 45

What's What in Football 115

General Index

What's What in Football Supplement 18

What's What in Football Yearbook 18

Whipper-Snapper, The 132

Who's Who in Football 28

Who's Who in Football on the Pacific Coast 231

Who's Who in Iowa Football 45

Who's Who in Minnesota Athletics 53

Why the Bulldog is Losing His Grip 251

Wilson Instructional Series 84

Wilson's Football Guide and Annual Review 9

Wing-T and the Chinese Bandits 101

Wing-T Fullback 150

Wing-T Multiple Offense for High School Football 203

Winged T, The 101

Wings Over West Point 139

Winning Football (Bierman and Mayer) 91

Winning Football (Roper) 88

Winning Football Plays 98

Winning Football with the Blockbuster Defense 205

Winning Football with the Strategic Slot 203

Winning Forward Pass, The 136

Winning High School Defensive Football 205

Winning High School Football 200

Winning Isn't Everything 66

Winning Play Sequences in Modern Football 203

Winning Quarterback, The 151

Winning Spirit, The 148

Winning Team, The 183

Winning Team of Centre College, The 183

Winning the Eagle Prize 127

Winning Touchdown, The 126

Wisconsin High School Coaches Summer Clinic 200

With Rockne at Notre Dame 46

Women's Guide to Football Watching 241

Wow Boys, The 185

Wright & Ditson Football Guide 7

Wright & Ditson's Rugby and Association Football Guide 7

Wrong-Way Neelen 151

Y

Yale Athletics 51

Yale Bowl, The 179

Yale Football Story, The 48

Yale-Harvard-Princeton Official Songs and Cheers 163

Yale-Harvard-Princeton Songs and Cheers Books, The 163

Yale, Her Campus, Classrooms, and Athletics 52

Yale-Princeton Song and Cheer Book 163

Yank Brown, Halfback 131

Yea, Coach! 68

Yea, Sheriton 131

Y.M.C.A. Boys at Football 130

You Are the Quarterback 208

You Are the Running Back 208

You Have to Pay the Price 65

Young Mr. Football 139

Young Readers Football Stories 155

Young Sportsman's Guide to Football, The 207

Your Future with the New York Jets 256

Z

Zuppke of Illinois 61

Professional Index

A

ABC's of NFL Football: A Primer, The   244

Action Sports Pro Football   33

AFL Dream Backfield   79

AFL TV Handbook   174

AFL vs. NFL (U.S. Court of Appeals)   180

AFL vs. NFL (U.S. District Court)   180

All-America Football Conference Record Manual   10

All-Pro Football (Maco Magazine Corp.)   30

All-Pro Football (Popular Library)   31

All-Pro Football Annual, Touchdown   31

All-Pro Quarterback   157

All-Star Sports Special   34

All-Time Records of the San Francisco Forty-Niners   56

Allie Sherman's Book of Football   112

Always a Winner   73

Always on Sunday   69

American Football Conference Media Information Book   22

American Football League   4

American Football League (Chrysler Corp.)   175

American Football League, The (The American Football League)   4

American Football League Championship Game   224

American Football League Constitution and By-Laws   255

American Football League Official Guide   11

American Football League Official History   11

American Football League Press, Radio, TV Guide   11

American Football League Record and Press Manual   11

American Football League Roster Guide   235

American Football League Titans of New York   190

American Football League TV Roster Round-Up   174

Professional Index

American Football League Yearbook 29

And Every Day You Take Another Bite 253

Annual Meeting, National Football League 255

Atlanta Falcons 189

Atlanta Falcons Press Guide 191

Atlantic Coast Football League Directory and Schedule 235

B

Backfield Play 108

Backseat Quarterback 70

Ball is Snapped, The 3

Ballentine Beer Pro Football Television Manual 175

Baltimore Colts, The (American Visuals Corp.) 187

Baltimore Colts (Golden Press) 189

Baltimore Colts, The (Wright) 56

Baltimore Colts Action Pictorial 187

Baltimore Colts Picture Album 187

Baltimore Colts Press Guide (All-American Football Conference 192

Baltimore Colts Press Guide (National Football League) 191

Baltimore Colts Roundup 119

Baltimore Colts Story, The 55

Baltimore Colts Tenth Anniversary Yearbook 187

Bart Starr 72

Bart Starr, The Cool Quarterback 72

Bear News 119

Bert Bell NFL Player Benefit Plan, The 181

Best Plays of the Year 4

Best Pro Football Games 38

Better Scramble than Lose 71

Big Play, The 242

Big Red 119

Blanda, Alive and Kicking 77

Block and Tackle 119

Blue Book of Professional Football, The 4

Bluffer's Guide to Football 243

Book of Football, The 107

Boston Patriots Press Guide 192

Boston Patriots Yearbook 190

Boston Redskins Press Guide 191

Boston Yanks Press Guide 191

Brian Piccolo: A Short Season 75

Brian's Song 75

Broadway Joe and His Super Jets 57

Broken Patterns 72

Broncos Corral 119

Brooklyn Dodgers Press Guide (All-American Football Conference 192

Professional Index

Brooklyn Dodgers Press Guide (National Football League) 191

Browns 189

Buffalo Bills Bulletin 119

Buffalo Bills Press Guide 192

Buffalo Bisons, Bills Press Guide 192

Bump and Run 75

C

Carroll Dale Scores Again! 73

Championship 224

Championship Quarterback 156

Championship Teams of the NFL 58

Chargers 58

Charley Conerly's All-Pro Football 31

Charley Charger Coloring Book 167

Chicago Bears (NFL Library) 189

Chicago Bears, The (Roberts) 55

Chicago Bears Press Guide 191

Chicago Cardinals Press Guide 191

Chicago Hornets Highlights 119

Chicago Rockets, Hornets Press Guide 192

Chicago Rockets Tales 119

Cincinnati Bengals Press Guide 192

Cleveland Browns 190

Cleveland Browns Press Guide (All-American Football Conference) 192

Cleveland Browns Press Guide (National Football League) 191

Coach: A Season with Lombardi 74

Complete Guide to Pro Football, A 30

Complete Handbook of Pro Football, The 13

Complete Televiewer's Guide to Pro Football, The 33

Confessions of a Dirty Ballplayer 75

Confessions of a Gypsy Quarterback 69

Conley's Pro Football Guide 12

Continental Football League Press, Radio and TV Guide 235

Cord Sportfacts Super Bowl Special Report 225

Cornerback, The 156

Countdown to Super Bowl 190

Cut 'n Run 159

D

Dallas Cowboys, The 189

Dallas Cowboys and the NFL, The 57

Dallas Cowboys Press Guide 191

Dallas Cowboys: Pro or Con? The 57

Dallas Cowboys' Super Wives 80

Dallas Cowboys: Winning the Big One, The 189

Professional Index

Dallas Texans Press Guide 191

Day of the Ram 156

Decade at the Met: The Twins and Vikings, A 57

Defensive Football 111

Dell Pro Football 30

Dell Pro Football Annual 30

Dell Sports 30

Dell Sports Magazine Pro Football 30

Dell Sports Pro Football 30

Dell Sports Pro Football Preview 30

Denver Broncos Press Guide 192

Detroit Lion Fanfare 119

Detroit Lions 190

Detroit Lions Facts and Team History 191

Detroit Lions Photo Album 187

Detroit Lions Press Guide 191

Dick Bass Story, The 73

Don Sidelines 119

E

Eagles Nest 119

Earl Morrall Story: Comeback Quarterback, The 73

Eastern Conference 190

Encyclopedia of Football, The 21

Everybody's Big Game: Professional Football 80

Exclusive – Paul Brown 235

F

Fabulous Green Bay Packers, The 54

Falcon Facts 119

Family Guide to Football, A 243

Family Pro Football TV Handbook, The 175

Famous Pro Football Stars 80

Field of Vision 167

Fifth Anniversary of the Super Bowl, The 225

Fifty Years of Professional Football 54

Fine Points of Ball Carrying 107

Fine Points of Football Defense 107

Fine Points of Football Offense 107

Fine Points of Line Play 107

Fine Points of Pass Receiving 107

Fine Points of Passing, Running, and Kicking 107

Fine Points of Playing Quarterback (Tittle) 107

Fine Points of Playing Quarterback (Waterfield) 107

First and Goal to Go 175

First Fifty Years, The 38

First NFL-AFL Illustrated Digest 12

Professional Index

First Official Illustrated Digest   12

Five-Yard Fuller   157

Five-Yard Fuller and the Unlikely Knights   157

Follow Those Detroit Lions   191

Football (Clark)   106

Football (Mosedale)   258

Football and the Single Man   71

Football as Champions Play It   106

Football Dictionary, The   244

Football Digest   118

Football Fundamentals for Feminine Fans   244

Football Graphic, The   117

Football: How to Play and Watch It   242

Football Kicking Techniques   111

Football Playbook, The   243

Football Register   21

Football Scouting   259

Football Stars of (year)   79

Football's Greatest Quarterbacks   81

Football's Miracle Men   56

Footsteps of a Giant   71

41st Packer, The   74

Forward Pass, The   109

Forward Passes from the Football Dodgers   119

$400,000 Quarterback, The   37

Fourth and One   70

Fran Tarkenton: The Scrambler   72

Frank Gifford Story, The   69

Frank Gifford: The Golden Year, 1956   69

Frank Gifford's All-Pro Football   31

Frank Gifford's NFL-AFL Football Guide   12

Frank Gifford's NFL CBS Football Guide   12

Frank Gifford's Pro Football Guide   12

From Football to Finance: The Story of Brady Keys, Jr.   76

From Out of the Huddle   246

Front Four, The   79

Future Is Now, The   77

G

Game, The   37

Gamemakers, The   78

Game Plan Pro Football   33

Game That Was, The   246

George Halas and the Chicago Bears   76

Get in the Game   71

Giant Quarterback   156

Giant Touchdown   119

Giants of New York, The   56

Professional Index

Gladiators, The   167

Glory Boy   156

Goal to Go   77

Golden Toes: Football's Greatest Kickers   79

Great Defensive Players of the NFL   79

Great Linebackers of the NFL   79

Great Moments in Pro Football (Berger)   38

Great Moments in Pro Football (Hollander)   38

Great Moments in Sports   31

Great Pass Catchers in Pro Football   79

Great Pass Receivers of the NFL   79

Great Pro Quarterbacks   78

Great Quarterbacks of the NFL   77

Great Quarterbacks Series   78

Great Running Backs, The   79

Great Running Backs in Pro Football   79

Great Running Backs of the NFL   78

Great Teams of Pro Football, The   58

Great Upsets of the NFL   39

Greatest Packers of Them All, The   80

Greatest Pro Quarterbacks   78

Green Bay Packer Personnel   191

Green Bay Packers, The (Johnson)   54

Green Bay Packers (NFL Library)   190

Green Bay Packers, The (Ward)   54

Green Bay Packers Press and Radio Guide   191

Green Bay Packers Press Book   191

Green Bay Packers Press Guide   191

Green Bay Packers Yearbook   188

Gridiron Baedeker, The   5

Gridiron Gourmet   262

Gridiron Guidebook   5

Gridiron Pro Yearbook   22

Guide for Visiting National Football League Publicity Directors   255

H

Half a Century   38

Hall of Fame Yearbook   258

Here's Why It Was the Best Football Game Ever   224

Heroes of the NFL   80

High for the Game   76

Historical and Statistical Data on the Redskins   55

History of the Duluth Eskimos   54

History of Professional Football, The   37

Professional Index

Home Stadium Program - Record Book 6

Houston Oilers 190

Houston Oilers Action Album 190

Houston Oilers Press Guide 192

How the Pros Play Football (Smith and Dudley) 107

How the Pros Play Football (Stainback) 108

How to Be an Armchair Quarterback 243

How to Be a TV Quarterback 242

How to Become a Quarterback 110

How to Pass, Kick, Run, Block 107

How to Punt, Pass and Kick 107

How to See Football 243

How to Watch and Enjoy Pro Football 242

How to Watch Football on Television 242

How to Watch Pro Football on TV 243

Huddle, The 118

I

I Am Third 75

I Can't Wait Until Tomorrow 73

I Pass! 70

Illustrated Digest of Pro Football 12

Illustrated History of Pro Football 39

In the Pocket: My Life as a Pro Quarterback 73

Inside Defensive Football 111

Inside Pro Football (Higdon) 108

Inside Pro Football (King) 3

Inside Pro Football (Smith) 6

Inside Quarterbacking 110

Instant Replay: The Green Bay Diary of Jerry Kramer 73

J

Jerry Kramer's Farewell to Football 73

Jet Stream 119

Jim 70

Jim Brown Runs with the Ball 70

Jim Brown, the Golden Year 70

Jim Brown, The Running Back 70

Jimmy Brown Story, The 70

Jock Sutherland's 20 Winning Football Plays 109

Joe Namath, a Football Legend 72

Joe Namath: Maverick Quarterback 72

Joe Namath, Superstar 72

Joe Namath's Sportin' Life 72

Johnny Unitas 81

Johnny Unitas and the Long Pass 69

Professional Index

Johnny Unitas Story, The (Greene) 69

Johnny Unitas Story, The (Unitas and Fitzgerald) 69

Joiner 159

K

Kansas City Chiefs Press Guide 193

Kansas City Chiefs Yearbook 191

Keep Off My Turf 77

Kicking the Football Soccer Style 111

Kicking to Win 111

L

Language of Pro Football, The (National Football League Properties) 244

Language of Pro Football, The (Rote and Winter) 242

Len Dawson, Pressure Quarterback 75

Len Dawson: Superbowl Quarterback 75

Life and Football History of Harold (Red) Grange 68

Life and Hard Times of the Super Heroes 158

Life in the Pit: The Deacon Jones Story 75

Life with the Dallas Cowboys in the National Football League 256

Life with the San Francisco 49ers 256

Linebacker, The 156

Locker Room Talk 6

Lombardi (Silverman) 74

Lombardi (Wiebusch) 74

Lombardi Era and the Green Bay Packers, The 54

Lombardi Era of the Green Bay Packers, The 54

Lombardi -- His Life and Times 74

Lombardi: Winning Is the Only Thing 74

Long Pass, The 57

Los Angeles Chargers Press Guide 193

Los Angeles Dons Press Guide 192

Los Angeles Rams, The 55

Los Angeles Rams Press Guide 191

Luckman at Quarterback 68

M

Mainliner: Pro Football Issue 33

Making of a Pro Quarterback, The 110

Making of a Rookie, The 108

Maroon Football Team 50th Anniversary 55

Medicine and the Green Bay Packers 249

Miami Dolphins, The (McLemore) 58

Professional Index

Miami Dolphins (Miami Dolphins) 119

Miami Dolphins Press Guide 193

Mighty Ones, The 38

Miller Falls Pro Football Fact Book 22

Minnesota Vikings Fact Book 188

Minnesota Vikings New Fact Book 188

Minnesota Vikings Official Cartoon Book 188

Minnesota Vikings Press Guide 191

Miracle in Miami 58

My Greatest Challenge 71

My Kind of Football 111

My Life with the Redskins 55

My Sunday Best 114

N

National Football Conference Media Information Book 22

National Football League, The 5

National Football League Action Stamp Album 167

National Football League Championship Game 224

National Football League Constitution and By-Laws 255

National Football League Digest of Rules, The 216

National Football League Football Up to Date 20

National Football League Guide 174

National Football League Guide to Physical Fitness 249

National Football League Handbook 174

National Football League Individual Statistics 21

National Football League Manual 10

National Football League Playoff Bowl 224

National Football League Professional Football Rules, The 10

National Football League Record and Rules Manual 10

National Football League Record Manual 10

National Football League Revised Rules 216

National Football League Roster Manual 20

National Football League/The NFL and You, The 3

National Football League World Championship Game 223, 224

National Football League Yearbook 29

National Pro Football Hall of Fame Dedication 258

National Professional Football Hall of Fame 258

NBC Sports Pro Football 11

Professional Index

Nelson's Encyclopedia of Pro Football 5

New American Football League, The 174

New Orleans Saints 189

New Orleans Saints Press Guide 191

New York Bulldogs Press Guide 192

New York Giants, The (Complete Sports) 188

New York Giants, The (Rubin and DeRogatis) 167

New York Giants (NFL Library) 190

New York Giants, The (Smith) 56

New York Giants Press Guide 192

New York Giants Yearbook 188

New York Jets, The 190

New York Jets Official Yearbook 190

New York Jets Press Guide 193

New York Yanks Press Guide 192

New York Yankees Press Guide 192

Next Year's Champions 189

NFL Action '72 168

NFL and AFL Pro Football Record Book 21

NFL and You, The 3

NFL Appointment Book 4

NFL Appointment Calendar 22

NFL Appointment Yearbook 22

NFL CBS Football Guide 12

NFL Football Flip-Up Line-Up 174

NFL Group Insurance Plan: The Bert Bell NFL Player Benefit Plan 181

NFL Library 189

NFL Man of the Year Award 80

NFL 1964 4

NFL Giants, The (Rubin and DeRogatis) 167

NFLP 180

N.F.L. Pro Football Yearbook 29

NFL Record Book 174

NFL Rookies to Watch 80

No Time for Losing 71

Norm Van Brocklin's Football Book 112

Now It Can Be Told 179

O

Oakland Raiders Press Guide 193

Off My Chest 70

Off-Season Football Training 249

Offensive Football 108

Official AFL Autograph Yearbook 33

Official American Football League Autograph Book 167

Official American Football League Guide 11

Official Encyclopedia of Football, The, 21

Professional Index

Official Football Rules of the National Football League 216

Official Guide, National Football League 10

Official Guide of the National Football League 10

Official Illustrated Digest 12

Official National Football League Autograph Book 167

Official National Football League Football Encyclopedia, The 20

Official National Football League Guide 13

Official National Football League Guide from 1935-38 216

Official National Football League Pro Record and Rule Book 10

Official National Football League Record Book 12

Official National Football League Record and Roster Manual 10

Official National Football League Record and Rules Manual 10

Official National Football League Roster and Record Manual 10

Official NFL Autograph Yearbook 33

Official Pro Football 32

Official Pro Football Almanac 11

Official Pro Football Record Book 21

Official Rules for Professional Football 216

Official's Manual 219

O. J.: The Education of a Rich Rookie 75

On Any Given Sunday 107

On God's Squad 76

100-Yard War, The 158

Only a Game 158

Organized Professional Team Sports 180

Other League, The 38

Otto Graham - "T" Quarterback 110

Our '64 Colts 187

Out of Their League 76

P

Pacemakers in Football 80

Pacific Coast Football League Constitution and By-Laws 235

Packer Dynasty 54

Packer Football News 118

Packer Hi-Lites 119

Packers of the Past 54

Paper Lion 71

Pass to Win 77

Passing and Kicking 109

Passing for Touchdowns 109

Passing Game, The 109

Paul Hornung 81

Paul Hornung's Football Magazine 32

Professional Index

Perspective on Victory, A   72

Philadelphia Eagles Press Guide   192

Pioneer in Pro Football   77

Pittsburgh Steelers Press Guide   192

Player of the Year   75

Players, The   5

Players' Choice   159

Playing Pro Football to Win   5

Playing the Line   111

Playoff   224

Poised for Action   108

Popular Sports Touchdown, All-Pro Football   31

Pottsville Maroons Testimonial and Reunion   56

Press and Radio Information Book   10

Pro Bowl Press Book   224

Pro Champion   158

Pro Coach   158

Pro File   119

Pro Football (Complete Sports Publications)   32

Pro Football (Editors of SPORTS TODAY)   33

Pro Football (Fawcett Publishing Co.)   31

Pro Football (Peterson Publishing Co.)   29

Pro Football (Pocket Books)   11

Pro Football (Smith)   37

Pro Football All-Stars   29

Pro Football Almanac   32

Pro Football Broadside   253

Pro Football Desk Diary   4

Pro Football Digest   118

Pro Football Encyclopedia   21

Pro Football Exclusive   118

Pro Football Factbook   21

Pro Football for the Fan   242

Pro Football Forecast   5

Pro Football Forecast for 1969   22

Pro Football Guide (Cord Communications)   33

Pro Football Guide (Goldwin Publications)   34

Pro Football Guide (Gridiron Publications)   118

Pro Football Guide (Masthead)   174

Pro Football Guide (Snibbe Sports Publications)   21

Pro Football Hall of Fame Appointment Calendar   4

Pro Football Hall of Fame Fact Book   38

Pro Football Handbook (Masthead Corp.)   174

Pro Football Handbook (Pocket Books)   11

Professional Index

Pro Football Heroes   80

Pro Football Illustrated (Complete Sports Publications)   31

Pro Football Illustrated (Elbak)   28

Pro Football Illustrated (Elbert)   117

Pro Football in the Days of Rockne   39

Pro Football, Its "Ups" and "Downs"   37

Pro Football Newsletter   117

Pro Football Playbook   108

Pro Football Plays in Pictures   109

Pro Football Record Book   21

Pro Football Report   33

Pro Football Review   23

Pro Football Rookie (Frankel)   157

Pro Football Rookie (Jackson)   156

Pro Football Schedule and Record Book   175

Pro Football Scouting Reports   4

Pro Football Sports Stars   33

Pro Football Stars   29

Pro Football Photostamp Album   33

Pro Football Strategy '71   6

Pro Football Tele-Spotter   242

Pro Football: The World of the NFL   6

Pro Football, U.S.A.   108

Pro Football Weekly   118

Pro Football Yearbook (Elk and Girsch)   29

Pro Football Yearbook (Rensart Publishing Co.)   29

Pro Football's All-Time Greats   258

Pro Football's Greatest Upsets   39

Pro Football's Hall of Fame   258

Pro Football's Passing Game   78

Pro Football's Rag Days   246

Pro Football's Unforgettable Games   38

Pro News   117

Pro Passer   158

Pro Pigskin   117

Pro, Pro, Pro   114

Pro Quarterback (Haines)   156

Pro Quarterback, The (Olderman)   5

Pro Quarterback (SCH Publications)   118

Pro Quarterback (Tittle and Liss)   157

Pro Quarterback Annual   22

Pro Quarterback Handbook (Drazkowski)   78

Pro Quarterback Handbook (Pro Football Weekly)   6

Pro Quarterback: My Own Story   69

Professional Index

Pro Quarterbacks, The (Devaney) 77

Pro Quarterbacks, The (Shapiro) 78

Pro Rookie 157

Pro Season, The 39

Pro: The Official National Football League Television Magazine 6

Pro Toughback, The 157

Professional Football 174

Professional Football Annual 30

Professional Football Highlights 174

Professional Football League Merger 180

Professional Football Player, The 180

Professional Football Yearbook of the National Football League 29

Professional Football's Greatest Games 39

Professionals Look at Pro Football, The 246

Profile of a Season 22

Prolog: The National Football League Annual 22

Promises to Keep: The Miami Dolphins Story 58

Pros, The 4

Public Calls It Sport, The 71

Punts and Dodger Passes 119

Q

Quarterback 118

Quarterback, The (Maule) 156

Quarterback, The (Milton) 159

Quarterbacking 110

Quarterbacking to Win 110

Quarterbacks, The 77

R

Ram News 119

Rams Yearbook 187

Receiver, The 156

Record and Roster Manual 10

Record and Rules Manual 10

Redskins, The 55

Remember the Time 38

Return to Glory 56

Rick Casares Story, The 69

Rookie, The 156

Roster and Record Manual 10

Run to Daylight 112

Running Back, The 156

Running Backs, The 78

S

St. Louis Cardinals Press Guide 192

St. Louis Football Cardinals 189

Saints Signals 119

Salute to the Packers 188

Professional Index

San Diego Chargers   119

San Diego Chargers Press Guide   193

San Francisco 49ers, The   56

San Francisco 49ers Press Guide (All-American Football Conference)   192

San Francisco 49ers Press Guide (National Football League)   192

San Francisco 49ers Yearbook   187

Semi-Tough   159

Seven Days to Sunday   189

So This Is What Happened to Charlie Moe   157

Somebody Called "Doc"   77

Spartan Yearbook   187

Specialist in Pro Football, The   108

Speed King: Bob Hayes of the Dallas Cowboys, The   76

Sport Heroes   32

Sport Magazine Biographical Series   80

Sporting News National Football Guide, The   12

Sports Action Magazine Pro Football Thrills   31

Sports All-Stars Football   30

Sports All-Stars Pro Football   30

Sports Extra: Pro Football   32

Sports Focus Yearbook, Green Bay Packers   188

Sports Focus Yearbook, Green Bay Packers, Wisconsin Badgers   188

Sports Forecast Football   30

Sports Hero Joe Namath   73

Sports Quarterly Presents Pro Football   32

Sports Quarterly Presents Pros Football   32

Sports Review Pro Football (Elbak Publishing Co.)   29

Sports Reviews Pro Football (M. F. Enterprises, Inc.)   32

Sports Review's Pro Football (Splendid Publications)   32

Sports Special: Pro Football   32

Star Pass Receivers of the NFL   79

Star Quarterbacks of the NFL   78

Star Running Backs of the NFL   79

Statistical Records of the Oakland Raiders   56

Stop-Action   76

Story of Pro Football, The   37

Story of Pro Football in Summary, The   180

Strategy of Pro Football, The   242

Street and Smith's Pro Football Yearbook   32

Sun at the Met   57

Super Bowl! (Devaney)   225

Super Bowl (National Football League Properties)   224

Professional Index

Super Bowl (Ralbovsky) 225

Super Bowl (Smith) 225

Super Bowl Press Guides 224

Super Bowl: Pro Football's Greatest Games and Stars 225

Super Joe Namath 72

Superjoe: The Joe Namath Story 73

Survey of Eleven 1939 National Football League Games, A 20

Survey of the 1940 National Football League Season, A 20

T

T-Formation Tips 110

Team Press Guides 191

Telecasting of Professional Sports Contests 180

Televiewing Guide 243

They Call It a Game 253

They Pay Me to Catch Footballs 69

Thinking Man's Guide to Pro Football, A 6

This Is NFL Football 5, 243

This Is Pro Football 244

This Is the American Football League 4

Throw the Bomb 158

Throw the Long Bomb 158

Tips on How to Punt, Pass and Kick 107

Touchdown (Popular Library) 31

Touchdown! (Sullivan) 37

Tricks in Passing 109

True Hearts and Purple Heads 57

TWA Official AFL TV Viewing Guide 175

Twenty Years with the Cleveland Browns 57

U

Union Oil Instructional Series 107

V

Vikings, The 188

Vince Lombardi Pro Football Guide, The 6

Vince Lombardi Story, The 74

Vincent Lombardi, Young Football Coach 74

Violence Every Sunday 71

Violence Game, The 190

W

War Whops 119

Washington Redskins Press Guide 192

We Came of Age 37

We Love You, Cowboys 57

We Play to Win! 112

Weeb Ewbank's Pro Football Way to Physical Fitness 249

Wehman's Book on Football 1

Professional Index

Western Conference 190

What a Pro Football Coach Does 77

Wheaties Pro Bowl Football Player Stamp Album and Fact Book 224

When All the Laughter Died in Sorrow 76

Who's Who in Major League Football 28

Who's Who in the Major Leagues Football 28

Who's Who in Pro Football 31

Wife's Guide to Pro Football, A 244

Winning Football 110

Winning It All 58

Witness for the Defense 188

Y

Young Sports Photographer with the Green Bay Packers 246

Your Future – The AFL 4

Your Future with the New York Jets 256

Your Guide to Monday Night Football 243

Your Guide to Professional Football 174

RAYMOND H. FOGLER LIBRARY

DATE DUE

BOOKS ARE SUBJECT TO
RECALL AFTER TWO WEEKS

RAYMOND H. FOGLER LIBRARY
UNIVERSITY OF MAINE

STUDENT AMUSEMENTS OF THE OLD WORLD
AND THE NEW WORLD -- "The American Way"